Praise for *The Irish in Illinois*

"This is an engaging account of the Irish and Illinois history. While Chicago predominates, Billings and Farrell have crafted a compelling story of the Irish role in shaping the region since European exploration and settlement of the state."

—Eileen M. McMahon, author of *What Parish Are You From? A Chicago Irish Parish Community and Race Relations, 1916–1970*

"This is a concise but very smart and rich history of the Irish in Illinois. It is particularly insightful in its treatment of the Illinois Irish in the early nineteenth century as well as their experiences downstate throughout the two or more centuries of their settlement in the state. It makes a fresh and critically important contribution not just to the history of Illinois or to the story of the Irish there but to our understanding of the broader history of the Irish in America."

—Timothy Meagher, author of *Inventing Irish America*

"This well-researched and well-written book highlights the richness and the diversity of Irish immigrants and Irish American life in Illinois from the colonial era to the present. Billings and Farrell have provided a comprehensive analysis of the large Irish American community in Chicago but also have shown us the significance of the Irish outside the Windy City. It will be a role model for other state studies of the Irish in America."

—David T. Gleeson, author of *The Irish in the South, 1815–1877*

THE IRISH IN ILLINOIS

THE IRISH IN ILLINOIS

MATHIEU W. BILLINGS
AND SEAN FARRELL

Southern Illinois University Press
Carbondale

Southern Illinois University Press
www.siupress.com

Printed in the United States of America

23 22 21 20 4 3 2 1

Cover design by Molly Kurtz

Library of Congress Cataloging-in-Publication Data
Names: Billings, Mathieu W., 1973– author. | Farrell, Sean, 1966– author.
Title: The Irish in Illinois / Mathieu W. Billings and Sean Farrell.
Description: Carbondale : Southern Illinois University Press, 2020. | Includes bibliographical references and index.
Identifiers: LCCN 2019057571 (print) | LCCN 2019057572 (ebook) | ISBN 9780809337996 (paperback) | ISBN 9780809338009 (ebook)
Subjects: LCSH: Irish—Illinois—History. | Irish Americans—Illinois—History.
Classification: LCC F550.I6 B55 2020 (print) | LCC F550.I6 (ebook) | DDC 977.3004916/2—dc23
LC record available at https://lccn.loc.gov/2019057571
LC ebook record available at https://lccn.loc.gov/2019057572

Printed on recycled paper ♻

To Our Parents

David and Gail Billings
and
Donald and Eleanor Farrell

CONTENTS

MAPS AND FIGURES

ACKNOWLEDGMENTS

This short book has been long in the making. In July 2014, Jeff Hancks of Western Illinois University approached us about writing a book on the Irish in Illinois. We are grateful that Southern Illinois University Press has stuck with the project, the first statewide history of the Irish. Particular thanks are due to Kristine Priddy and Jennifer Egan, who answered countless emails and helped us navigate the publication process. Copyeditor Joyce Bond and project editor Wayne Larsen were fantastic: prompt, thorough, and professional. We could not have done this without them.

The Irish in Illinois reflects the innovative and high-quality work that historians have published in Irish, Irish American, and Illinois history in recent years. While this research is acknowledged in the endnotes and throughout the text, we would like to thank the following friends and colleagues who have improved our understanding of the Irish American experience through countless conversations and presentations at academic conferences over the years: Charlie Fanning, David Gleeson, Larry McCaffrey, Eileen McMahon, Kerby Miller, Bill Mulligan, Gillian O'Brien, Matt O'Brien, Tim O'Neil, Jim Rogers, Ellen Skerrett, and David Wilson. Much remains to be done about the histories of the Irish in Illinois, but these pioneering scholars have made the Irish diaspora a dynamic and important field of study. They are not responsible for any errors of omission or interpretation in the pages that follow, but the book has greatly benefited from their input.

This project has been nurtured by friends and colleagues at the two institutions where we work: the University of Indianapolis and Northern Illinois University. At UIndy, Mat wishes to acknowledge James Fuller, Ted Frantz, and Lawrence Sondhaus for providing moral support and sage advice throughout the publication process. At NIU, Sean is grateful to Rosemary Feurer, Aaron Fogelman, Jim Schmidt, and Andrea Smalley for sharing their insights on a range of aspects of American and immigration history. We owe particular thanks to Beatrix Hoffman for reading and providing helpful critiques of some of the material on twentieth-century Chicago. The book is much better because of the intellectual communities in which we live.

Finally, we are appreciative of our families for their encouragement and support. It is a cliché that entire households have to live with a book throughout the research and writing process, but it is no less true for that. Mat would like to thank Christine, his wife and sounding board, for her willingness to listen and discuss all things Irish American. To his teenage sons, Leif and Enson, may this book serve as a testament to the value of perseverance. Sean's thanks go to Leila Porter, who took time off from her own frenetic academic schedule to learn about the Irish in Illinois. His son, Liam, now nine years old, has been no help whatsoever with this book but is a constant reminder that there is life beyond work. Both Mat and Sean have been fortunate to have parents whose love and support have made their careers and lives possible. This book's dedication is one recognition of that fact.

The Irish in Illinois

St. Patrick's Catholic Church, LaSalle, Illinois. Photo by Sean Farrell.

INTRODUCTION: THE IRISH IN ILLINOIS

William Byrne was an ambitious man. Born in Ireland, he came to the United States in 1812, settling down in Pittsburgh, where he met his wife, Sarah. Byrne became a contractor, hiring laborers to build the Chesapeake and Ohio Canal and other infrastructure projects in the rapidly expanding nation. Like so many Irish emigrants, the Byrnes followed the work west, eventually moving in 1837 to LaSalle County, Illinois, where Billy Byrne worked as a contractor on the Illinois and Michigan Canal. He was quite successful, building the largest log cabin in the Illinois Valley, near the confluence of the canal and the Illinois River. Byrne was determined to create a respectable community in LaSalle, which for him meant building a church, so he immediately set out to persuade Catholic leaders in St. Louis to send missionaries to the fledgling community. The initiative was successful, and Irish canal workers built the first Catholic church in the county the following year. Rebuilt and renamed after Ireland's patron saint in the late 1840s, St. Patrick's Parish Church currently is the oldest functioning parish church in the state of Illinois. Like the church they had helped found, the Byrnes remained in LaSalle, raising four children and playing an active role in the town's public life. William Byrne died in Chicago in 1873 at the age of 101. Illinois had become his home.[1]

Irish men and women played critical roles in the making of Illinois. They first came to the region in the eighteenth century, as soldiers in the British army and settlers in the state's first European communities. Irish immigration to the Prairie State increased dramatically in the nineteenth century, particularly after the Great Irish Famine of the late 1840s. By 1890, an estimated 278,729 Irish and Irish Americans lived in Illinois, the fourth-largest Irish population of any U.S. state. Many stayed. In 2010, 1.6 million Illinoisans described themselves as Irish, a good reflection of the cultural imprint that Irish men and women have made on the state. The Irish in contemporary Illinois are among the state's most affluent and best-educated residents. Nearly 72 percent owned their own homes, compared with a statewide average of just under 66 percent. Their median income stood just above $67,000, considerably more than the statewide median of $56,000. Exactly 40 percent of Irish Americans in Illinois age twenty-five and older held bachelor's degrees. This compares favorably with the state's average of a little more than 32 percent.[2]

The story of the Irish in Illinois thus is dominated by the gradual rise to relative success and respectability. This occurred unevenly and was by no means inevitable. Irish immigrants and their descendants have been involved in nearly every aspect of the state's history. They waged war against the state's indigenous peoples and fought against the British Empire in the Revolutionary War and against the Confederacy in the Civil War. They fought for the United States in two World Wars and in Korea, Vietnam, and Iraq. They farmed, dug canals, and peopled the state's growing communities. They founded churches, organized labor unions, and worked as teachers and police officers. They helped draft the state's first constitution, showing an aptitude for politics that quickly became an Irish hallmark. This was particularly true in Chicago, where Irish Americans created a political machine that dominated twentieth-century Illinois politics. As the Byrnes' story illustrates, however, Irish influence was not confined to the Windy City. If Irish communities in Bloomington, Champaign, East St. Louis, Rockford, Springfield, and the Quad Cities were too small to have the same political impact they had in Chicago, they played an outsize role across Illinois, retaining a powerful sense of ethnic solidarity expressed in the state's countless St. Patrick's Day festivals and parades. The Irish footprint in Illinois is a substantial one.

This is the first statewide history of the Irish in Illinois. Most of the excellent work that has been done on the history of the Irish in the state has focused on Chicago, an understandable emphasis, given its size and status as the quintessential American city. *The Irish in Illinois* takes a broader and longer view, detailing the critical roles played by eighteenth- and early nineteenth-century Irish immigrants in the settlement and creation of the Prairie State, as well as recounting the more familiar stories about working-class struggle and the rise of the political machine in twentieth-century Chicago. The book combines the insights of existing scholarship with original research, making particular use of often underutilized local histories. *The Irish in Illinois* is written in a narrative format and features short biographies that underscore both the human complexity and rich diversity of the Irish experience in Illinois. These accounts portray such diverse figures as James Shields, an army general and politician from Kaskaskia; Mary Harris (Mother Jones), the famed labor activist; and Liz Carroll, a successful fiddler and composer from the South Side of Chicago.[3]

If there is no single Irish story in Illinois, a number of common themes stand out. Historian David Emmons argues that Irish migrants had greater opportunities as they pushed west, where they were able to take advantage of cheap land and more fluid economic and political structures to obtain higher standards of living and improved social status. This was certainly the case in Illinois, where Irish men and women grasped their chances for advancement through the Catholic Church, the Democratic Party, and labor unions. These opportunities should not be romanticized; conflict and struggle were at the heart of the Irish experience in Illinois. Irish men and women often lived in poverty and faced the same racialized animosity as their fellow immigrants in Boston and New York, particularly in the second half of the nineteenth century. What is striking, however, is how effectively the Irish in Illinois used their numbers and the political opportunities afforded them to mobilize to effect change.[4]

By the early 1930s, Irish American politicians controlled municipal politics in Chicago and played leadership roles in Illinois communities from Rockford to Rock Island. Political control in Chicago was particularly important. Named mayor of Chicago in 1933, Edward Kelly was the first of five Irish American political bosses in that city, giving supporters access to jobs and resources that shielded them from the worst of the Great Depression and set them up for postwar success. On a broader level, the Irish rise to respectability and relative success in Illinois did not occur until after 1945. The Great Depression of the 1930s, along with the Hollywood films that captured its miseries, helped break down the once-potent ethnic and religious barriers that had separated Irish Catholics from Protestants and rival ethnic communities. Irish American service in World War II further eroded suspicions, and the GI Bill that followed the war provided new opportunities for improvement.

Simultaneously, the Chicago Irish took control of a political machine that dominated municipal politics until the late 1970s and helped elect the nation's first Catholic president, John F. Kennedy. Many continued to clash with African Americans over jobs and housing, but others went to college and gradually entered the professional classes. By the 1960s, they were moving to the suburbs, a shift fueled by both increased prosperity and racial anxiety. Despite fears of a postwar "ethnic fade," these communities have retained or reinvented their interest in their Irish heritage, a fact underlined by the popularity of cultural forms such as Irish dancing and traditional music, as well as St. Patrick's Day parades and Irish festivals across the state. "It's chic to be Irish," as one (admittedly Irish American) historian puts it.[5]

Although the Irish experience in Illinois is a predominantly Irish American story, it is one that is inextricably connected to Irish history. Modern Ireland's global diaspora is a direct legacy of colonial conquest and its economic and political impact on the island. Anglo-Normans invaded Ireland in the late twelfth century and established a measure of English control in an ever-shifting zone around Dublin. Irish society as a whole was transformed in the seventeenth century, when an expansionist English and Protestant state defeated its Irish and Catholic foes in three dramatic international conflicts: the Nine Years' War of 1594–1603, the Great Irish Rebellion and Cromwellian Reconquest in 1641–52, and the Williamite Wars of 1688–91. In the aftermath of each of these wars, land and power moved from Catholic to Protestant hands. By the time the Treaty of Limerick was signed in 1691, it was an English official, the lord lieutenant, who governed all of Ireland from Dublin Castle, and Protestant landlords owned nearly all Irish land. Between 1697 and 1750, the Irish Parliament, an all-Protestant body that had little independent authority from the British government, passed a number of Penal Laws to restrict Catholic economic, political, and religious power. While these laws failed to curtail the expansion of the Catholic Church in Ireland, the Penal Laws effectively restricted Catholic landed and political power. Perhaps their most powerful legacy, however, was the role they played in strengthening a powerful sense of Irish Catholic grievance against both British and Irish Protestant elites. This is something that Irish emigrants took with them to the New World.[6]

By formalizing Ireland's place within the British Empire and accelerating the island's entrance into a dynamic Atlantic economy, British conquest and colonization had yet another legacy in Ireland: emigration. Between fifty thousand and one hundred thousand people, mostly Irish Catholics, left Ireland for the American colonies in the seventeenth century. Little evidence has survived about these settlers, who seem to have been largely young, single males who blended into the general population. Irish emigration surged after 1700, with an estimated five hundred thousand men and women crossing the Atlantic for the American colonies in the eighteenth century. Roughly 75 percent of these were Presbyterians from Ulster, who left the northern province for better economic opportunities and greater political and religious liberties. While not as well known as the massive Irish emigration of the nineteenth century (an estimated 5.2 million people left Ireland for the United States between 1820 and 1920), eighteenth-century emigration had a huge impact on both Ireland and the American colonies. The 250,000 to 300,000 men and women who left Ulster amounted to roughly 50 percent of the population there. Many were recent emigrants from Scotland, settlers who found the rising rents of an Anglican-dominated Ireland less than congenial. Later they would be known as the Scots-Irish, a term that Protestant Irish Americans embraced only after Irish Catholic emigration increased dramatically in the 1830s and 1840s. In 1790, Irish men and women constituted roughly 14 to 17 percent of the white population in the fledgling United States. These new Irish Americans played a disproportionate part in the American Revolution, and in the radical politics of the early Republic, particularly after the failed Irish Rising of 1798.[7]

Much changed with the advent of the new century. Frustrated by the failure of the Irish Protestant elite to provide security and stability on the island, the British government successfully pressured the Irish Parliament into voting itself out of existence. In its stead, the British passed an Act of Union in 1800 that brought Ireland under more direct control from London. This made the British government the focus of Irish nationalist grievance, particularly after the Pitt government failed to pass a proposed measure giving Catholics full civil and political rights. Catholic Emancipation was only achieved in 1829, after Daniel O'Connell and the Catholic Association mobilized hundreds of thousands of Irish supporters in a massive public campaign. The lesson was clear:

British justice for Ireland could be achieved only through threat or revolt.

Patterns of emigration also shifted. Much of the change was rooted in the island's unprecedented population growth. In 1750, the Irish population was around 2.5 million; by the early 1840s, it had risen to nearly 8.5 million, an increase fostered by economic growth and the widespread use of the potato, which allowed Irish tenant farmers and laborers to live on small plots of land. Population growth put increasing pressure on an Irish land system that was ill suited to support the island's rural population; land and resources were poorly distributed, and poverty was widespread. After 1800, and particularly after 1820, it was increasingly Irish Catholics who immigrated to North America, aided by money sent by already established immigrant communities and cheaper transatlantic passages. Between 1815 and 1845, between eight hundred thousand and one million men, women, and children crossed the Atlantic. In his pioneering study of Irish emigration, Kerby Miller shows that it was more commercially oriented tenant farmers who left prefamine Ireland in an effort to maintain their independence and escape the poverty trap. Smallholders in the west of Ireland and other less modernized regions stayed, breaking up their farms into smaller and smaller fragments to support their children. In an argument that has been hotly contested, Miller maintains that these decisions were partially shaped by cultural ties to the land, as well as a lack of resources or incentives to leave.[8]

The Irish famine broke these connections, turning Ireland into a society that depended on substantial levels of emigration for its economic and political stability. Between 1845 and the early 1850s, partial or complete failures of the potato crop led to the death of a million people and the departure of nearly two million more for North America. The sheer inadequacy of the British response sharpened Irish nationalist sentiment, reinforcing the idea that emigrants had been exiled from their native Ireland. As the nationalist leader John Mitchel famously puts it in *The Last Conquest of Ireland (Perhaps)*: "The Almighty, indeed, sent the potato blight, but the English created the Famine." While few historians agree with this genocidal interpretation, Mitchel's emotional charge captured the anger at the heart of what one historian has termed the collective memory of the famine. This sense of anger reverberated across Irish emigrant communities, leading many to continue to fight for Irish freedom from British rule.[9]

Between 1856 and 1920, nearly 3.5 million Irish men and women left Ireland. Most went to the United States. By 1890, there were 5 million first- and second-generation Irish Americans—five hundred thousand more than lived in Ireland. It was these years that saw the creation of modern Irish America, a distinct ethnic community built through participation in the Catholic Church, the Democratic Party, labor unions, and Irish nationalist organizations such as Clan na Gael and the Ancient Order of Hibernians. Many were active supporters of nationalist causes in Ireland, providing funding and resources for the revolutionary politics of the Irish Republican Brotherhood, the Irish Land War and the campaign for Irish Home Rule in the late 1870s and 1880s, and the struggle for Irish independence from 1912 to 1922. But it was not only their support for Irish nationalism that made postfamine immigrants stand out. Irish women outnumbered their male counterparts—a unique feat among immigrants to America in this era. They took up positions in domestic service and teaching, with Irish women like Margaret Haley of Chicago leading the fight for improved pay and status for female teachers.[10]

Irish immigration to the United States slowed after 1920, curtailed by American legal restrictions and the creation of Northern Ireland and the Irish Free State. It resumed after World War II, with as many as two hundred thousand Irish coming to the United States from 1945 to the present, although undocumented and illegal immigration has undoubtedly distorted those numbers. The postwar years saw a dramatic increase in Irish American prosperity, as thousands took advantage of improved economic conditions and the GI Bill to firmly establish themselves in middle-class America. They continued to play an active role in Irish politics, particularly with the controversial declaration of the Irish Republic in 1949 and the onset of the Troubles in Northern Ireland in the late 1960s.[11]

The Irish American rise to success and respectability has not led to a loss of Irish identity. If anything, the popularity of Irish and Irish American cultural practices has surged since 1960, marked by countless St. Patrick's Day parades and Irish festivals of dance and music across Illinois. And yet for Irish Americans (and certainly those in Illinois), their greatest contributions lie not in their relative material success or cultural vitality, but in marking a path that other immigrants have followed. Ardent patriots, both Protestant and Catholic, the Irish of Illinois helped win the American

Revolution—and they defended the Union during the Civil War. As veterans, they won the admiration of their contemporaries. As immigrant patriots, they recruited and welcomed new waves of Irish to join them in the Prairie State. The Irish Catholics who followed, however, were regarded with far more suspicion than their predecessors, and it took longer for them to gain respectability in their new homeland. Nevertheless, they populated the cities and built the institutions that greeted new waves of immigrants from around the world. In Chicago, they forged the multiethnic political coalitions that ran one of the largest cities in America. To be sure, Irish Americans contributed to the racial divides that long have plagued the United States. But without the Irish, it is difficult to imagine how Illinois communities would have accepted, however unevenly, the immigrants who followed: Italians, Poles, Jews, Mexicans, Filipinos, and West Africans, to name but a few. In 2017, one of every seven people living in Illinois was an immigrant. This is the greatest legacy of the Irish in Illinois.[12]

1

FROM IMPERIAL SOLDIERS TO PRAIRIE PATRIOTS: THE IRISH IN THE ILLINOIS COUNTRY, 1750–1818

Somewhere between 250,000 and 500,000 men, women, and children left Ireland for America between 1700 and 1820. By 1790, the Irish made up 14 to 17 percent of the white population of the United States—the single largest group of European immigrants on the North American continent. They differed significantly from later waves of Irish immigrants: a majority were Protestant and disproportionately Presbyterian. Most came from the north of Ireland in search of affordable land and a greater measure of political and religious liberty, although approximately 100,000 Irish Catholics—almost all indentured servants—made the voyage as well. From the beginning, the Irish population in America was both substantial and diverse.[1]

Relatively few of these early immigrants came west to the Illinois Country, although they did play key roles in the history of the region. According to the census of 1800, Illinois had 2,458 residents, at least half of whom lived in villages along the Mississippi River south of St. Louis. This area later became known as the American Bottom, a thin stretch of old Mississippi floodplain that ran south from Alton to Kaskaskia and Chester. The Irish constituted a relatively small proportion of the soldiers and settlers who came to eighteenth-century Illinois. In terms of religion, some were Catholic, but more were Presbyterian and other Protestant denominations. The documented story of the Irish in Illinois during this period is in many ways a disparate collection of remarkable biographies. Many occupied positions of power and prestige. Irish political allegiances were fluid. Some served in the French army, administering the Upper Louisiana territory. Others fought for the British Empire, which acquired Illinois from the French after winning the Seven Years' War (1754–63). When the

American Revolution broke out, Irish patriots helped wrest the territory from British control. Following independence, the Irish were among the first Europeans to settle the Illinois Country. Irish Americans immediately got involved in state politics, helping draft the state's first constitution in 1818 and participating in contentious debates over slavery. The number of Irish men and women in early Illinois may have been small, but their impact was not.[2]

Serving Two Empires

The first Irishman recorded in Illinois history was Chevalier Charles MacCarthy, a French army officer and governor of Upper Louisiana. Born in Ireland in 1706, MacCarthy first appears in American records in New Orleans in 1731. His rise through the ranks of the French Empire makes him an American counterpart of the Wild Geese, Irish soldiers who fought for European armies from the sixteenth century. A number of contemporary accounts allow us to reconstruct his administrative and military career. MacCarthy was made commandant of the Illinois Country in 1751, governing from Fort de Chartres, roughly forty-five miles south of St. Louis on the Mississippi River. The Irish chevalier oversaw the fort's reconstruction in 1752, and the structure was later described by a British observer as "the best built fort in North America." He was known as MacCarthy McTaig (Irish for the son of Taig or Tadhg) or Barthelemy de Macarty-Mactigue and was the leading French civil and military administrator for the area from 1751 to 1760. The Franco-Irish leader maintained largely peaceful relations with nearby Illini, Miami, and Shawnee nations while protecting French settlements against potential attacks. Fort de Chartres brought a measure of stability to the immediate area, and the French settled several new villages, where the Jesuits built rudimentary churches and schools.[3]

French control of the Illinois Country, however, was coming to an end. MacCarthy's Illinois was perched on the western edge of the French and Indian War, the American front of the Seven Years' War. In 1758, the French abandoned Fort Duquesne, a crucial eastern frontier outpost at the confluence of the Allegheny, Monongahela, and Ohio Rivers. Together with British victories at Louisburg in Nova Scotia and at Fort Frontenac in what is now Ontario, the British capture of Fort Duquesne (rebuilt and renamed Fort Pitt) marked a turning point in the American theater of the Seven Years' War. Two years later, MacCarthy stepped down as commander of Fort de Chartres and focused his energies on administering the territory. France surrendered its North American claims to Britain at the Peace of Paris in 1763, and the Irish chevalier retired to Point Coupee in present-day Louisiana. In 1764, the French government conferred on him the Cross of St. Louis "as a reward for his fidelity and services." He died shortly thereafter.[4]

When the French handed over their Mississippi Valley possessions to the British Empire in 1763, Irish soldiers paved the way. The first of these, ordered to take possession of Fort de Chartres, were members of Britain's 22nd Infantry Regiment. Before they could reach the Illinois Country, however, a band of Tunica warriors ambushed and killed many of them along the Mississippi River several hundred miles north of New Orleans. British relations with indigenous peoples quickly deteriorated. The renowned Ottawa war chief Pontiac led the resistance to British rule, putting together a coalition of tribes from the Illinois and Ohio Countries, including Potawatomi, Kickapoo, Miami, Shawnee, and others. In military terms, Pontiac's War was essentially a stalemate, as Pontiac and his allies failed to drive the British from their lands. At the same time, British forces could not conquer their tribal foes.[5]

Attempting to bring a diplomatic end to the conflict in 1765, British administrators called on Irish diplomats to negotiate with Pontiac and secure passage to Fort de Chartres. The first of these was an experienced public servant, trader, and negotiator named George Croghan, a forty-seven-year-old native of County Sligo, Ireland, who immigrated to America in 1741. During the 1740s and 1750s, Croghan managed the often-contentious relations between settlers and indigenous peoples for the Council of Pennsylvania in the western reaches of the colony. He married a Mohawk woman, and they had a daughter. Croghan also used his position to his own economic advantage, developing a profitable fur trade with a number of other Irish merchants. This came to an end with the onset of the French and Indian War in 1754, when British authorities viewed Irish traders as potential French sympathizers. Croghan soon resigned from his position.[6]

It was another Irishman, the famed Indian agent Sir William Johnson, who rescued his career, naming Croghan as deputy agent for the Allegheny and Susquehanna nations in 1756. A native of

County Meath, Johnson descended from a long line of Irish Catholic dignitaries, although he had been raised Protestant to ensure his upward mobility in the British Empire. At the age of twenty-three, he immigrated to North America and settled in New York. Johnson soon established himself as a prominent fur trader in the Mohawk Valley, where he acquired a reputation as a fair-minded merchant and Mohawk ally. For nearly a decade, Johnson and Croghan successfully navigated the multiethnic Great Lakes region, known to contemporaries as the French *pay d'en haut* and later described by historian Richard White as the "middle ground," a place where Europeans and indigenous peoples forged cultural alliances as much as they fought one another. By 1765, the reputations of these Irishmen preceded them. Johnson had recently negotiated the Fort Niagara Treaty, and Croghan was recognized by British officials as "the fittest person in America" to negotiate an end to the hostilities with Pontiac.[7]

In the spring of 1765, at Johnson's behest, Croghan led a contingent of soldiers and Shawnee diplomats westward from Fort Pitt. In June, they were attacked in present-day Indiana by a band of eighty Kickapoo and Mascouten warriors, who had misidentified Croghan's indigenous escorts as rival Cherokees. Two British soldiers and three Shawnee chiefs were killed. Croghan was hit in the skull by a tomahawk, and all were captured. The attack, however, proved to be a stroke of luck for Croghan. By mistakenly killing Shawnee chiefs, the Kickapoo and Mascouten tribes risked war with their powerful allies in the Ohio Country. They desperately needed the Irishman to intervene. Upon recognizing their mistake—and accepting a bribe of sixty-four gallons of rum—the captors treated their prisoners' wounds and begged Croghan's forgiveness. The veteran envoy conceded, but not before insisting on a meeting with his "old acquaintance" Pontiac.[8]

Croghan's efforts succeeded, but they also marked the beginning of the end of the "middle ground." In July, he met with the Ottawa war chief at Fort Ouiatenon near the present city of Lafayette, Indiana. There he initiated negotiations that eventually secured the peaceful possession of de Chartres and the entire Illinois Country. According to Croghan's journal, the fear of Shawnee reprisal, as well as his own rapport with Pontiac—who commanded "more respect amongst those Nations, than any Indian . . . could do amongst his own Tribe"—ensured a negotiated end to the conflict. Yet with the American Revolution, in which Croghan became an ardent patriot, the tribes of the Great Lakes Region declined in the face of expansion. Americans had little interest in establishing a new middle ground after securing independence. Tecumseh's defeat during the War of 1812 eventually brought about its end, and the Black Hawk War of 1832 in Illinois was but a lingering wisp of the age. According to Croghan's foremost biographer, Nicholas B. Wainwright, the Irishman should be remembered as a symbol of the American West during the colonial

William Croghan and Lucy Clark Croghan in portraits by John Wesley Jarvis.
Courtesy of Historic Locust Grove, Inc., Louisville, Kentucky.

William Croghan (1752–1822), and Lucy Clark Croghan (1764–1838)

George Croghan encouraged family members to emigrate from Ireland to North America. His nephew William Croghan, born in Dublin in 1752, left home at the age of sixteen and became a merchant in New York with his uncle's assistance. When the American Revolution broke out, William supported the patriot cause. He enlisted with the 8th Virginia Regiment and later served under George Washington. At Valley Forge, he was promoted to the rank of major. Captured by British forces in South Carolina, Croghan met Jonathan Clark, brother of George Rogers Clark, with whom he was later assigned the task of surveying portions of the Illinois Country. Croghan received payment for his services in land deeds and eventually settled near Louisville, Kentucky, where he met his future wife, Lucy Clark, a Virginia native. It was her brothers who introduced her to William Croghan, whom she married on July 14, 1789. The couple founded an estate outside of Louisville named Locust Grove, where they raised eight children. William died in 1822, and Lucy died in 1838.[9]

period: "It was he who pacified Pontiac. He was tomahawked, shipwrecked, alternately rich and poor, despised and praised, rejected and sought after. He walked with the great and humble of his day. He forcibly expressed the democratic spirit which was to be America." Yet one also might remember George Croghan as a harbinger of darker days for indigenous tribes—and among the last of those wilderness diplomats of the middle ground.[10]

The American Revolution

If Irish diplomats and soldiers secured the Illinois Country for the British Empire, Irish patriots played an integral role in acquiring the territory for the United States during the American Revolutionary War. British efforts to create postwar stability in the American West failed, creating problems and resentments that played a critical role in the onset of the American Revolution. In 1763, the British government issued a royal proclamation prohibiting settlement west of the Appalachians. Settlers largely ignored the edict, flooding into the Ohio River Valley. Relatively few came to Illinois, however, and the British reduced their military presence in the Illinois Country. Fort de Chartres was abandoned and destroyed in 1772, with troops moving to Fort Gage near Kaskaskia. When hostilities broke out in 1775, the fighting was largely confined to the East, having relatively little impact on life in the American Bottom.

Yet Illinois was not entirely forgotten. Many Americans had a keen understanding of the importance of western land and resources, and they made efforts to secure the region from both the British and indigenous tribes. Conflict there intensified dramatically in 1777, as the British commander at Fort Detroit, Lieutenant Colonel Henry Hamilton, encouraged the Shawnee and other tribes of the Ohio Valley to raid American settlements. An Irish native, Hamilton was known by his opponents as the "Hair Buyer General" because he purchased white scalps. Warfare in Kentucky, known to indigenous tribes as the "Dark and Bloody Ground," had been so vicious that at one point in 1777, only eighty-one riflemen could be mustered in Kentucky's defense.[11]

A young Virginian named George Rogers Clark pitched an idea to Governor Patrick Henry to break this stalemate: invade key British outposts in the Illinois Country and then take Detroit, thus preventing further attacks on vulnerable western settlements. As an officer in the colonial militia, Clark had led a successful effort to make Kentucky part of Virginia in the years immediately before the revolution. He was also well connected. Obtaining funding from an Irish Catholic financier in New Orleans named Oliver Pollock, Clark managed to persuade the Virginia governor. In June 1778, George Rogers Clark and roughly 175 volunteers, perhaps half of whom were Irish by birth or blood, crossed the Ohio River near Louisville. The first phase of the expedition succeeded in dramatic fashion. On July 4, Clark's forces captured Fort Kaskaskia along the Mississippi River without firing a shot. Three days later, they took Cahokia. The following month, they turned eastward and captured Vincennes along the Wabash River—again without bloodshed. British forces under Hamilton recaptured Vincennes in December, but Clark and his men retook the fort in a surprise winter assault two months later. Clark never took Detroit, but his victories in the Illinois Country gave the United States leverage in the negotiations that followed. In 1783 at the Treaty of Paris, Britain formally recognized American independence and ceded the Northwest Territory to the new nation.[12]

George Rogers Clark later commended several Irishmen who served in his campaign for their bravery. Among those officers recognized were Major Thomas Quirk, Captain John Montgomery, Captain Richard McCarthy, Lieutenant Martin Carney, and Lieutenant Thomas Dalton. Enlisted men of the expedition each received 108 acres of Illinois land for their services, and many of these had decidedly Irish surnames: Lyne, Mahoney, Manifee, Marr, Martin, McDermott, McDonald, McGar, McMannus, McMullen, McNutt, Moore, Murphy, and Murray, among others. Given the small number of combatants at Clark's disposal, it seems reasonable to suggest that Irish volunteers played a conspicuous role in the Illinois campaign. One prominent Clark biographer certainly believed so: "Had it not been for the Irish in Clark's command," William H. English later commented, "the latter would never have whipped the British and the Indians."[13]

Although few documented Irishmen lived in the Illinois Country before the Revolution, migrants began to trickle in during the conflict. Almost all settled in the American Bottom. They came from poor and disadvantaged backgrounds. Most avidly supported the American cause, and many participated in Clark's northwestern campaigns. One such figure was Thomas Brady, a Cahokia resident who led a small contingent of sixteen volunteers in October 1777 against Fort St. Joseph, a British trading post along the southeastern rim of Lake Michigan. The party was initially successful, overwhelming the fort's defenders and decamping with a large quantity of goods—valued at perhaps as much as $50,000. The victory proved fleeting, however, as several British officers and about one hundred Potawatomies regrouped and overcame Brady's expedition near the present city of Chicago. Two of his men were killed and two others wounded. Brady and roughly a dozen men were captured, although the Irishman later escaped to support George Rogers Clark the following year. Another Irish volunteer was Richard McCarty, a Franco-Irish captain from Cahokia who joined Clark's 1779 winter campaign to retake Vincennes. He and his comrades endured, as Governor John Reynolds put it three quarters of a century later, "the fatigues and perils of the campaign . . . thro high water and ice; and almost in a starving condition."[14]

Other, lesser-known Irish veterans of the Revolution played key roles in the making of an American Illinois. In 1779, a Virginian named John Todd—whose parents, David Todd and Hannah Owen Todd, had emigrated from Ireland—arrived in Kaskaskia to organize the Illinois Country. Commissioned by Patrick Henry to take the position of lieutenant colonel and civil commandant of the Illinois Country, he established the first county governments in the state. Among the first to promote statehood in the territory, Todd later died at the Battle of Blue Licks in 1782, near Mount Olivet, Kentucky. He is better remembered as the distant uncle of Mary Todd Lincoln, wife of Abraham Lincoln. John Doyle, a schoolmaster who served under George Rogers Clark, established a settlement east of Kaskaskia in 1780. John Dobbin, a former hired hand and veteran of the Battle of Bunker Hill, joined him there—as did families by the names of Anderson, Camp, Curry, Dodge, Hughes, Montgomery, Pickett, Seybold, and Tiel. Others soon followed.[15]

Settling an American Illinois

Following independence, the U.S. Congress began organizing the Illinois Country into a governable territory. It passed the Northwest Ordinance of 1787 to stave off competition among states vying for control of the region. It established a system of survey and appointed Arthur St. Clair as the first governor. It prohibited slavery. Five states—Ohio, Indiana, Illinois, Michigan, and Wisconsin—were eventually carved out of the territory. The U.S. Congress also funded the Northwest Indian War, which raged across the region after the Revolution for more than a decade, as indigenous tribes resisted Britain's illegitimate concession of their ancestral lands at the Treaty of Paris. In 1794, General "Mad Anthony" Wayne defeated a coalition of Miami, Shawnee, and Delaware warriors at the Battle of Fallen Timbers near present-day Toledo. The ensuing Treaty of Greenville awarded lands as far west as present-day Chicago and Peoria. More settlers headed west.[16]

The Irish migration, which had begun as a trickle, turned into a stream. It is unclear how many arrived before Illinois became a territory in 1809, but the United States Census of 1810 counted a grand total of 12,282 residents—a fivefold increase since 1800. Undoubtedly, hundreds if not thousands of these were of Irish stock. Most Irish, like most migrants, continued to settle in the American Bottom. Many served as judges and politicians, thus presaging future generations of Irish Illinoisans in politics. Others founded new communities and religious institutions. Some succeeded in business. For those individuals recorded to history, it is clear that they made important contributions to the political, economic, and cultural foundations of early Illinois.[17]

The most prominent Irishman of the era was General John Edgar. A former officer in the British navy, this Catholic immigrant was persuaded by his wife to promote the American cause secretly among the king's soldiers during the Revolution. Edgar was eventually discovered, and the couple relocated to Kaskaskia in 1784. For many years, he was the wealthiest man in Illinois, with as many as nineteen people—including twelve free persons of color and two slaves—residing on his Randolph County estate. Later described by Governor Reynolds as "intelligent," as well as "large and portly," Edgar made his fortune partly through fraudulent land deals. Civil cases against him dragged out in the courts for years. Ironically, he served as chief justice for the Illinois Territory in the 1790s and as a judge for the Court of Common Pleas and justice of the peace for Randolph County. He stands out in retrospect among the first in a long line of colorful Irish politicians in the Prairie State. Edgar County is named for the general.[18]

Others of Irish descent contributed to the development of Kaskaskia, which served as the territory's capital until 1819. Among these were James Lemen Sr., who, along with his wife, Catherine Ogle, and their eldest son, Robert, survived a perilous journey to the fledgling capital in 1786. James Lemen's grandfather had emigrated from Ulster to Virginia earlier in the century. His father was Episcopalian, but James was raised a Presbyterian. He served under Washington during the Revolution and traveled westward after the war. In 1814, the Lemens and a handful of other residents organized the community's first Bible Society. Another family, the Whitesides, relocated from Kentucky to a settlement near Kaskaskia in 1793. Governor Reynolds remembered them as inheritors of "the Irish character," meaning "warm-hearted, impulsive, and patriotic." Two brothers, William and John, were veterans of the Revolution, the former having served at King's Mountain. In Illinois, the Whitesides battled hostile Kickapoos, until peace was made throughout the Old Northwest in 1795. William also served as justice of the peace, judge for the Court of Common Pleas, and again as a colonel in the U.S. Army during the War of 1812.[19]

In the late eighteenth century, Irish men and women pursued commercial opportunities in the American Bottom. In 1797, a son of Irish immigrants and native of Virginia named William Scott established a new settlement in present-day St. Clair County at a

Major John Whistler. B. J. Griswold, *The Pictorial History of Fort Wayne, Indiana* (Chicago: Robert O. Law Company, 1917), 1:233.

Major John Whistler (ca. 1756–1829)

John Whistler, an Irishman by birth who remained loyal to the Crown during the American Revolution, immigrated to the United States in 1790 following his elopement with Ann Bishop. The couple settled in Hagerstown, Maryland, where John enlisted in the U.S. Army. He served in the Northwest Indian War, fighting at the Battle of Fallen Timbers in 1794. Meanwhile, Ann, described by one historian as "a woman of rare charm and force of character," relocated to Fort Wayne, Indiana, where she gave birth to the first of the couple's fifteen children. In 1803, Whistler was recommissioned to the Illinois Territory, where he established Fort Dearborn (later Chicago) at the mouth of the Chicago River. According to the late historian John P. McGoorty, Whistler—not the notorious murderer John Kinzie—should rightly be regarded as "the real father of Chicago." Ann and John Whistler moved to St. Louis in 1816. John died in 1829.[20]

place called Turkey Hill. Following in the paths of successful French merchants, Scott and his family achieved a measure of prosperity by trading with the nearby Kickapoo tribe. Scott later served on the commission to select the county seat of St. Clair, and Turkey Hill became an important colony in southwestern Illinois.[21]

Perhaps the most renowned political family to settle in Illinois in this era was that of Vermont congressman Matthew Lyon. A native of Ireland, veteran of the American Revolution, and staunch Jeffersonian, Lyon abhorred John Adams and the Federalist Party. In 1798, he had been imprisoned under the Alien and Sedition Acts, which extended the waiting period for naturalization from five to fourteen years and made it illegal to defame the government. Framed as a national security measure, the laws were primarily political, as Federalists feared that new immigrants (including the Irish) would back Jefferson's Republicans. These fears proved to be well founded. In 1798, while still in prison, Lyon was elected to the House of Representatives. Around the turn of the century, he and his family moved to Kentucky, where Lyon further served multiple terms in Congress. In 1802, his daughters and their husbands continued on to the Illinois Country, where his sons-in-law John Messinger and Dr. George Cadwell became a prominent legislator and judge, respectively. Irish politics in Illinois had deep roots.[22]

Settling the Illinois Territory

As thousands of migrants headed west during the early nineteenth century, Illinois politicians began pressing Congress for territorial autonomy. John Edgar clashed with Governor William Henry Harrison, accusing him of ignoring western interests. Land prices remained too high, as most could not afford the set price of $2 per acre. Speculation ran rampant. Some residents lobbied to repeal the prohibition of slavery, while others demanded that it remain firmly in place. When Congress approved the Louisiana Purchase in 1803, which more than doubled the size of the republic, Edgar and other prominent individuals began to organize. In 1805, 1806, and 1808, residents petitioned Congress to create a separate entity. On March 1, 1809, the Illinois Territory was born.[23]

At the same time, the promise of available land, the capitulation of hostile tribes, and the opportunity to begin anew beckoned even more Irish immigrants westward. New settlements were created across the territory. In 1802, a thriving Irish community cropped up east of the Kaskaskia River in Randolph County. Settlers named it Plum Creek. Its population hailed primarily from Abbeville, South Carolina. The founder of this largely Presbyterian settlement, James Patterson, had Irish immigrant parents, and his father had served under Washington during the Revolution. Over forty families of the South Carolina Irish, as they came to be known, settled at Plum Creek. These included families with names such as Anderson, Couch, Cox, Erwin, McBride, McDonald, Miller, and Thompson. In 1805, Samuel O'Melvany pioneered a new settlement in present-day Pope County along the Ohio River. O'Melvany had emigrated from Ireland in 1798, and his parents and siblings followed the next year. A successful farmer and dealer of hogs and corn, O'Melvany went on to represent Pope County at the Illinois State Convention of 1818.[24]

Irish educators were a common sight in the American Bottom. Students at Plum Creek studied under an Irish schoolmaster named Halfpenny. The only teacher in the region for years, Halfpenny was later remembered as the earliest "school-master general of Illinois." Another educator by the name of William Bradsby, whose father had emigrated from Ireland in the eighteenth century, came to the Illinois Country in 1804. For years, he taught throughout the region, including at Turkey Hill. A relative of the Bradsbys named Thomas Higgins, ironically remembered as having "not much love for a schoolhouse," came to St. Clair County in 1807. He later made his mark during the War of 1812 as an "Indian fighter." Higgins eventually moved to Fayette County, where he and his wife raised a large family. In 1808, another Irish-born teacher, an immigrant by the name of William Mears, moved to Cahokia from Philadelphia. Of humble origins and possessing few material goods, he had a strong mind and a potent memory. Mears pursued a career in law, later married, and in 1814 accepted an appointment as the attorney general of the Illinois Territory.[25]

Talented and educated Irish women settled in the American Bottom. In 1805, Eliza Lowry of Baltimore accompanied her brother Colonel Donaldson to St. Louis, where he had been commissioned to investigate land titles in the West. Of Irish ancestry, Lowry possessed, in the words of the late historian P. T. Barry, "a mind gifted with originality, imagination, and romance." She wrote poetry, commented on politics, and contributed to scientific publications. She also deeply contemplated her faith. Lowry was at one time a Presbyterian, but "on further research and much reflection," she joined the Roman Catholic Church, becoming "a very warm and zealous member." In 1806, Eliza married Robert Morrison, an up-and-coming Kaskaskia politician whose father had emigrated from County Cork during the 1790s. The wedding was held at the estate of a wealthy fellow Irish Catholic, John Edgar. The Morrisons had three sons, all of whom became notable lawyers. One of them, James Lowry Donaldson Morrison, went on to serve with distinction in the Mexican-American War and as a member of the Illinois House and Senate. Throughout the nineteenth century, the family achieved a reputation for being "one of the best known politically and socially in the state."[26]

Ambitious Irish Americans continued to move west, founding new communities and serving in public office after Illinois was officially organized into a territory in 1809. Thomas Forsyth, whose father, Robert, was Irish, had been imprisoned with John Edgar in Detroit during the early years of the Revolution because of his sympathy for the American cause. Forsyth relocated to Peoria in 1809, where he became a "founder and leading citizen" of the community. Dr. John Logan, a native of Ireland, came to southern Illinois during the early 1800s and settled along the Big Muddy River. He later married Elizabeth Jenkins, sister of Alexander M. Jenkins, a lawyer who was later elected lieutenant governor of Illinois in 1834. The Logans had eleven children, including John A. Logan, who went on to serve in Congress and the U.S. Senate and was an unsuccessful candidate for vice president in 1884. Another Irish American by the name of Zadok Casey, whose father had emigrated from County Tyrone in the mid-eighteenth century and fought under Francis Marion during the Revolution, settled in present-day Jefferson County in 1817. He later served Illinois as a congressman and was elected lieutenant governor in 1830.[27]

The War of 1812: Forge of Future Irish Governors

Illinois residents saw comparatively little action during the War of 1812, but the violence could nevertheless be brutal. Nationalism was on the rise, and many westerners no doubt supported President Madison's war. The British navy had long been guilty of kidnapping American sailors on the high seas, while Shawnee warriors had renewed their attacks on settlements in the Ohio Valley. In the Illinois territory, the indigenous population continued to outnumber whites by a ratio of ten to one. Potawatomi, Kickapoo, and Winnebago warriors raided settlements across the territory.

On August 15, 1812, hostile tribes ambushed and killed more than seventy men, women, and children evacuating Fort Dearborn, the site of present-day Chicago. Terror spread. Many white residents sought revenge and formed a militia in hopes of ridding the territory entirely of its native inhabitants—part of a process scholars have labeled "settler colonialism." The militia devolved into a mob, razing Miami and Kickapoo villages near Springfield and Peoria. The territorial government offered bounties for captured or killed warriors. Still, expeditions against Sauk and Fox strongholds near Rock Island failed, just as the country at large had failed to defeat British Canadian forces. Americans stood by helplessly as Redcoats ransacked and burned the White House in August 1814. Only Andrew Jackson's victory over British forces at New Orleans on January 8, 1815, fought two weeks after the War of 1812 officially ended and peace had been concluded, seemed to restore a sense of national pride.[28]

While the war spurred a renewed sense of patriotism among Americans in the Illinois Territory, it also reminded potential migrants of the risks in settling there. As Governor Reynolds later remembered, "In the war of 1812, the exposed situation of the country, the weakness of the population, and the strength of the Indian enemy brought into actual operation the whole capacities of the country, physical and mental, for its defence." Between the onset of the war and statehood in 1818, the population according to one federal count increased to a paltry 34,620—less than one-quarter that of neighboring Indiana. Yet for those stalwart pioneers who had defended the Illinois Territory during the War of 1812, political futures awaited. Two prominent Irishmen stood among them.[29]

The first of Illinois's future Irish governors forged in the War of 1812 was Pennsylvania native John Reynolds. John was born in 1788 to Irish immigrants Robert Reynolds and Margaret Moore, who were from County Monaghan and County Louth, respectively. Young John's father "caught the mania" to move to the "Far-West" in 1800. Concerned that Spanish law would require them to raise their children Catholic, they set their sights on the American Bottom. Decades later, John Reynolds recalled the journey: "Our traveling caravan consisted of my two parents, six children (I the oldest), one negro woman, three hired men, eight horses, two wagons, and the appropriate number of dogs for a new country." Hunger, severe weather, flooding, and privation plagued

Governor John Reynolds. *McClure's Magazine*, January 1896.

them throughout their "dreary and desolate journey," in which they crossed over one hundred miles of "wilderness" before reaching Kaskaskia. Reynolds was astonished by his new environs when they arrived. He recalled seeing buffalo, members of the Illini Confederation outnumbering white settlers two to one, and French-speaking residents who "did not consider themselves *dans l'Amerique*, as they termed it."

The Reynoldses were proudly Irish and ardent American patriots. Robert Reynolds, as his son later put it, "was a great admirer of Jefferson and hated the government of Great Britain with a ten-horse power." "I never saw any man," John declared, "who loved the government of the United States more than he did." Presumably, John Reynolds adopted his father's love and appreciation for American politics. After his family moved in 1807 to the "Goshen Settlement," some four miles south of Edwardsville, he immersed himself in classical studies and became a lawyer. When the War of 1812 broke out, John served as a U.S. ranger, fighting against the Sauk, Fox, and Kickapoo tribes. It was here that Reynolds acquired the epithet "Old Ranger." And it was here that he began his political career.[30]

After the war ended, Reynolds served on the Illinois Supreme Court in 1818 and was elected to the Illinois House of Representatives in 1826. He served as the Prairie State's fourth governor from 1830 to 1834. While in office, he commanded the state militia during the Black Hawk War. A Democrat and supporter of Andrew Jackson, Reynolds represented his home state in Congress from 1834 to 1837. He thereafter returned to the Illinois House and eventually took up newspaper work. In 1852, he published *The Pioneer History of Illinois*, an immensely valuable record of the state's early years. During the election of 1860, he favored Douglass over Lincoln. And he remained a Democrat through the Civil War. According to one biographer, Reynolds "evinced a clear sympathy for the Southern secession." Despite having been married twice, John Reynolds died childless in 1865.[31]

The state's second Irish governor, Democrat Thomas Carlin, also had served in the War of 1812. Just one year before the conflict, the twenty-two-year-old Carlin left his home in Kentucky for the Illinois Territory. His parents were both "of Irish extraction" and poor, and young Thomas arrived with little means. The war brought him recognition and opportunity for advancement. He made a name for himself fighting hostile Potawatomies and Kickapoos under Governor Edwards in the Lake Peoria campaign. At the war's end, he married Rebecca Huitt of Madison County. The following year, they moved to Greene County, where the Carlins raised a "large and respectable family." His record as a veteran and reputation as an "Indian fighter" proved to be a political asset. Carlin went on to become the first sheriff of Greene County, serve in the Illinois Senate, command a battalion during the Black Hawk War, and accept an appointment from Andrew Jackson as receiver of public moneys. In 1838, he was elected the seventh governor of Illinois, presiding in the wake of the country's worst financial panic and overseeing the relocation of the state capital to Springfield. Thomas Carlin lost his final electoral race against Stephen Douglas in 1844. He died in 1852.[32]

For Reynolds and Carlin, service in the War of 1812 helped advance their political careers, just as the military records of future generations assisted Irish politicians. Both governors were proudly American and unabashedly Irish. Both were Democrats. Neither had to contend with the xenophobic vitriol that later generations of Irish immigrants did in the mid-nineteenth century. Just the same, Illinois politics eventually rewarded those Irishmen whose service had protected the territory's isolated populations during the war. A long line of Irish prairie politicians followed.

Irish Culture and Folklore in Illinois's Egypt

Nearly all the Irish men and women who came to the Illinois Territory prior to statehood settled in Egypt, an early nickname for the lower third of Illinois. Cities and towns in the region were also given Egyptian place names, such as Cairo and Thebes. According to historian Roger Biles, over 70 percent of these migrants came from Kentucky, Tennessee, Maryland, Virginia, the Carolinas, and Georgia. More often Presbyterian than Catholic, they have often been remembered as Scotch-Irish or Scots-Irish. Yet contemporaries rarely if ever referred to them as anything other than Irish. This continues to be the case today. Even in the 2010 census, where Scotch-Irish was a choice, Illinoisans routinely described themselves as Irish. Southern Illinois still has the counties with

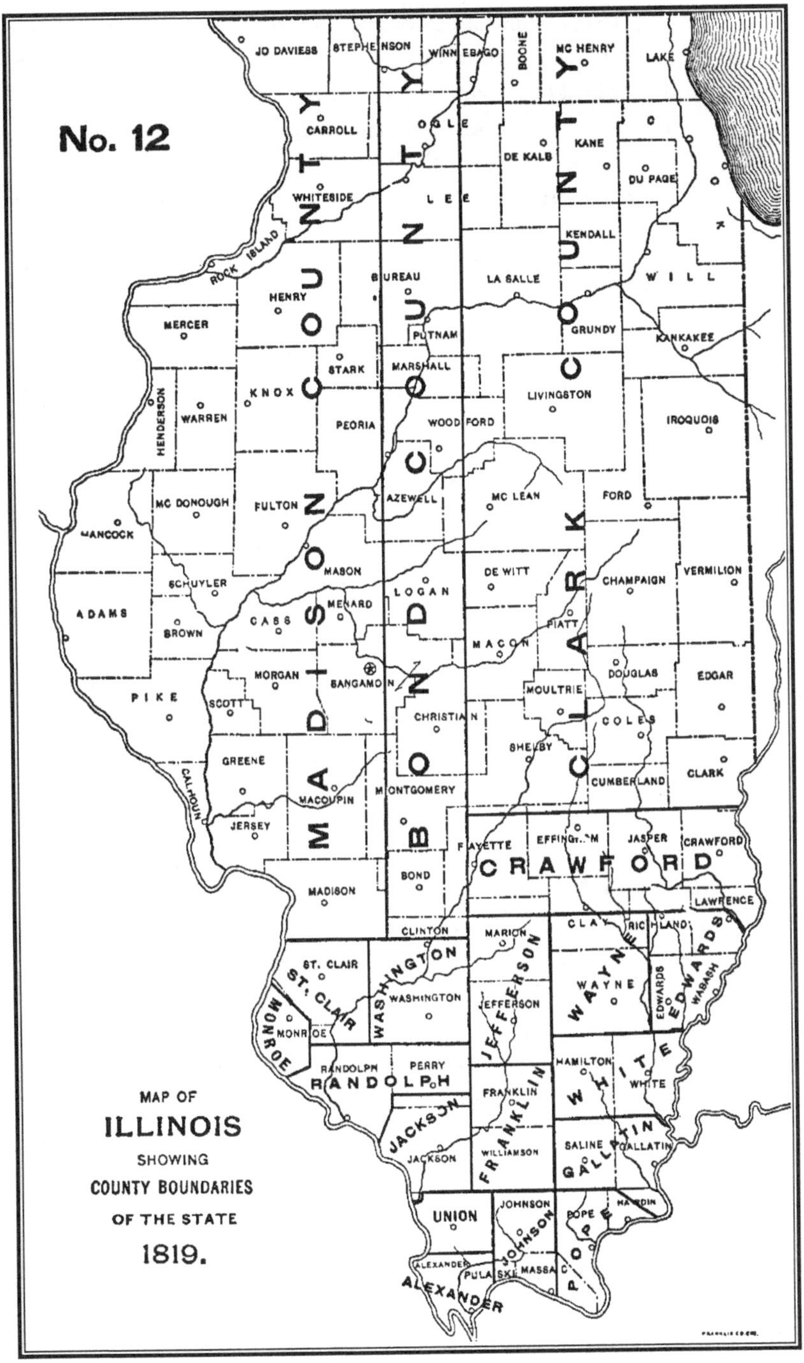

Map of Illinois counties, 1819. Illinois Office of Secretary of State, *Counties of Illinois: Their Origin and Evolution* (Springfield: Illinois State Journal, 1919).

the highest concentrations of Irish Americans in the Prairie State: Pope (19 percent), Hamilton (20.7 percent), Gallatin (23.7 percent), and Hardin (27 percent).[33]

Early nineteenth-century Irish immigrants brought music, stories, and folk customs with them that in some ways have endured. Their music, in particular, could be heard throughout the region. John Reynolds remembered a tune called "Willy Reilly"—a song about tragedy, forbidden love, and exile—as the most popular of its day. Often, he recalled, it "was sung so loud that it could be heard to a considerable distance." Other ballads, such as "The Hold-Up," "Peg's Spinning-Wheel Song," "St. Patrick's Day Parade," and "Brennan on the Moor," were popular during this period in Illinois. Many of these songs addressed issues of justice and revolution. Willie Brennan, for example, was a fabled highwayman who faced the gallows for robbing an unjust mayor of his gold. The Irish of "St. Patrick's Day Parade" donned green cockades and green neckties, symbols of Irish nationalism and independence.

Most songs expressed loss—unsurprising, given the fact that many had fought in, or at least lived through, the American Revolution or Ireland's failed Rebellion of 1798. As John Reynolds put it, "It must be recollected that these times were but a few years after the Revolution, and all the transactions of that terrible conflict were fresh in the minds." During the 1940s, folklorists traced the popularity of these and other tunes throughout the southwestern reaches of the Illinois Country, including St. Clair, Randolph, Monroe, and Jackson Counties. They concluded that all the songs predated the vast Catholic Irish migrations of the 1840s, and many were popular in the early nineteenth century, substantiating Reynolds's account. The continuity of these Irish ballads and others later helped bridge the generational and religious gaps that separated immigrants of the 1840s from those Irish Americans whose families had immigrated earlier.[34]

Irish tales and customs introduced during this period have long persisted in southern Illinois. According to the late historian John W. Allen, St. Patrick's Day has had a particularly mystical appeal. Well into the twentieth century, residents held that sweet peas and Irish potatoes grew most bountifully if planted on March 17. Others claim on dreary nights to have heard the wail of the banshee—a female spirit in Irish folklore whose "keening" portends the death of a loved one. Among the people of

Lamb, an unincorporated community located at the Prairie State's southeastern tip, the banshee's scream has been heard since the earliest days of the Illinois Territory. In 1811, Irishman Hugh McConnell and his wife immigrated to Hardin County, where they started a family. Both had been visited by the banshee in Ireland, after Hugh witnessed a young girl burn to death in a church. The spirit, they claimed, followed them to Illinois, where one of the McConnell's daughters married a man named Brown and later claimed to hear the banshee's cry whenever there was a death in the family. In her twilight years, "Old Granny" Brown allegedly saw the banshee with her own eyes. According to legend, she died fighting it off in her bed. Tales of the banshee of Lamb continue to captivate audiences today.[35]

Irish Liberty, Illinois Statehood, and the Question of Race

In many ways, Illinois was made for the Irish—at least, several prominent early nineteenth-century Irish immigrants believed as much. Following the American Revolution, ordinary people throughout the Atlantic World—from France to Haiti to Latin America—attempted to throw off the yoke of oppression. Ireland witnessed a similar rebellion in 1798, when the Society of United Irishmen, a revolutionary organization dedicated to creating an independent Irish republic, rose up in an effort to win independence from the British Empire. Irish men and women of all denominations and stations joined forces in a poorly coordinated and ultimately failed uprising. As many as thirty thousand died. Leaders of the United Irishmen, as well as rank-and-file participants in the rebellion, were exiled or fled their homeland. During the 1790s alone, some sixty thousand immigrated to America, while thousands more followed in the early 1800s.

In the United States, sympathetic countrymen and women, as well as some native-born Americans, established benevolent societies to help new immigrants begin their lives in the young republic. In 1816, relief associations in New York, Philadelphia, Baltimore, and Pittsburgh petitioned Congress asking that a section of the Illinois Territory "be set apart for the purpose of being settled by emigrants from Ireland, to whom it is requested the lands may be sold on an extended credit." As historian David Wilson notes, this venture "was very much a United Irish affair." Congress rejected the measure by twelve votes in 1818, but the seeds of generational migration had already been sown. In subsequent years, Illinois became the premier destination for Irish immigrants with their sights set on the American West.[36]

On August 3, 1818, thirty-three delegates convened in Kaskaskia to organize the Illinois Territory into a state and draft a constitution. Residents from fifteen counties selected electors from a variety of occupations: three physicians, three attorneys, two peace officers, a land official, a minister, and several farmers and laborers. Of these delegates, at least three were Irish or came from Irish families. The aforementioned Samuel O'Melvany, a 1798 exile and now county treasurer, represented Pope County. James Lemen Jr., a Baptist minister who was the great-grandson of Ulster emigrants, was elected as a member of the St. Clair delegation. And John Messinger, a surveyor whose immigrant father-in-law, Matthew Lyon, had been imprisoned under the Alien and Sedition Acts, likewise represented St. Clair County.

The proceedings ran smoothly—at least, until the topic of slavery was introduced. Although the Northwest Ordinance of 1787 had expressly prohibited the institution, French merchants had been using slave labor in the region for nearly one hundred years. Neither the British nor the Americans who followed protested its existence, in large part because slave labor was used in salt manufacture near Shawneetown. With the issue before the convention, three factions emerged: one strongly in favor of slavery, one strongly opposed, and one "more numerous class," as Carpenter and Kitchell put it, in favor of compromise. On August 18, the delegates voted on a measure that protected the status of current slaves and indentured servants while maintaining their use at Shawneetown until 1825.[37]

Some Irish Americans supported compromise, while others rejected slavery altogether. James Lemen Jr., an outspoken abolitionist, voted nay. Messinger and O'Melvany cast their votes in favor of the measure. Outside of the convention, it is impossible to discern what most Irish men and women thought about slavery, although one nineteenth-century author maintained that many Irish throughout the state opposed the institution—perhaps presaging Irish support for Lincoln in 1860. Nevertheless, the yeas prevailed by a count of seventeen to fourteen. In the end, Illinois entered the Union as a state that protected slavery where it existed but formally opposed its expansion. On December 3,

1818, President Monroe signed the resolution officially admitting Illinois as the twenty-first American state.[38]

The obscured history of an abandoned Illinois community sheds further light on the complicated race relations between Irish and African Americans prior to statehood. In 1816, a Kentuckian and Irish descendant by the name of John McCreery relocated to southern Illinois. He brought with him several slaves worth over $10,000. One of McCreery's four sons, a young man named Allen, made off with the slaves in an attempt to sell them in neighboring Missouri. Two of his brothers, Robert and Alexander, pursued and eventually overcame Allen. Soon after, Robert and Alexander freed the slaves and built homes for them in a new settlement called Africa, in what eventually became Williamson County. Freed slaves and runaways sought shelter there. According to local lore, Alexander McCreery even purchased slaves and relocated them to this settlement to prevent families from being split up. Years later, black veterans of the Union army settled in the community. At its peak in the mid-nineteenth century, white and black people, as well as immigrants, could be found there. Yet urbanization and industrialization soon took their toll. By the 1940s, scarcely two dozen people resided in Africa. Today all that remains is a cemetery.[39]

Conclusion

Research opportunities abound for historians interested in the pioneering generation of Irish immigrants who settled in Illinois. Given our relative lack of knowledge about these men and women, much of this work must begin by identifying exactly who these people were. What were their occupations? What percentage became farmers? Politicians? How many were Catholic? Protestant? Did they convert? What were their political affiliations? What specific roles did they play in settler colonialism? To answer these questions, researchers will have to dig deep into census records, local histories, and newspaper databases to construct social profiles of the Irish in eighteenth-century Illinois. This work will have implications for larger historical questions—namely, the degree to which Irish American Protestants helped or hindered future generations of Catholic immigrants. After all, if the Irish in Illinois fared better than their eastern counterparts, the earliest waves of immigrants may have been crucial to their success.[40]

From the colonial period to the onset of statehood, Illinois's Irish defied the negative stereotypes that plagued later generations of immigrants. To be Irish in Illinois could mean a variety of things. To begin with, the majority of immigrants to the region were Protestant. Nearly all of George Rogers Clark's soldiers came from Kentucky, where a sizable Irish Presbyterian community had settled. The same held true for Plum Creek. Even Eliza Lowry, who married Robert Morrison and enthusiastically converted to Catholicism, was at one point a Presbyterian. Many others, notably including the Baptist minister James Lemen Jr., joined popular denominations that swept through the young republic—unsurprising, given the fact that there was not a single Presbyterian minister in Illinois at the time of statehood. As a practical matter, religious affiliation could be very fluid in the West. The few Catholic Irish who did settle in the territory, such as John Edgar, hardly fit later stereotypes. Clearly, many Irish came to the Illinois Country poor, if not destitute, but so did the vast majority of their fellow pioneers. Most staked their future on farming. Some Irish Illinoisans owned slaves, such as the wealthy Edgar, although he also employed freed African Americans. Others, such as James Lemen Jr., passionately opposed the institution. Samuel O'Melvany and John Messinger evidently regarded compromise on slavery, in the name of statehood in 1818, as a greater virtue. Race relations worsened later in the century.[41]

These variations aside, some general conclusions can be made about what it meant to be Irish in the Illinois Country during the eighteenth and early nineteenth centuries. First and foremost, to be Irish simply meant that one or one's family came from Ireland. Ulster Presbyterians, like their Irish Catholic counterparts, were simply referred to as Irish, not Scots-Irish. Documents from George Rogers Clark and George Croghan substantiate this point, as does Reynolds's account from the 1850s. Some contemporaries likely called themselves Irish, apart from religious denominations, because they shared a fierce antipathy for British rule. After all, Protestants and Catholics alike fought for independence during the American Revolution, just as they fought for Irish freedom in 1798. Robert and Margaret Reynolds may have expressly chosen to raise their children Protestant, but they, like so many others who settled in the American Bottom, despised the British Empire "with a ten-horse power." Along with the isolation and privation that accompanied life in the Illinois Country, their shared revolutionary experiences largely transcended religious differences. Yet to be Irish also signified that one was *not* British—an important identifier during *and* after the war for independence. Loyalist Irishmen, such as Henry Hamilton, Simon Girty, and countless others, avoided settling in Illinois. They had, after all, sided with the Crown while encouraging Indian raids on American settlements. Risking life and limb if they stayed, most Loyalists retired to Canada.

Meanwhile, the Illinois Country attracted Irish patriots for another reason: it offered land. Practically unavailable in Ireland, expensive in the American East, and increasingly falling into the hands of speculators in Kentucky, land was more plentiful and cheaper on the prairie (if for no other reason than that people simply squatted on it). Granted, this land had belonged primarily to the Kickapoo, Potawatomi, Sauk, and Fox tribes. European empires and the American republic took it from them, and the Irish were part of this dispossession. The Whitesides won fame in nineteenth-century Illinois history by fighting hostile Kickapoos during the 1790s. Thomas Higgins and Thomas Carlin again battled the Kickapoo and Potawatomi tribes during the War of 1812, and Irishmen later fought in the Black Hawk War of 1832. Yet as many contemporaries saw it, they were securing land, at the expense of a vanquished foe and British ally, for themselves and subsequent generations of immigrants. Most Irish chose to farm the land that they settled. But many went on to become lawyers, civic leaders, and politicians as well—another opportunity historically unavailable to Catholics and Presbyterians alike in Ireland.

What is more, during the 1790s and early 1800s, southern Illinois, much like Kentucky, served as a refuge for Irish patriots, those fleeing the authoritarian policies of John Adams and the Federalist Party. When Matthew Lyon and his family left Vermont, he chose Kentucky and his family southern Illinois as places of residence and refuge. After all, the state of Kentucky, along with Virginia, had passed resolutions challenging the constitutionality of the Alien and Sedition Acts. Even into the nineteenth century, contemporaries in the early national period did not distinguish Irish from Scots-Irish. As historian Kerby Miller notes, "Most of the new immigrants, Protestants and Catholics alike, assimilated as 'Irish' into a party system that either validated (by the Republicans) or stigmatized (by the Federalists) the political principles and the bitter memories of British oppression that made them, albeit temporarily, 'united' Irishmen in the New World." Yet in Illinois, this process of assimilation lasted well into the nineteenth century. A longtime bastion of support for the politics of Thomas Jefferson and later Andrew Jackson, Illinois remained the home of electors who chose a Democratic candidate in every presidential election from the state's inception until Abraham Lincoln won office in 1860. In short, the Irish in Illinois became Irish American patriots—hostile to the British Empire and prepared to take advantage of the distinct opportunities that the Prairie State offered them.[42]

The Irish played crucial roles in the development of Illinois. Irish political loyalties proved to be quite fluid, as they served the French and British Empires and then the new American state. Whatever their allegiance, Irish immigrants to eighteenth- and early nineteenth-century Illinois seized the opportunities available to them, with many notable individuals rising to positions of status in their new home. As the next chapter shows, statehood meant new economic opportunities throughout the Prairie State, which in turn attracted emigrants from across the Atlantic World. As for the Irish, the poorer and mainly Catholic emigrants who came to Illinois in the mid to late nineteenth century often appalled the sensibilities of newly arrived Yankees. Unlike the Irish of the American Bottom, most of these individuals faced discrimination. Yet like their predecessors, many acquired political power, founded religious institutions, and struggled to coexist peacefully with indigenous tribes and African Americans. Still others would fight in a Civil War to defend the American union that previous generations of Irish Illinoisans had fought to establish.

2

FROM IRISH EXILES TO PADDY POLITICIANS: THE IRISH IN ILLINOIS, 1818–65

Chorus—The Irish homes of Illinois,
The happy homes of Illinois;
No landlord there
Can cause despair,
Nor blight our fields in Illinois.

'Tis ten good years since Ellen *bawn*
Adventured with her Irish boy
Across the sea, and settled on
A prairie farm in Illinois.
The Irish homes of Illinois, etc.

. . . .

And yet some shadows often steal
Upon our hours of purest joy;
When happiest we most must feel
"If Ireland were like Illinois!"
The Irish homes of Illinois, etc.[1]

—*Thomas D'Arcy McGee,*
"The Irish Homes of Illinois"

Few Irishmen advocated westward migration more than Thomas D'Arcy McGee, the Catholic poet and revolutionary exile who clashed with fellow countrymen over his vision of Irish America. For McGee, the American West, and Illinois in particular, offered immigrants a prospect almost unimaginable in Ireland or the eastern United States: independent landownership. To the Young Ireland exile, the urban Northeast trapped immigrants in filthy, dead-end communities, where bigotry and discrimination ran rampant. Anti-Catholic prejudice no doubt existed in rural Illinois, but it was hardly as toxic as it had become in Boston, New

York, or Philadelphia. In 1856, McGee spearheaded a convention in Buffalo, New York, to promote Irish "colonies" in both the American West and Canada—a concept that, he soon discovered, appalled most attendees. As historian David Wilson puts it, "Irish republicans denounced him as being anti-Irish, American Democrats condemned him as being anti-American, and Irish American nationalists attacked him as being both anti-Irish and anti-American." McGee left the United States the following year for Montreal, where he and his family settled permanently. Tragically, in 1868, Thomas D'Arcy McGee was assassinated by an Irish Canadian nationalist.[2]

Tens of thousands of Irish men and women settled in Illinois during the decades that followed statehood. Between 1820 and 1865, politics, privation, and a horrific famine compelled at least 2.5 million Irish men, women, and children to leave their homeland. By 1850, at least 27,800 had settled in the Prairie State. Ten years later, that number had skyrocketed to 87,600, making the Irish the second-largest immigrant group in the state. In Ireland, most had leased relatively small farms from landlords and middlemen who charged exorbitant rents. In Illinois, they could afford to purchase sizable farms. Some continued to settle in the American Bottom, although most chose homes in the northern prairie. Many took up residence in Galena to work the lead mines, in Ottawa to dig the Illinois and Michigan Canal, and in Chicago to find employment on railroads and later in meatpacking. Remarkably, by midcentury, Illinois had become the fifth most popular destination for immigrants in the United States. Thomas D'Arcy McGee may not have chosen to settle in the Prairie State, but thousands of Irish men and women followed his advice and began their new lives in Illinois.[3]

As many as one-third of these immigrants went on to become farmers on the Illinois prairie, but others settled in an environment—increasingly urban, anti-Catholic, and antiforeigner—not entirely different from that in the Northeast. Those who settled in burgeoning Chicago faced discrimination from ambitious Yankees who wanted to "modernize" the American West. Mostly Anglo-American and Protestant, Yankee migrants regarded Irish Catholics, particularly the destitute victims of the Great Famine, with suspicion or outright hostility. Irish laborers who did the dangerous and backbreaking work along canals and railroads occasionally confirmed these stereotypes. The insecurity of temporary employment, low pay, disease, and hypermasculine work environments sometimes led to drunkenness and violence. Yet privation and factionalism were nothing new to most Irishmen. More frequently, they leveraged their numbers and political experience to become power brokers and elected officials in Illinois. More than anything else, their keen political skills, typically but not exclusively used on behalf of the Democratic Party, drew the ire of rivals—including Abraham Lincoln. By the 1850s, anti-Catholic and anti-Irish sentiment had achieved such heights that the people of Chicago elected an anti-immigrant mayor.[4]

When the Civil War broke out, however, Irish Americans throughout Illinois embraced the opportunity to demonstrate honor and loyalty to their adopted country—a sacrifice that did not go unnoticed. Between 1861 and 1865, the Prairie State fielded two Irish regiments, which included more than twelve thousand first-generation immigrants. Casualties ran high, and their courage and sacrifice convinced many skeptics that even Irish Catholics could become worthy Americans. Chicago's first war hero was an Irish Catholic: James Albert Mulligan, colonel of the 23rd Illinois Infantry. To be sure, emigrants from the Emerald Isle faced social exclusion and outright bigotry during the decades that followed the war, but not to the extent that they had before the war—and not to the same extent that their compatriots did in Boston or New York. With the conclusion of the Civil War, the Irish of Illinois, more Catholic than previous generations, had begun to obtain levels of wealth, power, and respectability equal to those of their Irish predecessors during the Revolutionary era.[5]

An Increasingly Catholic Migration

Immigrants who came to Illinois between the 1820s and mid-1840s faced an extraordinary four-thousand-mile, two-month journey. Some sailed from Ireland through Liverpool to the United States, usually arriving in Philadelphia or New York. After 1825, many continued westward on the Erie Canal, the famous waterway built in part by Irish laborers. Others disembarked in New Orleans, where they took a steamboat up the Mississippi River. Yet most arrived through the port of Quebec, mainly because fares from Ireland to British Canada were less expensive than those to American ports. From there, they sailed 180 miles up the St. Lawrence River, across Lake Champlain, and finally to Buffalo. The immigrants then crossed Lake Erie, from Cleveland to

Toledo, where they commenced the final leg of their journey to Illinois—usually via the Ohio and Indiana canals or the Great Lakes. In 1840, fares from Buffalo to Chicago cost $20. Less than a decade later, prices fell by half, and the journey took less than nine days. Nevertheless, most Irish men, women, and children who immigrated before the Great Famine, described their journey as tedious. By the time they reached Illinois, most undoubtedly were ready to settle down.[6]

During the 1820s, the most vibrant Irish community in Illinois was at Galena, in the northwestern corner of the state. While Chicago remained but a trading post of twelve to fifteen houses, Galena attracted thousands of ambitious individuals hoping to strike it rich by mining lead. In 1825, two anonymous Irishmen became the first mineral speculators along the Fever River. A year later, another nameless pair became the first to receive a Galena mining permit. In 1827, Irish Americans convened as members of the community's first grand jury: James and John Foley, Michael Murphy, P. Hogan, Michael Coe, Michael Finley, James Lynch, and Owen Riley. John Foley obtained the Fever River's first ferry license. Patrick Markey filed the county's first will. An Irishman by the name of Michael Dee became the first person to be indicted by the local circuit court.[7]

The Irish community of Galena thrived, anchored by Democratic politics and Catholic institutions. Many residents became outspoken supporters of Irish independence. The Foleys named the township in which they settled Vinegar Hill, after the famous battle of the Irish Rebellion of 1798. During the late 1820s, Galena boasted an active Friends of Ireland Society, organized to promote and fund Daniel O'Connell's crusade for Catholic emancipation. After learning that $1,000 had been raised for the cause, one English traveler to Galena derided the accomplishment as "a fund for an Irish rebellion under the guise of civil and religious liberty." Such sentiments reflected fear and prejudice more than reality. In 1832, the Irish of Galena founded the town's first Catholic school. And many actively supported the Democratic Party. During the late 1830s, when antiforeign politicians and newspapers accused Catholics of voter fraud and disloyalty, the *Galena Democrat* denounced them as antiforeign bigots and dangerous abolitionists. "The same party who would make the *negro a freeman*," the paper declared in reference to the Whig Party, "would make the *Irishman a slave*." Such rhetoric was common in states with large Irish populations during the antebellum period. By the 1840s, some five thousand miners, many of whom were Irish, made Galena the wealthiest community in Illinois. Today the town of Galena and its surrounding county boast an Irish population of nearly 20 percent—the fifth highest in the state.[8]

Southern Illinois continued to attract Irish immigrants, increasingly Catholic as well as Protestant, to rural communities. Many became subsistence farmers in places such as Shawneetown, Enfield, Piopolis, Waltonboro, and New Haven. Devout in their faith, most helped establish new churches and parishes during the 1830s. Itinerant priests such as Father Elisha Durbin, known to local Protestants as "Daddy Durbin," provided sermons and sacraments to parishioners. Irish Catholics prioritized religion as they established communities in Illinois.[9]

Irish politicians played integral roles in driving indigenous peoples from the state. In 1832, members of the Sauk and Fox tribes began skirmishing with the U.S. Army and the Illinois militia. The leader of this confederation, a Sauk warrior known to whites as Black Hawk, attempted to organize a pantribal movement against white expansion. His followers, known as the "British Band" because of their twenty-year alliance with the British Empire, included over a thousand men, women, and children. Andrew Jackson's Indian removal policy, signed into law early in 1832, had forced them to relocate west of the Mississippi River. In April, however, Black Hawk believed that if he returned to Illinois, warriors from the Potawatomi, Mascouten, and Winnebago peoples would join him in support. He was mistaken. The Sauk had made too many enemies with other tribes, and Governor John Reynolds, the state's first Irish American governor, had anticipated conflict, calling for federal reinforcements. Reynolds was all too eager for a war that might enhance his reputation. He liked being called the "Old Ranger," a moniker he had been given during the War of 1812, and he frequently put himself in harm's way in battle. As historian Kerry Trask puts it, Reynolds "seemed caught up in a perpetual quest for personal attention."

Irish Americans of all ranks helped defeat Black Hawk. The governor's acquaintances, including General Samuel Whiteside and Thomas Carlin, fought in the war—as did an unknown number of enlisted men of Irish descent. Throughout the summer, the two sides fought across northwestern Illinois and southwestern Wisconsin, but the outcome was never in doubt. In August, Black

Hawk abandoned his people and fled north. The war ended at Bad Axe, in present-day Wisconsin, where some three hundred men, women, and children were brutally massacred by militiamen from Illinois and Indiana. It was a grisly end to a vicious conflict. In all, seventy-seven Americans and an estimated five hundred Sauk and Fox tribe members died.[10]

Anti-Catholic Sentiment

With the remaining tribes subdued, a new wave of American migrants from the Northeast headed west. Before the 1830s, most people who settled in the Prairie State came from the South. No matter their religious affiliation, most preferred traditional rural lives as farmers. They drank heavily and tolerated slavery. Their worldviews contrasted sharply with those of the Yankee newcomers from the Northeast. Most new settlers were Protestants and American nationalists. They believed in the perfectibility of human beings and abjured vice. They opposed alcohol consumption and denounced slavery. They abhorred Catholicism, which they deemed incompatible with American liberty and a republican form of government. As prominent reformers such as Samuel Morse and Lyman Beecher saw it, Irish immigrants were little more than foot soldiers in the pope's army. Nationally, tensions reached a fever pitch in 1834, when an angry mob burned the Ursuline Convent in Charlestown, Massachusetts, to the ground. With increasing numbers of Irish Catholics migrating alongside this new wave of Yankee reformers, conflict appeared increasingly likely.[11]

That conflict soon became manifest in the American Bottom. In 1833, Elijah P. Lovejoy, a fiery Presbyterian minister from Maine, established a religious newspaper in St. Louis that claimed a readership in southwestern Illinois. With characteristic vitriol, Lovejoy famously editorialized about the sin of alcohol, the threat of "popery," and the evils of slavery. Remembered for his uncompromising support for abolition—indeed, Lovejoy was killed by a proslavery mob in 1837—he was disliked by Irish immigrants for his anti-Catholic rhetoric. In the *St. Louis Observer*, Lovejoy targeted Catholics as enemies of the republic. He referred to the typical "Roman priest" as a "surprising ignoramus." He described the Virgin Mary as "the goddess of the papist." He delighted in the fact that "public sentiment" had finally begun "arousing itself to the dangers which threaten our institutions from the influence of foreign Papists." In 1835, when pressed by co-owners of the *Observer* to cease his attacks on slavery, Lovejoy responded, "Think not that it is because I am an abolitionist that I am so persecuted. . . . The true cause is the open and decided stand which the paper has taken against the encroachments of popery."[12]

Irish Catholics retaliated in characteristic fashion, using their strength in numbers. In December 1835, a vigilante committee met in St. Louis to confront Lovejoy. The assembly alarmed many newspaper editors, who noted that "at least one half of [the committee] was composed of Irishmen!" The newspaper further argued that the power wielded by such immigrants should "arrest the attention" of citizens—particularly their "assembling in a hall consecrated to the execution of American constitutional law and justice, to deprive a native-born American citizen of the exercise of his constitutional privilege of the liberty of speech and the press." The vigilantes were, however, successful. Six months later, Lovejoy announced plans to move his operation to Alton, Illinois. The task proved difficult, as mobs repeatedly vandalized his equipment. Yet by the time Lovejoy established his new press, he had abandoned his crusade against "popery." If Irish Catholics faced discrimination in the 1830s, their opponents soon discovered their potent faculty for organization and resistance in their adopted land.[13]

In hindsight, Lovejoy's anti-Catholicism serves as a reminder of how difficult it can be to disentangle Irish hostility toward abolitionism from the religious bigotry of abolitionists. With few exceptions, this point has been lost on historians. Long recognizing the racial antipathies that Irish Catholics had for African Americans, some historians have argued that the working classes emphasized their own "whiteness" in order to distinguish themselves from blacks, both slave and free. Others have ignored the historical context of Irish immigration, focusing instead on abolitionism's intellectual antecedents and its relationship with the development of "race" in America. Yet for Irish Catholics who came from a land plagued by sectarian violence and religious discrimination, most were determined to defend themselves from an all-too-familiar prejudice. It is important to remember that when Yankee Protestants pushed for abolition and racial equality, most prominent advocates did so while disparaging Catholics—as Lovejoy's journalism reveals. In the long history of the Irish in Illinois, one fraught with racial conflict, historians would do well to keep this perspective in mind.[14]

Digging the Illinois and Michigan Canal

Despite increasing anti-Catholic sentiment, Irish immigrants continued to pour into the Prairie State during the 1830s, with most seeking work on the Illinois and Michigan (I&M) Canal. The ninety-seven-mile waterway, eventually completed in 1848, connected Lake Michigan to the Mississippi River. As early as the 1820s, politicians of Irish descent, such as Congressman Zadoc Casey of Jefferson County, envisioned the enterprise in the image of New York's Erie Canal. An 1827 federal land grant allotted 290,915 acres to the project, but engineering concerns and rising costs delayed construction. Planners, meanwhile, divided the canal into three sections: the Summit, which began at the new town of Chicago; the Middle, which ran through Will County; and the Western, where the canal finally linked with the Illinois River in LaSalle County. In the early 1830s, the state had platted communities such as Chicago and Ottawa along the proposed route, in anticipation of the canal's eventual construction. In 1836, Governor Joseph Duncan secured a loan of $500,000, and excavation began on the Fourth of July that same year. At $26 per month, the I&M offered the highest wages of any canal project in the country. What is more, the state actively recruited experienced canallers in the eastern United States, Canada, and even Ireland. By December 1836, some 350 laborers were at work on the I&M. The vast majority were Irish.[15]

Irish canallers and their families lived hard lives. The work was physically demanding. Provided that the ground or the waterway was not frozen, laborers dug year-round, sunup to sundown. Their tools included little more than a pickax and a shovel. Canallers began by "grubbing" the land. Bands of laborers chopped down hardwoods with axes and pulled out the stumps with teams of oxen. After cutting through the trees and undergrowth, workers began the seemingly endless process of digging. Typically, six to eight men scratched away at the earth, constantly filling horse-drawn carts. Upon loading one cart, a driver would lug away the dirt as another cart immediately took its place. Each section typically required a base of twenty-six feet, a depth of four feet, and an upper width of forty feet. The towpath rose two feet above the waterline and measured ten feet across. Once they finished digging a section, workers tamped down the base with long rods and their feet. Pay could be sporadic, and no work meant no pay.

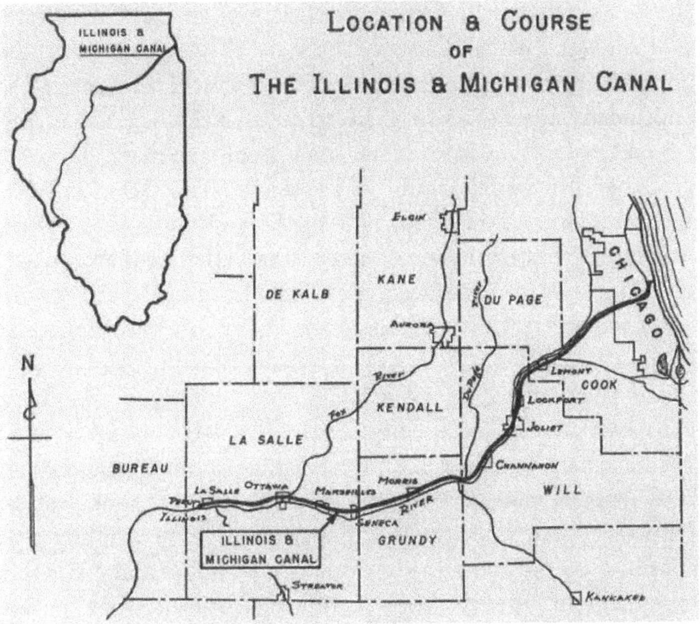

Map of Illinois and Michigan Canal. Courtesy of the Lewis University History Center.

Unscrupulous contractors, some of whom were fellow Irishmen, notoriously underestimated their costs and then shorted common laborers. Disease was a constant threat, particularly malaria and cholera. Most of the workmen consumed alcohol on a daily basis, often while on the job. Violence was not uncommon, as faction fights broke out regularly. Women were not entirely absent from canal camps and worksites, although men outnumbered them significantly. Most were married to canallers. They ran boarding shanties, did the laundry, prepared food, and raised families. The Irish men and women who lived and worked along the I&M lived a Spartan existence.[16]

Such working conditions often marginalized immigrant laborers and their families, but these communities did not live in isolation. To be sure, many of the vices that Protestant reformers attributed to Irish Catholics—drunkenness, rioting, and domestic turmoil—were not entirely the inventions of critics. Yet such behaviors were often the result of a foreign population adjusting to an alien land where available employment was dirty and difficult. In this climate, some Protestants eagerly noted the foibles of Catholic immigrants. In 1842, the Cornish journalist James Silk

Buckingham described the Irish canaller community of Ottawa as "drunken, dirty, indolent, and riotous." "I never saw anything approaching to the scene before us, in dirtiness or disorder," he concluded. "It is not to be wondered at, that the Americans conceive a very low estimate of the Irish people generally."[17]

Other commentators were more positive. In 1837, the German-born Roman Catholic Francis Grund maintained that despite "prejudice" created by vice and poverty, "The Irish are, by the great majority of Americans, considered as an oppressed and injured people, which is sufficient to entitle them to the sympathies of freemen." Illinois newspapers, such as LaSalle County's *Free Trader*, often echoed this point. "We hope, honestly and sincerely," the newspaper editorialized in 1841, "that Ireland will become what she CAN be, a liberal, brave, intelligent and prosperous nation. Every American will wish her God speed in the good work." Irish immigrants, including canallers, became upstanding citizens in the Prairie State. They founded churches and charitable organizations. They served as sheriffs and coroners. They became doctors and teachers. Many faced prejudice, but many more found communities that welcomed them. Throughout the farmlands of Illinois, Grund's account was the better prediction of the relationships formed between immigrants and their neighbors.[18]

Relations proved more tenuous in Chicago. On the very day that the state broke ground on the I&M, a handful of immigrant laborers engaged in a dramatic fight that foreshadowed future hostilities. On July 4, 1836, members of the city's high society celebrated Independence Day with toasts and gun salutes aboard a steamship on the Chicago River. When they reached a quarry near the canaller community of Hardscrabble (later Bridgeport), several workmen began hurling rocks at the men and women on the ship's upper deck. The captain steered the ship aground, and a brief melee ensued. According to the *Chicago American*, "Some fifty passengers leaped ashore, some with bludgeons," and apprehended the "heroes of the Emerald Isle," as the paper facetiously labeled the Irish canallers. Twelve were sent to jail. It should be noted that some of the celebration's dignitaries included Irish Americans. Dr. William B. Egan, an accomplished Kerry-born physician who came to Chicago in 1833, delivered the address for the groundbreaking ceremony. Nevertheless, the incident signaled rising tensions between Chicago's Yankee elites and the town's primarily Catholic immigrant workers.[19]

Meanwhile, in 1837, economic panic rocked the financial system. The year had begun pleasantly enough, with Illinois legislators voting to move the capital to Springfield. Chicago was incorporated as a city. The general assembly approved a massive public-spending bill for roads, canals, and railroads. The Whig Party, in particular, supported by a young Abraham Lincoln, actively promoted such "internal improvements," as public works projects were commonly known. On top of the half million in debt already accrued on behalf of the I&M, legislators borrowed another $3.5 million for a statewide railroad network. Then calamity struck. On St. Patrick's Day in New York City, a prominent financial firm by the name of Joseph & Joseph went bankrupt after the Bank of England curtailed loans. State banks throughout the United States, heavily dependent on British funds, began to fail. Industry plummeted. Over 90 percent of the country's factories closed. Panic spread westward. Public spending ground to a halt. Canal workers were hit particularly hard. The Bank of Illinois halted specie payments. Chicago resorted to issuing its own paper notes. Residents continued to feel the weight of the collapse into the 1840s, with the state treasurer eventually refusing payments in any currency other than silver or gold. The state's economic woes continued for a decade.

The Panic of 1837 hit Irish canallers particularly hard. The state reduced wages from $26 per month to $20 and eventually remunerated workers in scrip that could be exchanged for land. All along the canal, contractors could not afford to pay their workers. Some laborers took their employers to court. Others destroyed property. On the night of June 7, several unidentified individuals in Chicago, most purportedly Irish, vandalized sections of the I&M—a common mode of retaliation along canals in Ireland. Their contractor, a man by the name of Dodson, attempted to intervene. A brief altercation ensued. Dodson killed one of laborers, described simply as "an Irishman" by one local newspaper. Most canallers throughout the state either sought new opportunities elsewhere or accepted reduced wages and land scrip. For the next eight years, construction on Illinois's internal improvements projects virtually halted. Railroad construction stopped in 1839, when the state nearly defaulted on its loans. For many Irish workers and their families, the Illinois and Michigan Canal suddenly failed to provide the opportunities that it had but a few years earlier.[20]

To make matters worse, Irish factions fought one another along the line of the canal. The most renowned of these clashes were between the Fardowns and Corkonians. The latter faction derived its name from County Cork and generally included immigrants from the southwest of Ireland. The Fardowns typically were composed of individuals from the Irish midlands, but its name confounded contemporaries just as it has historians, although it probably was an Anglicized corruption of the Irish words *Fear aduain*, meaning "stranger." The two parties, both predominantly Catholic, held each other in fierce contempt. Their conflicts dated at least to 1834, when they waged war along the line of the Chesapeake and Ohio Canal in Maryland. From there, the clashes spread to internal improvements projects in Pennsylvania, New York, Indiana, and eventually Illinois.[21]

On June 11, 1838, nearly five hundred Corkonians, led by a contractor named Edward Sweeney, overwhelmed a much smaller number of Fardown laborers and their families in LaSalle County. An Italian priest who observed the incident firsthand was shocked that the Corkonians "were resolved to burn all the houses along the Line that belong[ed] to people of the hated province." Some of the Fardowns rallied behind the leadership of William Byrne, a Leinster native and veteran contractor who had come to Illinois with his wife, Sarah, the previous year. Respected and well connected, Byrne appealed to Sheriff Alson Woodruff and Deputy Zimri Lewis for help. The following day, Lewis led a posse of some eighty Fardowns and local citizens against the Corkonians, many of whom were hung over after their exploits the day before. When the two parties faced off along the Illinois River near an island bluff called Buffalo Rock, the deputy foolishly announced that he intended to arrest the Corkonian ringleaders. Violence ensued. Lewis ordered his men to fire a volley into the ranks of the opposition. Ten Corkonians were killed. The rest fled. Two members of the posse fell wounded. Deputy Lewis arrested sixty men and sent them to jail in Ottawa, although the meager facility could not accommodate such numbers. All were soon released. The "Irish Rebellion," as one contemporary described it, had come to an end.[22]

Irish American Politics

The "Irish Rebellion" of 1838 provided Illinoisans with a glimpse of what "politics" meant to the Irish working classes. To be sure, the Corkonians of LaSalle County attacked their Fardown adversaries for a variety of reasons—to control wages, to enact revenge, and to defend their honor. But the manner in which they did so reflected how Irish laborers viewed power and its acquisition. Put simply, most Irish Catholics believed in majority rule. In their homeland, they had made up roughly 80 percent of the population. Yet they were governed by a Protestant minority, illegitimate rulers in the minds of most. Corkonians along the I&M regarded their numbers as the key legitimizing factor in determining employment. In 1838, the number of men working the canal leaped from 790 to 3,200. With a failing economy, Corkonians recognized that their Fardown adversaries were depressing wages. Since the former constituted a majority, the latter had to go. Moreover, they attempted to enforce their legitimacy by overpowering their adversary. As true majoritarians, working-class Irish Catholics believed that numbers determined not only who should rule but also how those with power should put it to use. In Jacksonian America, and Illinois in particular, these political attitudes benefited Irish immigrants.[23]

Irish laborers arrived in Illinois already equipped with skills to leverage power. Emigrants who left Ireland during the late 1820s and early 1830s were experienced in electoral politics. This began in 1824, when Daniel O'Connell organized a national political movement to win Catholic emancipation. Irish Catholics had been barred from holding office for nearly 150 years. When the British passed the Act of Union in 1800–1801, many Irish Catholics supported the merger because Westminster had promised emancipation. King George IV balked at the concession, and Catholics were still disbarred from parliamentary office in the 1820s. They did, however, have the right to vote—provided that they were adult males who owned or rented land that was worth at least 40 shillings. Since 1793, when suffrage was first extended to Catholics, voters had typically supported candidates favored by their landlords. After all, polling was conducted in public, and few tenant farmers wanted to risk eviction. This changed in 1826, when O'Connell's Catholic Association conducted a massive campaign to unseat antiemancipation candidates in parliamentary elections. The association, Catholic priests, liberal Protestants, and courageous members of the working classes led an effective revolt against conservative landlords in five counties, electing supportive Protestants to serve in Parliament. Ireland's Catholic masses had stunned the political establishment. They did so again in 1828, when O'Connell won a staggering victory in a by-election in County Clare. Although it was illegal for the Catholic O'Connell to take his seat, the victory helped to force Westminster's hand. A year later, the British government passed the Roman Catholic Relief Bill of 1829. The Catholics of Ireland had won a key victory—and in so doing honed critical skills in "machine politics" that served them well in the Prairie State.[24]

Illinois suffrage laws favored Irish laborers with political experience. The Constitution of 1818, drafted and ratified in part by immigrants, extended the vote to any adult white male with at least six months' residence. The state's laws were among the most liberal in the country. In neighboring Indiana, for example, the law required voters to become U.S. citizens before they could register, a process that took a minimum of five years to complete. Farther east, laws were frequently even stricter, requiring state citizenship, tax payments, or even property ownership in order to cast a ballot. For Irish laborers, Illinois was a political land of milk and honey.[25]

Beginning in the late 1830s, Irish canallers became a potent voting bloc, a fact soon recognized by Illinois politicians. In the 1838 campaign for the 3rd Congressional District, John T. Stuart, a two-time Whig candidate and Abraham Lincoln's legal partner, faced off against Democrat Stephen A. Douglas. Both supported continued funding for the canal, and both courted the Irish vote. Stuart touted his support for Irish freedom and accused his opponent of secretly desiring to suspend work on the I&M. Douglas proclaimed that his ancestors, the "McDooglases," hailed from Ireland. With the state's liberal suffrage laws and thousands of immigrants at work on the canal, Whigs and Democrats expected a high turnout. Nevertheless, both parties were shocked by the number of votes cast—thirty-six thousand in all, more than double the turnout in the previous congressional election. Even more surprising, merely three dozen votes separated the two candidates. After weeks of counting and recounting, it was finally determined that Stuart had prevailed.

Nevertheless, the Irish made their presence felt. The state's Whig Party had anticipated a greater margin of victory, and Whig newspapers blamed canallers. The editor of the *Jacksonville Illinoisan* described the contest as "a terrible display of Irish politics and foreign influence." The *Quincy Whig* accused "*Pat*-riots and other unnaturalized foreigners" of having voted illegally. Grafton's

Backwoodsman insisted that Irish laborers had no business participating in state politics: "It is not a crime that the laborers on our canal, fresh from 'Ould Ireland,' should still be Irishmen, without one American feeling.—Nor will we interfere with their bloody fights between 'Corkonians and Fardowners,' but we issue a PROTEST against such men going to the *polls.*" Springfield's *Sangamon Journal* echoed these sentiments, arguing that "these foreigners," who in June had been "subjected by military force," now had "given law to the citizens of LaSalle County." Nativists continued to lodge similar complaints against the Irish into the 1840s.[26]

Irish successes came much earlier for immigrants in Illinois than they did for their fellow countrymen back east, who generally broke into the political scene during the 1840s. In Illinois, Irishmen voted their own interests, ran their own candidates, and won office. As early as 1838, Cook County voters elected Isaac R. Gavin as sheriff. Three years later, Gavin ran for mayor of Chicago as a Whig but was defeated by Francis Cornwall Sherman. In 1839, laborers working on the Summit and Middle sections of the I&M organized an independent Canaller Party, even electing an Irishman to the office of recorder. The pro-Whig *Chicago American* warned its readers of the Irish and their political influences: "Already an Irish representative and an Irish sheriff . . . two Irish candidates for recorder and five Irish candidates for the offices of county clerk, county surveyor and constables. In the name of all we love most, our country and our liberty, shall we submit to such dictation?" A year later, the *American* continued to sound the alarm about Irish politics in Illinois: "It is also known that this foreign influence is perverted to the election of men unfit for office, and that the foreign population in Cook and Will Counties have asserted the right, as they hold the power, to elect officers for the sole reason that they are Irishmen." Irish politicians also enjoyed success in LaSalle County. In 1839, William J. Reddick became the county's first Irish sheriff. One year later, Christopher Bailey became the county's first Irish coroner.[27]

Despite their disadvantaged social and economic status, the Irish frequently outmaneuvered their political opponents. Occasionally, these included fellow party members. In 1842, Chicago's Irish voting bloc had become so influential that the Democratic Party replaced Isaac N. Arnold with Irishman William B. Egan for the Illinois General Assembly—although Arnold had defeated Egan during the county convention. Nor did immigrants blindly

How the Irish Became Democrats

The Irish of Illinois did not blindly support the Democratic Party. This was particularly evident during the presidential election of 1840, which pitted the Whig challenger, William Henry Harrison, against the Democratic incumbent, Martin Van Buren. During the campaign, Whigs attempted to shake off their image as the party of moneyed interests by promoting their candidate as a rugged westerner—the hard cider–drinking hero of the Battle of Tippecanoe. Parades across the country honored "Tippecanoe and Tyler Too," as Harrison and his running mate were called, with catchy songs and slogans. Courting the Irish vote, Whigs promised government spending for new canals and railroads, while denouncing their opponent, whom they dubbed "Martin Van Ruin," as an opponent of the working man. For laborers who had felt the brunt of the Panic of 1837, the Whig slogan, "No Reduction of Wages," sounded awfully appealing. Indeed, Whigs across Illinois believed that they could win the Irish vote. Writing to his law partner John T. Stuart, Lincoln optimistically noted, "I believe we will carry the state." "A great many of the grocery sort of Van Buren men," he continued, "are out for Harrison. Our Irish Blacksmith Gregory, is for Harrison."

In May, Whig enthusiasts headed to Springfield's "Tippecanoe Convention," where mobile log cabins drawn by teams of oxen paraded before thousands of spectators. Among them, according to one newspaper, was a conspicuous delegation of more than two hundred "sons of ERIN," who paraded before a "banner of GREEN SILK, with streamers of the same color." The "gallant band of Irishmen," as the reporter described them, waved a banner with the words "Harrison and Tyler," as well as the motto "Where Liberty dwells there is my country." On the reverse, the delegates had printed the words "Where is there a battle field for freedom, where Irish blood has not been spilt?" "The effect," the reporter concluded, "was thrilling." In June, a Whig visitor passed through an immigrant community near Peoria called Irish Grove, where he witnessed a woman swinging her shawl and shouting, "All Whigs in this grove!" Perhaps, as Lincoln had predicted, the "grocery sort" of Irish could be counted on to support Harrison.

Less than a month later, however, 250 prominent Chicago politicians, most of whom were Whigs, issued a petition to the U.S. Congress demanding that the federal government amend its immigration and naturalization laws. In short, they argued that foreign-born citizens should not be allowed to vote. This proved catastrophic for Harrison and the Whigs. The Democratic press insisted that Whigs at the state and national levels planned to eliminate immigrant suffrage. Van Buren won the state of Illinois by 2 percentage points, although Harrison won nationally. Nevertheless, the state's Democrats won a valuable ally that year. After 1840, the Democratic Party became the default choice for Illinois's Irish immigrants.[28]

support a single party. In 1846, Chicago's Irish defected from the Democratic Party over concerns that the mayoral candidate, Charles Follensbee, harbored antiforeign prejudices. Outspoken opponents of Irish immigration had a point: the Irish were skilled in the art of American politics. As Orestes Brownson put it in

1845, the real "offence" committed by the Irish, at least in the eyes of anti-foreign nativists, was in their "being democratic, and in wishing the government to be administered on truly democratic principles." It was not their "ignorance of the real nature of our institutions" that bothered the antiforeign party, "but their intelligence of them that constitutes their disqualification."[29]

Irish American Nationalism: The Repeal Movement

The Irish of Illinois also put their political skills to use in supporting freedom for their homeland. This support was first manifested during the early 1840s in Daniel O'Connell's campaign to repeal the Act of Union. After failing to persuade fellow Members of Parliament to support Repeal, O'Connell decided to take his case directly to the people of Ireland. At the Dublin Corn Exchange in 1840, he formally announced a new movement modeled on the Catholic Association and dedicated to ending the Union. Later named the Loyal National Repeal Association, the organization offered membership for as little as one penny per month. The Repeal Association was not confined to Ireland; thousands of Irish Americans rallied behind O'Connell. Advocates established Repeal Associations in Boston, New York, Philadelphia, New Orleans, Savannah, St. Louis, and Dubuque. The Irish of Chicago followed suit, founding a branch in 1842. None other than William B. Egan presided over the organization. To promote the cause, Chicago's Irish held a St. Patrick's Day parade the following year. The city's Montgomery Guards—a uniformed militia company named after Richard Montgomery, an Irish-born general killed during the American Revolution—led the procession. Dr. Egan delivered a speech. Mass was held at the Catholic church, and the choir sang. Ireland's repeal movement had come to Illinois.[30]

Pro-Democratic presses with Irish readerships gave their support for repeal. Between 1841 and 1843, LaSalle County's *Illinois Free Trader* posted multiple editorials on the subject. On one occasion, it denounced Britain for subjugating the Irish to "the fetters and insults of forty years of tyranny." "Ireland with a population of eight millions," the paper railed, "will look rather to the living example on this side of the water, and perhaps make a last stand against the tyrant." On another occasion, the *Free Trader* echoed the sentiments of O'Connell, who credited Ireland's "exiled children" for raising "the cry for the restoration of the liberties of Ireland." As the repeal movement grew, reports of vast "monster meetings" in Ireland, which attracted tens of thousands of spectators, reached Illinois. "Public opinion," the newspaper celebrated in 1843, "has become a mighty engine in controlling the movements of all nations."[31]

Yet support for repeal, in both Ireland and Illinois, eventually waned. Fearing disorder and trying to undermine O'Connell's momentum, British authorities outlawed a scheduled "monster meeting" at Clontarf, where Brian Boru had defeated the Danes in 1014. Just a month before, in September 1843, the *Free Trader* had predicted crisis. Fearing bloodshed, O'Connell canceled the October meeting and eventually served two months in prison for threatening the peace of the kingdom. The movement never recovered. In the United States, O'Connell's firm opposition to slavery did not help his cause. Throughout his campaign, O'Connell had called upon his fellow countrymen abroad to denounce slavery. The cause of Irish freedom, he argued, was a cause shared by all people in bondage. By repeatedly criticizing the institution, he irritated Irish American repealers, many of whom lived in slave states or were suspicious of abolitionists.[32]

O'Connell's attitude toward slavery did not kill repeal in the United States or in Illinois. As late as June 1844, the recently renamed *Ottawa Free Trader* held out hope for success. Rather, O'Connell lost his popularity with most Irish Americans the following year, when the British Empire and the United States stood at the brink of war. In a speech before Dublin's Repeal Association, he announced that if Britain gave Ireland its own parliament, the Irish would in turn oppose American expansion into Oregon and Texas. Unwilling to risk disloyalty in their adopted homeland, Irish repealers in Baltimore and Philadelphia disbanded their associations. Others soon followed, including Chicago's own branch. The *Free Trader* echoed these sentiments, describing O'Connell in August 1845 as a mere "charlatan, who pretends to, but cannot see into the great heart of things." "It is expected that all repeal associations," the *Free Trader* concluded, "will be dissolved immediately." Commitment to Irish nationalism did not perish in Illinois that year, but support for Daniel O'Connell did.[33]

An Gorta Mór: The Great Hunger

If the year 1845 marked the decline of O'Connell's influence in America, it also marked the beginning of the most horrific calamity in modern Irish history. Late that summer, a milky gray film appeared on the leaves of potato plants throughout the Emerald Isle—a manifestation of the blight known as *Phytophthora infestans.* As the rains began to fall, the plants decayed. The smell of rot soon filled the countryside. Fifty percent of the crop was lost. The following year was almost a total failure. Between 1847 and 1851, harvests rarely yielded more than 50 percent. For the vast majority of Irish peasants, many of whom already lived on the edge of survival, the blight proved deadly. For nearly a century, the potato had been the primary staple of Irish households. It had catapulted Ireland's population of less than 4 million in 1750 to 8 million people in 1845. Where the potato gave, however, the blight took away. By eliminating half of the country's food supply, the fungal disease deprived most ordinary Irish people of their daily source of nutrition.

The British government failed to provide adequate relief for Ireland's starving population. Many Irish men and women believed that this failure was intentional and, in their own language, began referring to the Famine as *an Gorta Mór*, meaning the Great Hunger. As Irish exile John Mitchel later proclaimed, "The Almighty, indeed, sent the potato blight, but the English created the Famine." Between 1845 and 1852, up to 1 million Irish men, women, and children died of starvation or related diseases. At least 1.5 million others left Ireland, overwhelmingly for the United States. Most considered their departure an involuntary exodus. Some left their homeland, albeit unwillingly, at the expense of their landlords—better to pay for their passage to the Americas than to have to provide for them in Ireland. Others relied on family members in the United States. The price of a one-way transatlantic passage fell below 3 pounds, but this was still a great deal of money to peasant and working-class families. For the men and increasing numbers of single women who made the trip, tickets amounted to a single year's rent. Many Irish relatives, believing that they would never see their loved ones again, mourned their departure with an "American wake," a solemn occasion replicating the tradition of sitting with the body of a deceased family member on the eve of burial.

Voyages often were deadly. The ships that transported these emigrants often carried disease and despair. As many as fifty thousand passengers died. Thousands more contracted typhus and faced lengthy quarantines when they arrived. When emigrants landed in ports such as Quebec, New York, or Boston, they often owned little more than the clothes on their backs. One contemporary in New Orleans described famine exiles as "mere living skeletons." Indeed, practically all were at the mercy of their new homeland.[34]

Thousands of famine emigrants settled in Illinois, where the existing Irish community provided aid and comfort for the afflicted, as did Americans across the country. In November 1845, the *American Almanac* reported that sixteen U.S. cities had contributed $651,712 to famine relief. The following year, donations topped $1.2 million. Chicago's Irish community—which included city dignitaries, the middle classes, female domestic servants, and male laborers—sent money to assist in the survival or emigration of their beleaguered families. As the late historian George Potter put it, "They wanted to get their own out of Ireland to America. The most enduring effect of the famine's cruel purge was the emigration of Ireland's sons and daughters who fled to other lands, principally America, which made the small and isolated Atlantic island one of the great motherlands of the Western World."[35]

Many found work on Illinois's resuscitated internal improvement projects. Renewed construction on the I&M began in 1845. By 1847, the canal employed thousands of laborers, including more than two thousand Irishmen on the eastern end of the line near Chicago. Pay improved as well, increasing to $1.25 per day. Following the canal's completion in 1848, immigrant laborers sought work on the state's many railroad projects: the Quincy to Springfield line, the Galena and Chicago Union Railroad, the Chicago Rock Island line, and the Illinois Central Railroad, which stretched from Cairo to Galena. By 1860, these workers helped make the Prairie State second only to Ohio in terms of railroad mileage.[36]

Still, most famine emigrants were happy to get work wherever they could find it. Many became hired hands on Illinois farms, which by the 1850s housed one-third of the state's Irish population. Some, such as Michael Lawler and Patrick Duffy, settled in Williamson County in southern Illinois—where some of their descendants continue to live. Others, particularly along the line of the I&M, purchased their own land with canal scrip. These included former laborers, such as John Brown, Roger Waters, and Thomas McCormick in Will County. Most, however, took their chances in Chicago. Irish women made money in service, accepting roles as live-in maids for well-to-do families there. Irish men found work with the city. Others barely scraped by. By the 1850s, Irish Catholics constituted a majority of the applicants seeking assistance at the Cook County Poor House—a fact that Yankee reformers were all too quick to note. Nevertheless, they kept coming. By 1850, Illinois was home to 27,800 Irish men and women.[37]

Bringing Catholicism to the Prairie: Bishop Quarter and the Sisters of Mercy

With thousands of migrants pouring into the state during the 1840s, missionaries of all denominations rushed toward Illinois. Newcomers were desperate for religious leadership. "Now is the seed time of this territory," one missionary wrote in 1841. "Now, the people everywhere want and demand the Gospel." Methodists, Baptists, Presbyterians, Catholics, and others competed to be the first to "plant" their distinct brand of faith throughout the state. Even Mormons, under constant threat of vigilante violence throughout the period, established a thriving enclave in Illinois before a mob at Carthage murdered founder Joseph Smith in 1844. Yet Catholics posed the greater concern to Protestant missionaries, just as Protestantism caused fear among Catholic prelates. Yankee associations funded Protestants; European societies funded Catholics. Both argued that the stakes were high. Outspoken Protestant theologian Lyman Beecher described the struggle as "a conflict of institutions for the education of her sons, for the purposes of superstition, or evangelical light; of despotism, or liberty." German Catholic Father Boniface Wimmer countered, "Here if anywhere, the destiny of the Catholic church, yea of the whole world, will be decided."[38]

Irish Catholics throughout the Prairie State thirsted for religious institutions. Many had never known regular church services and sacraments. In rural Ireland, Catholics attended mass infrequently and saw a priest merely a few times per year. Others, reminded perhaps of sectarian strife in Ireland, feared the power and influence of Protestantism. "The amount of money employed [by Protestants] in this ceaseless campaign against the Christian faith," one anonymous Irish Catholic forewarned, "is almost incredible." Yet in 1836, only one priest, Father St. Cyr, was available to attend to the spiritual needs of canallers on the I&M. It was no wonder, then, that when William Byrne reached out to Bishop Rosati to organize the first Catholic church in LaSalle County, the Irish financed the effort. Still, even Protestants such as the Reverend J. G. Porter, who settled in Will County along the I&M, lamented that the Irish along the canal too often lived "without God and without hope in the wish."[39]

Chicago's spiritual needs came first. For much of the Irish population there, as historian Ellen Skerrett puts it, "Catholicism remained their primary loyalty." Chicago's first bishop, the Irish-born William J. Quarter, arrived in the city in 1844. He faced a monumental task. Only one church, St. Mary's, the interior of which had never been completed, served an Irish Catholic population of several hundred. Quarter busied himself with finishing the construction of the church, paying off the debt, and establishing parishes based on language rather than territory. This important decision not only divided Catholics according to nationality but also gave the Irish command of Chicago's English-speaking parishes. With one exception, every bishop of Chicago between 1844 and 1915 was Irish or Irish American.[40]

If Irish men ran the Catholic Church, it was Irish women who were at the forefront of providing social and spiritual care for the poor. The first order of nuns in Chicago was the Sisters of Mercy, founded by Catherine McAuley in Dublin in 1831. Mother Frances Xavier Warde brought the order to the United States, and in 1846, she and five nuns—all under the age of twenty-five—came to Chicago, where they tended to the needs of the city's poor, a population swollen by famine emigrants from Ireland. Under the formidable leadership of the Carlow-born Mother Agatha O'Brien, the Sisters of Mercy set up schools, sheltered young women, nursed the afflicted, and cared for orphans. The Sisters later expanded their outreach, establishing St. Francis Xavier Female Academy and founding branch houses and ministries in Aurora, Galena, and Ottawa. By the early twentieth century, an area throughout the Midwest known as the Chicago Regional Community comprised eight independent Mercy communities. Their legacy continues into the twenty-first century.[41]

Irish immigrants established parishes and built Catholic churches, institutions that helped ease their transition into permanent Illinois residents. The earliest of these could be found along the corridor of the I&M Canal. The parish of St. James at Sag Bridge was founded in 1837 near present-day Lemont. Local farmers and two Irish-born carpenters completed a limestone church there in 1858. St. Augustine Parish was founded in 1836 in what later became the city of Bushnell. St. Patrick's of LaSalle was established in 1838.

Parishioners in Ottawa founded St. Columba that same year and laid the cornerstone for Trinity Church in 1841. The French cleric Father Hypolite Du Pontavice led masses in Grundy County, where parishioners built a school and church. In 1847, Catholic residents of Peoria established St. Mary's Church. Farther west, the Irish of Galena had built a Catholic church as early as 1832. In the American Bottom, the Irish of Madison County founded the Immaculate Conception of the Blessed Virgin Mary in 1843. By the time famine emigrants began pouring into Illinois during the late 1840s, Catholic institutions from across the state were already in place.[42]

Ordinary Irish Catholics in Illinois developed a somewhat adversarial relationship with the Church hierarchy during this period. Far from being devoted *Roman* Catholics, as many Protestants imagined, the Irish of Illinois were becoming independent *American* Catholics. A brief glimpse at the early history of the Catholic Church in Chicago exemplifies this point. In 1844, Bishop Quarter established St. Mary of the Lake University. Upon his death in 1848, Quarter endowed the head of the institution, a priest by the name of Father Jeremiah Kinsella, with the authority to make independent decisions. Father Kinsella did more than

St. James Church at Sag Bridge, Lemont, Illinois. Photo by Sean Farrell.

Bishop William Quarter (1806–48)

William Quarter, born in 1806 in County Offaly (formerly King's County), immigrated to the United States in 1822. He entered the seminary at Emmetsburg, Maryland, where he trained for seven years. Ordained in 1829, Father William Quarter served under Bishop John Hughes in New York, establishing schools and assisting the needy. In 1834, the church established a new diocese in Chicago, where Father Quarter took up his new position. He was appointed bishop in 1844 and worked tirelessly to build churches, schools, a university, and a seminary for the city's growing Catholic population. Bishop William Quarter died in 1848 at the age of forty-two, due in no small measure to the amount of work that he undertook.[43]

Bishop William Quarter. Courtesy of the Portraits Collection, University of Notre Dame Archives.

this; he set about building a grand gothic cathedral for the Holy Name parish. Bishop Anthony O'Regan resented the breach of command and dismissed Kinsella. But local parishioners protested, and lay leaders in the Irish community pledged to complete the church themselves—which they did (although it was later destroyed in the Great Chicago Fire).

Another example of lay independence involved Father Denis Dunne, a native of County Laois. Dunne was known to his flock for being attentive to the needs of Chicago's poor. He founded the city's first St. Vincent de Paul Society, turned St. Patrick's Parish into a model community, and served as vicar general at St. Mary of the Lake University. Yet Bishop James Duggan, another Irishman, begrudged Dunne's success. He stripped the priest of his title and closed the university. Irish parishioners turned against the bishop. A public controversy ensued, which led to the exposure of Bishop Duggan's unwarranted absences and financial misdeeds. Father Dunne died before the issue was resolved, but Church officials in Rome intervened and replaced Duggan with the quiet yet effective Bishop Thomas Foley, the city's first American-born bishop. In both situations, the Irish of Chicago valued the independence of their priests and parishes. They desired, in the words of the *Chicago Times*, that "the checks and balances of constitutional freedom" apply to their church as well as their government.[44]

Collective Action and Violence in the Workplace

The 1840s also witnessed Irish workers engaging in collective action against their employers. In 1847, workmen on the I&M, led by the Corkonian leader Daniel Lynch, petitioned state trustee Charles Oakley for improved hours and pay. In a written notice, they implored Oakley to "have such regulations Established" providing them with "time for sleep and rest, $1.25 per day, or one dollar per day & board, with hours of work from 6 oClock AM. to 7 PM. Saving 2 hours for Breakfast and Dinner." As "white Citizens," the petitioners concluded, they did not deserve to be "drove Even worse than Common Slave Negroes." Chief Engineer William Gooding considered their demands, taking note of their nonviolence as well as their appeal to "whiteness." He also warned his superiors of the influence that Irish workmen might exercise at the polls. The strike dragged on for two weeks. Yet Gooding could not be persuaded. He did not want to establish a precedent that would encourage further organization. The workmen eventually backed down.[45]

Their demands dismissed and voices ignored, Irish laborers were left with few options. To be sure, some left the line for farm work. Most, however, stayed. In 1853, violence erupted on the Illinois Central Railroad. Antiforeign newspapers throughout the state had been spewing anti-Catholic vitriol. In June near Decatur, locals were heard shouting insults at Irish trackmen. Rumors abounded that the immigrant laborers planned to retaliate by setting fire to the town. Citizens called upon a local militia, which soon took to the field. Meanwhile, a gang of German laborers attacked an Irish faction on the Great Western Railroad. Irish trackmen from the Illinois Central marched to the defense of their countrymen. The Decatur militia quickly intervened and temporarily prevented bloodshed, but the incident portended trouble.[46]

LaSalle County was less fortunate. In December, following wage cuts across the Illinois Central, contractor Albert Story lowered wages from $1.25 to $1.00 per day. Story's men, roughly 450 in all and mostly Irish, worked a particularly dangerous section of the line. Many quit in protest. Most remained patient—at least, until a clerical mistake halted pay entirely. Outraged workers rushed the contractor's office. One by the name of John Ryan demanded his wages immediately. Story told him to wait. Ryan advanced. When Story reached for his revolver, several Irishmen rushed to Ryan's aid. As one eyewitness put it, they "drove him from his store to his house, thence to his barn, where they most brutally knocked him down, beat his brains out, dragged him to the door, and then with large stones crushed his skull to a mummy." LaSalle County citizens called upon Shields' Guards—a militia company named after the acclaimed Irish-born General James Shields of the Mexican American War—which consisted of eighty volunteers, some of whom were Irish American. Thirty-two individuals were detained. Eleven were tried. Six were sentenced to hang, although Governor Joel Matteson, widely known to have Irish political ties, pardoned those convicted. Incredulous Yankee newspapers claimed that the governor had "bowed to Irish arrogance and outrage."[47]

The LaSalle riot of 1853 foreshadowed tensions between a growing number of antiforeigners and immigrant communities, but it also marked a turning point for Irish laborers. No longer did Fardowns and Corkonians regard each other as principal adversaries. No longer did they go to war. To be sure, Irish laborers only rarely engaged in large-scale acts of violence during the antebellum years. Yet when they did, they increasingly targeted employers—and only because they had exhausted other options. The era of intra-Irish faction fighting had passed. A nascent labor union movement was emerging.

Nativism

During the early 1850s, a powerful wave of antiforeign hysteria swept through the United States. Nativism had arrived. In part, this was a product of unprecedented levels of immigration. Between 1840 and 1860, over 4.3 million predominantly Irish and German individuals resettled in the young republic, constituting a staggering 14.5 percent of the total population. In New York during the 1840s, ardent anti-Catholic leaders such as Thomas R. Whitney founded the Order of United Americans, dedicated to curtailing the political power of new arrivals. As Whitney and other nativists saw things, immigrants lacked the morals or intellect to participate in governance. "If democracy implies universal suffrage, or the right of all men to take control of the State," Whitney railed, ". . . I am no democrat." With disagreements over slavery undermining the Whig Party, politicians in

James Shields (1806–79), Hero of the Mexican-American War

Born in Dungannon, County Tyrone, in 1806, James Shields came to the United States in 1826, settling in Kaskaskia four years later. There he found work as a schoolteacher and later practiced law. He also honed his skills in politics, winning a seat in the Illinois General Assembly in 1836 and later ascending to the position of state auditor. In 1842, Shields nearly fought a saber duel with Abraham Lincoln over a public rebuke, but mutual friends persuaded them to set aside their grievances. When war with Mexico broke out ten years later, Shields raised an Illinois regiment—which included many Irish canallers—and served at the rank of colonel. He distinguished himself in combat on numerous occasions and was wounded twice. Shields was eventually promoted to general and honored by communities around the United States for his gallant service. From 1849 to 1855, he represented Illinois in the U.S. Senate, the only Catholic at the time. Shields went on to serve as a senator for Minnesota and Missouri. He died in 1879.[48]

James Shields. Courtesy of the Brady-Handy Photograph Collection, Library of Congress.

the Order of United Americans sensed an opportunity. In 1854, Whitney's organization merged with several other nativist institutions, forming the Know-Nothing Party. The organization allegedly earned the appellation because its clandestine leadership instructed members to reply, "I know nothing," when asked about the association. The party received support from all classes, and its membership soon swelled to more than ten thousand lodges and 1 million members. That same year, nativist candidates won key elections in New York, Pennsylvania, Ohio, Indiana, and throughout New England. "The 'Know nothings,'" as one Midwesterner noted, "are as thick as locusts in Egypt."[49]

Chicago effectively served as the northern headquarters of Illinois nativism, although Know-Nothing conventions were also held in Springfield. Chicago's Yankee population rallied around the issue of immigration, which they feared had grown out of control. Indeed, a veritable tidal wave of famine refugees continued to pour into Chicago, helping push the city's population from 30,000 in 1850 to nearly 110,000 a decade later. More than half of the city's population was foreign-born. Nativist newspapers warned readers of impending calamity. In 1853, the *Chicago Tribune* relentlessly questioned Catholic loyalty to the United States, describing them as ignorant followers of a distant church "whose head [the Pope] is in a foreign land . . . but the institutions and laws of their adopted home may be set aside with[out] scruple and without a crime." "Who does not know," howled the *Tribune* two years later, "that the most depraved, baseless, worthless and irredeemable drunkards and sots which curse the community, are Irish Catholic?" The *Chicago Literary Budget*, a weekly magazine owned by William W. Danenhower, attacked immigration so consistently that by 1854, it had become, in the words of one historian, "the city's authoritative vehicle for nativist propaganda." With good reason. The *Literary Budget* regularly singled out the Irish as the most dangerous foreign community in the city: "They have formed plans for the control of the polls; and they have organized themselves into bands through whose misconduct perpetual disorder and tumult disturb our streets, and

A Saber Duel Averted

In 1842, while James Shields was serving as state auditor, the Bank of Illinois failed and no longer accepted the state's printed money to pay off private debt. Shields, a Democrat, supported the measure. Abraham Lincoln, a Whig, did not. Lincoln submitted an anonymous letter condemning Shields to the *Sangamon Journal*, Springfield's top Whig newspaper. In it, a fictional farmer named Jeff and his wife, Rebecca, attacked the state auditor's personal and political shortcomings. They referred to him as a "fool as well as a liar" and derided him for the vanity he characteristically displayed around women. "Dear girls, *it is distressing*, but I cannot marry you all," Lincoln mocked in imitation. "Too well I know how much you suffer, but do, *do* remember it is not my fault that I am *so* handsome and *so* interesting." What is more, Lincoln had shown the letter to his fiancée, Mary Todd, who not only approved of it but also decided to join in the fun. On September 16, a poem by Mary Todd, signed "Cathleen," appeared in the *Sangamon Journal*. In it, she ridiculed Shields as an Irishman, referring to him as "the pride from the north of the emerald isle" and "Erin's son." Shields demanded that the editor of the *Journal* identify who was behind the letters. Upon learning that it was Lincoln, he challenged his rival to a duel. It was Lincoln, however, who chose the weapons, "broadswords of the largest size," primarily because he believed that Shields would kill him if he chose pistols. Fortunately for both politicians, mutual friends intervened and persuaded them to reconcile.[50]

our prisons are filled." To be clear, other publications such as the *Chicago Democrat*, the *Sangamon Journal*, the *Chicago Times*, and the newly established Catholic *Western Tablet* opposed nativism. Nevertheless, by the mid-1850s, anti-immigrant newspapers gave voice to anti-immigrant politics.[51]

A national crisis over slavery soon emerged, providing nativists with further momentum. In 1850, the country nearly came to the brink of civil war. Proslavery advocates wanted to see the institution spread into the new western territories. Opponents of slavery, such as Abraham Lincoln, preferred that the institution remain in the South. Illinois senator Stephen Douglas, a Democrat, worked with Whigs such as Henry Clay to avoid catastrophe. Douglas introduced the concept of "popular sovereignty," whereby residents of an aspiring state could decide for themselves whether slavery should be legal. The passage of the Kansas-Nebraska Act of 1854 put Douglas's concept into law, but it also left antislavery Northerners without a political party. Meanwhile, the Whig Party split over the issue of slavery along sectional lines, effectively ending its role as a national party. Sensing opportunity, Know-Nothing delegates reorganized and rebranded their movement as the American Party.

In Chicago, as in the rest of the country, former Whigs looked for a new political home. Many found it in the American Party, as did their ideological counterparts in cities such as New York, Boston, Philadelphia, New Orleans, Cincinnati, and St. Louis. In Chicago, Dr. Levi Boone, the grandnephew of the legendary Daniel Boone, ran as the city's American Party candidate in 1855. Proponents of temperance, abolition, and nativism, Boone and his allies won the mayorship and several city council seats. In his inaugural speech in March, Boone charged the city's Catholics with being "under an oath of allegiance to the temporal, as well as the spiritual supremacy of a foreign despot." This type of language was not new; the mayor's victory marked the continuation of decades of nativist politics in Chicago. In 1840, 250 residents of Cook County, nearly all Whigs, had unsuccessfully petitioned the U.S. House of Representatives to repeal the current naturalization laws and replace them with native-born citizenry. But before Boone, none had won this kind of power and seeming mandate. The election of 1855 marked the first time that Chicago politicians had declared open warfare on the city's immigrant population.[52]

Boone and the American Party's successes provided common cause for the city's German and Irish Catholics. Barely a month after the mayor's inauguration, the city council increased liquor license fees and decreased the terms of the licenses from a year to three months. Boone also ordered taverns closed on Sundays, openly acknowledging that the policy targeted Irish and German saloonkeepers. Anticipating blowback, he tripled the size of the police force. Blowback soon came. On April 21, saloonkeepers challenged the legality of the mayor's actions in court. German and Irish protestors flocked to the Cook County Courthouse, battling with police for three days in the city's infamous Lager Beer Riot. One person was killed and three were seriously injured. Boone's police arrested sixty. In the wake of the violence, the city's experiment with Know-Nothing politics declined rapidly. Boone stopped attending council sessions, and the nativist coalition split further over the issue of slavery. Just the same, the movement fully exposed the anti-Catholic and antiforeign prejudices with which the Irish would have to contend for decades to come.[53]

The American Party found only pockets of support in Illinois. Voters in Springfield enthusiastically backed the new party, hosting its convention every other year. Voters in Belleville and Galesburg, both of which contained marginalized Irish minorities, embraced the nativist platform. Democratic newspapers such as the *Illinois State Register* (Springfield) warned readers, "Democrats, Beware of Secret Societies." Many nativists waxed optimistic about their chances of electing an American Party governor or president in 1856. But the movement's culture of secrecy, which had been an asset in local campaigns, did not translate into larger victories. And Catholic newspapers such as Chicago's *Western Tablet* gave new voice to immigrants and their allies. Former Chicago mayor Buckner S. Morris garnered just over 8 percent of the vote and carried but one county. Millard Fillmore, former U.S. president and the American Party's national nominee, won a mere 6 percent of the vote. By 1856, many former Know-Nothings had already begun shifting their loyalty to the Republican Party. Most regarded slavery, not temperance or immigration, as the pivotal issue of the day. In counties with large Irish populations, such as Jo Daviess (Galena) and those along the line of the I&M (Will and LaSalle), neither Fillmore nor Morris claimed more than 1 percent of the vote—a sign that Ireland's exiles in the Prairie State continued to exercise power at the polls.[54]

Happy Homes of Illinois

Despite the nativist controversies of the 1850s, Irish men and women continued to seek new homes on the prairie. Land beckoned. Between 1850 and 1870, the percentage of the state's Irish population who lived on farms increased from 33 to 36.1 percent. Land agents such as Irishman William Scully were instrumental in bringing immigrant families to rural Illinois. Later accused of absenteeism and overcharging tenants, he created a veritable farming empire by purchasing scrip that had been given to veteran canallers who fought in the Mexican-American War. He then rented plots to newly arrived immigrants. Scully's landholdings eventually exceeded two hundred thousand acres across the Midwest.[55]

The experiences of Irish farmers often varied across the state. In the canal town of Lemont, roughly thirty miles southwest of Chicago, the Irish viewed farming as a commercial enterprise and tended to be more financially successful than their German and Yankee neighbors. Irish farmers on the rural edges of Cook and McHenry Counties, anxious to put memories of the Great Famine behind them, profited from farming in ways that contrasted with life in Chicago's urban ghettos. Meanwhile, those in the town of Hartland, over sixty miles northwest of Chicago, preferred stability to commercial success. Lending resources and equipment to immigrant newcomers, the people of Hartland built a veritable Irish farming community—an "island," as Eileen McMahon puts it, "in a hostile Yankee sea." Many of the Irish of the Prairie State saw a distinct opportunity in farming in these mid-nineteenth-century years.[56]

Opportunity and appreciation were common themes found in letters sent back to Ireland. "I think on the hole you would better your self mutch by coming to this country," a westward migrant wrote to his brother in 1845. "Here every man is Lord of the soil he owns, there is no rent yearly. It is his and hairs for ever." William Porter, a County Down Protestant who came to Illinois in 1850, later reported to relatives in Ireland, "We would never think of going back to live in that misruled land again . . . for here you can hold up your head and not take off your hat to any man." William Williamson of County Armagh wrote his brother about having come to the "Good land of Illinois," where shortly after his arrival, he had met a fellow Irishman who owned "fifty acres of as good land. . . . It is what is called here prairie, no trees or any [amount] of timber on it." Irish travel books reinforced the point: "The American farmer, Patrick, never pays any rent. When he takes a farm he buys it for ever." To be sure, Irish-run newspapers such as the *Boston Pilot* and influential figures such as New York's Archbishop John Hughes opposed westward movement, just as they had opposed Thomas D'Arcy McGee's vision of an Irish community in Illinois. But others, including New York's *Truth Teller* and William J. Quarter, first bishop of Chicago, encouraged migration to the Prairie State. Those who came west tended to agree. As one priest noted in 1855:

> Indeed, there appears to be a happy blending of kindly influences, and a disposition in all to submerge minor differences of country and race, and to become in manners, as well as in fact, Americans and men of the West. And this has a happy effect in promoting charity and the absence of those senseless outcries against foreigners which have become the disgrace of other cities. This change of feeling is refreshing to one who has lived for years in the East, and had to feel the cutting lash of persecution, and the sting of anti-Catholic prejudice.

By 1860, Irish-born individuals represented over 5 percent of the state's population. Illinois had become the fifth most-popular destination for Ireland's exiles. As McGee had predicted, "Irish homes of Illinois" were indeed "happy homes of Illinois."[57]

Toward Civil War

In the 1850s, renewed debate over an old issue threatened to tear apart the country, which for over eighty years had become home to millions of Irish immigrants. Slavery and its expansion into western territories divided people and institutions across the United States. The Compromise of 1850—which admitted California as a free state, organized Utah and New Mexico under the provisions of popular sovereignty, and established the Fugitive Slave Act as federal law—had held the nation together uneasily at best. Stephen Douglas's plan to allow residents of new states to decide the legality of slavery for themselves had backfired. In Kansas, antislavery pioneers and proslavery advocates poured into the territory, intent on drafting the laws of the land, only to meet one another in pitched battle. Churches split over the theology of slavery. Senator Preston Brooks of South Carolina physically assaulted Charles Sumner of Massachusetts on the floor of the U.S. Senate, nearly beating him to death with his cane. The Supreme Court had declared in *Dred Scott v. Sandford* that black Americans could not become citizens. Members of the newly founded Republican Party, including Abraham Lincoln, vehemently protested. An impending crisis loomed. For immigrants who had braved hardship, famine, and prejudice, they had no desire to see the United States destroyed by civil strife.[58]

To the Irish of Illinois, Stephen Douglas appeared to be the one politician capable of restoring unity to the divided nation. Known to voters as the "Little Giant," Douglas had long courted and won the Irish vote in Illinois. In 1836, Douglas had emphasized his Irish ancestry in speeches, and with Irish support, he nearly won the U.S. congressional race against Stuart. His stiff opposition to tighter naturalization laws and suffrage rights endeared him to immigrants. Douglas ran again in 1843, and with Irish votes, he won this time. He would do so again. In 1852, while running for U.S. Senate, he delivered a speech in honor of the visiting Hungarian revolutionary Lajos Kossuth, which spoke more to his Irish audience than to his guest. England "must do justice to Ireland [applause], and to the Irish exiles [great applause]," he began. "So long as she imprisons and banishes for life, Irish patriots for no other crime than that which has made the illustrious Hungarian our national guest, she must look elsewhere for allies and assistance." To be clear, state legislatures voted for U.S. Senators in the nineteenth century, not the body politic. Yet the Illinois General Assembly appreciated Douglas's popularity and sent him to Washington in 1852. The Irish in Illinois loved the Democratic politician, and he loved them back. When Douglas remarried after the death of his first wife, General James Shields served as his best man. He also was a close friend of the editor of the *Chicago Times*, an Irish American by the name of Jim Sheahan. As Potter observes, "No political figure since Andrew Jackson had so won the affection, even the love, of the Catholic Irish as Stephen Douglas."[59]

Consequently, when Lincoln and Douglas met in the town of Ottawa on August 21, 1858, for the first of seven debates over the issue of slavery, the "Little Giant" had plenty of supporters. Both men were running for U.S. Senate, and both recognized the importance of winning over the Irish. LaSalle County, after all, boasted one of the largest Irish communities in the state. Douglas began by accusing Lincoln of being an abolitionist and attempting to make Illinois "a free Negro colony"—a point intended to strike fear in the hearts of white laborers, whose wages would decrease with competition from African-Americans. Lincoln retorted that Douglas was proposing to nationalize slavery, something white farmers in Illinois did not want to see either. From the perspective of most Irish immigrants, however, the debates were clearly about preserving the union, a word employed by both candidates nearly three dozen times. It was Douglas who eventually won the seat. In his remaining debates with Lincoln, he made it plain that he neither supported nor opposed slavery. What mattered to him was the right of the voters to choose. This argument spoke clearly to the Irish. According to George Potter, "They believed he had found the formula to save the Union in his principle of popular sovereignty, which, after all, was what the Irish in Ireland asked of the English government—the right to make their own domestic decisions."[60]

In LaSalle County, as in Illinois more generally, Irish voters mattered. Echoes of nativism often reverberated in Republican papers, which claimed that the "two despotisms" of Catholicism and slavery threatened liberty. The Democratic press was quick to respond. Nearly two weeks before the election, the *Ottawa Free Trader* had warned readers, "The republican party is preparing to reenact the outrages of Baltimore," whereby "bands of bullies . . . permitted nobody to vote who did not openly show and as openly vote the 'American' ticket." "We ask our citizens of foreign birth," the paper continued, "to mark this threat." Another headline ran, "The Last Card—Danenhower for Lincoln," an effort to tie Lincoln to the political scheme of Chicago's most prominent nativist. On the eve of the contest, the *Free Trader* answered Republicans' claim that several hundred Irish laborers from LaSalle had voted in multiple counties. After dismissing the illogic behind the charge—after all, Douglas needed all the votes he could get in LaSalle County—the paper warned readers of "a gigantic scheme of fraud by the republicans . . . and other bullies in the republican ranks to drive Irish and German voters from the polls." Indeed, on the day of the election, rumors began to stir that fifty Irishmen from Ottawa had forcibly taken possession of the polls in the town of Rutland and refused to allow Republicans to vote. The *Free Trader* disagreed. Rather than fifty illegal voters, it was "ten or twelve voters, principally Irishmen," who had hitched a ride with an "honest" man named John Sweeney on his way to the polls. "There was not a man in the load," the paper concluded, "but was known to be a resident of the town, and a legal voter." In hindsight, it is unclear whether Republicans or Democrats voted illegally in the election. It is clear, however, that Stephen Douglas won the Illinois Senate seat with Irish support.[61]

Irish American Nationalism: The Fenian Brotherhood

Another political development in 1858 had a profound impact on both the United States and Ireland. That year, in Dublin and New York, James Stephens and John O'Mahony founded separate wings of a single association dedicated to Irish independence. The Irish Republican Brotherhood, known in America as the Fenian Brotherhood (so named for the "soldiers of Finn," an ancient Irish warrior chief), attracted members from across the globe who believed that constitutional efforts to achieve Irish nationhood were doomed to failure. Short of an armed revolution, they reasoned, the British Empire would never concede to a free Ireland. The Catholic Church, an institution with increasing power in Ireland, loudly opposed Fenianism, arguing in favor of nonviolent and constitutional methods of political action. Yet the Church had less influence in America. The revolutionaries who came to the United States, men such as O'Mahony, Michael Doheny, and Jeremiah O'Donovan Rossa, quickly discovered a budding community of nationalists with memories of the famine and a desire to do their part for Ireland.[62]

Irish Americans from across Illinois responded enthusiastically to the Fenian call—to both the criticism and praise of their contemporaries. By 1863, at least forty separate branches of the organization were active in the state, with prominent associations in Chicago and Ottawa. Illinois's Fenians, like others around the country, officially belonged to a secretive, oath-bound society. Not only did they pledge "to strike for the independence of Ireland whenever an opportunity arises," the *Ottawa Free Trader* reported, but they also urged "younger members of the Brotherhood to study military tactics, so as to be prepared to aid 'the United States, by land or by sea, against England's myrmidons.'" Most served in the Union army during the Civil War. Many were commissioned officers.[63]

In 1863, Chicago hosted a national meeting for the organization, which the press labeled the "Fenian Fair." Some three hundred delegates from sixty-three branches across North America attended. Most were members of the working classes and bore ties with the emergent labor movement. Irish women sold tickets, played music, served meals, and directed the concourse. Representatives elected John O'Mahony as head of the organization, and they drafted a Declaration of Independence for a new Irish Republic. Bishop James Duggan of the Chicago Diocese excoriated the Fenians, arguing that they constituted a secret society and had therefore violated a papal ban on such associations. Newspapers such as the *Chicago Tribune* and the *Rock Island Daily Argus* routinely criticized them as well. In 1865, the *Tribune* referred to the Brotherhood as "the most laughable, as well as absurd, project which at present amuses the public." The *Daily Argus* called them "thieves and swindlers." Yet the *Ottawa Free Trader*, ever sympathetic to the nationalist cause, defended against charges that Fenians had planned to "assist Jeff Davis to become the dictator of an American Nation." "The gallant members of our organization who are now in the army," the *Free Trader* countered, "is a sufficient refutation of this charge." Even the *Cairo Evening Times*, a self-described "advocate of religious as well as political tolerance," confessed to "a large share of esteem for the Fenian Brotherhood."[64]

In both Ireland and the United States, the organization failed to spark a successful revolution, but the Irish of Illinois again showed their dedication to independence. In 1866, American Fenians launched an ill-fated invasion of Canada, hoping to hold its government hostage while bargaining for Irish independence. In 1867, the brotherhood attempted a similarly doomed uprising in Ireland. Both insurrections failed, but not for the last time.

The Irish of Illinois and the American Civil War

In 1860, with the United States on the brink of a civil war and Abraham Lincoln pledging to preserve the union, many Irish voters in Illinois threw their support behind the Republican candidate. In Chicago's predominantly Irish community of Bridgeport, over two-thirds of the vote went to the "Rail Splitter," as Lincoln was commonly called. In LaSalle County, where Douglas had been so successful two years prior, Lincoln defeated the "Little Giant" by a count of 5,342 to 4,288. Across Illinois, counties with sizable Irish populations, particularly those in the northern half of the state, went for Lincoln. Jo Daviess County (Galena) went for Lincoln by 1,000 votes. Both Will and Grundy Counties, which bordered the I&M, chose the Republican candidate by strong majorities. To be sure, the Democratic *Ottawa Free Trader* of LaSalle County expressed disappointment, but it also proved prescient: "The great battle is over, and the Republicans have won. For the first time, in the history of our country, a president has been elected upon a sectional issue, by one section of the Union over another. Taken in the light of Washington's Farewell Address, where such solemn warnings are given against sectional politics, and arraying one section against another, the event of Lincoln's election is one that may well excite reckless thought." Indeed. Lincoln's election, secured in part by Irish voters across the Northern states, convinced Southern politicians that the union was lost. South Carolina seceded from the United States in December 1860 over the issue of slavery. Other states followed. In April, rebel forces fired on federal troops at Fort Sumter. Lincoln called for 75,000 volunteers. The American Civil War had begun.[65]

The Irish of Illinois overwhelmingly backed the Union war effort. Heeding Lincoln's call, as well as that of Stephen Douglas, who reminded citizens that in war that there were "only patriots—or traitors," thousands enlisted. In all, 12,041 immigrants of the Prairie State served in the Union army, over 8 percent of all Irish-born soldiers. Irish militias from the towns of Earlsville, Morris, and Ottawa, many with Fenian ties, volunteered en masse. Illinois fielded two specifically Irish units, the 23rd and 90th Illinois Infantry Regiments. The latter, known as the "Irish Legion," mustered in September 1862 with the support of Father Denis Dunne, who provided Catholic chaplains for the outfit. It served under Grant at Vicksburg and under Sherman in Georgia and the Carolinas, and its casualties were high. Of the 980 men who fought in the unit, only 221 returned. The former, known as "Mulligan's Western Irish Brigade," was named after James A. Mulligan, a devout Catholic and the first graduate of St. Mary of the Lake. Composed primarily of volunteers from Cook, Wayne, Grundy, and LaSalle Counties, the unit mustered in July 1861. It saw action in Kentucky, before being stationed the following year at Chicago's Camp Douglas, the state's notorious facility for Confederate prisoners of war. The unit fought in Virginia throughout the rest of the war and served under Grant when Lee surrendered at Appomattox. In July 1864, Mulligan was shot and killed at the Second Battle of Kernstown. His men rushed to save him, but the colonel reportedly insisted, "Lay me down and save the flag." He died two days later. On August 1 and 2, thousands of

Chicagoans honored Mulligan, "the city's first and most beloved Civil War hero," in the words of Lawrence McCaffrey.[66]

Irish women strove to preserve the union as well. In Chicago, "Female Patriots," as the *Tribune* termed them, formed a Ladies' Association, "organized for the purpose of assisting and encouraging the [Irish] Regiment." Marian Nugent Mulligan, wife of the famed colonel, often accompanied her husband in the field and raised money for his brigade. She also organized an expedition of twenty Sisters of Mercy, all of whom were Irish-born, to tend to the wounded veterans of the 23rd Regiment in Kentucky. During the journey, they faced gunfire from Confederate forces. Later in 1861, these "angels of the battlefield," as the Sisters became known, helped establish a field hospital in Jefferson City at the behest of the U.S. Sanitary Commission. Irish women in Chicago led the campaign to raise money for the 23rd Regiment's American flag. Scores of Irish women served as army laundresses in the state's regiments, and some may have served among the estimated four hundred women who disguised themselves as male soldiers and fought in combat. The Irish of Illinois sacrificed much to preserve the union.[67]

The attitudes of Irish Americans around the country changed, however, when abolition became part of the Union plan for victory. In January 1863, Abraham Lincoln issued the Emancipation Proclamation, which ended slavery in those states in open rebellion. For many soldiers who had volunteered to preserve the union, the cause of the conflict appeared to have shifted. To compound matters, the U.S. Congress passed a conscription law in March 1863 intended to fill the depleting ranks of the Union army. The law permitted draftees the opportunity to purchase a substitute for $300. Both decrees incensed working-class Irish communities across the North, but none like that of New York City, which erupted in violence on July 13, two days after the implementation of the draft. Predominantly Irish Catholic mobs—men, women, and children—targeted abolitionists, Republicans, and any black person who dared appear in public. They attacked the mayor's house, looted wealthy homes on Lexington Avenue, and burned an orphanage for black children. They beat and killed police officers, many of whom were also Irish. By some estimates, more than one thousand people were killed. Draft protests also occurred in other cities with significant Irish Catholic populations—Boston, Milwaukee, Troy, and Dubuque, to name a few—although none quite like the four-day riot in New York.[68]

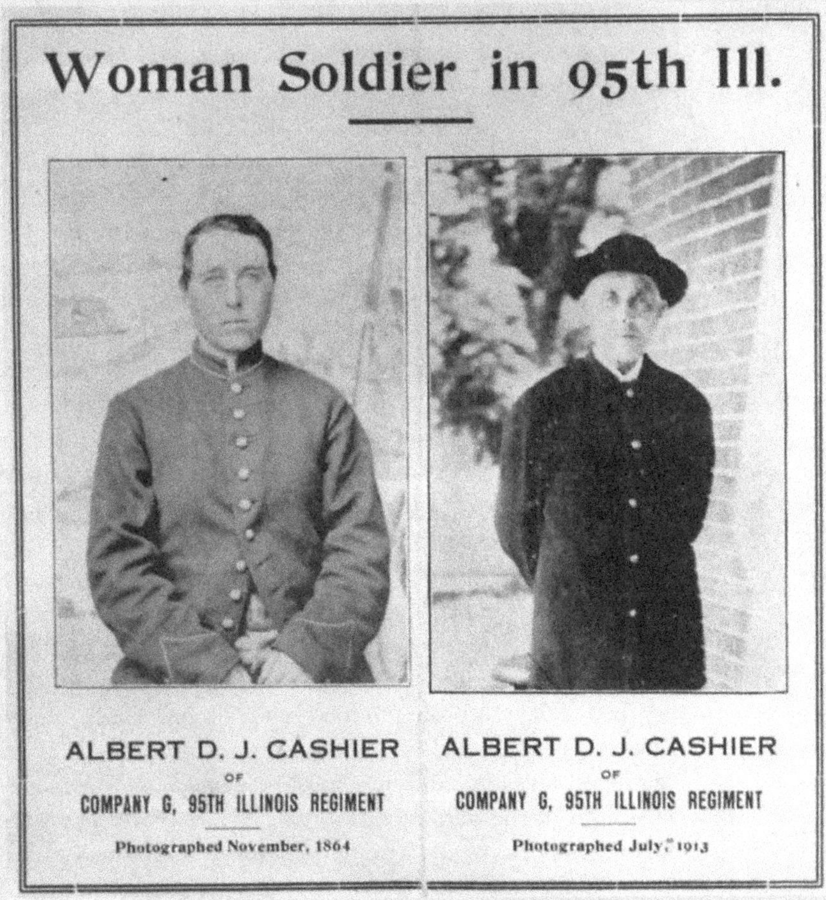

Jennie Hodgers, also known as Albert Cashier. Courtesy of the Abraham Lincoln Presidential Library and Museum.

Jennie Hodgers, aka Albert Cashier (1843–1915)

Jennie Hodgers was one of the most remarkable Irish women to participate in the American Civil War. Born in Ireland, she immigrated in her youth to Belvidere, Illinois. In 1862, she donned a man's suit, adopted the pseudonym Albert Cashier, and enlisted in the 95th Illinois Infantry. Like hundreds of similar women throughout the country, she fought in battle, most notably during the Vicksburg Campaign. Following the war, Hodgers retained the last name Cashier and continued living as a man, even voting in elections and collecting a pension in 1899. Only after an automobile accident in 1911 was Cashier's secret transgender identity unmasked. In 2017, Jay Paul Deratany, Joe Stevens, and Keaton Wooden wrote and produced a folk-country musical titled "The Civility of Albert Cashier," which ran in Chicago and Los Angeles.[69]

Many of Illinois's Irish chafed at emancipation and conscription. This held true across the state, even before either policy became law. In September 1862, African American "contrabands," former slaves turned soldiers, bivouacked at Camp Defiance near Cairo. Witnessing the hostility of common laborers toward black enlistees, a man by the name of H. Oscar documented the enmity. In a letter to his friend and esteemed abolitionist Frederick Douglass, Oscar observed that "PARTICULARLY *the* Irish, are raging intensely and fiercely here against those poor unfortunate and innocent people. I believe the Irish would murder every man and woman of them if they thought they dare do it." A month later in Chicago, an Irish woman by the name of Mrs. Mulrooney, who owned and operated a boardinghouse in Bridgeport, refused to disclose the names of her boarders until the police took her into custody. In June 1863, a woman by the name of Mrs. Ellen McCafferty threatened to stab Chicago draft marshals with a butcher knife. In other cases, Irish men simply fled to Canada. Some became "bounty jumpers," men who enlisted for cash bonuses and then quickly deserted. The most serious incident of draft violence occurred on June 6, 1863, when a crowd assailed several enrollment officers in an impoverished neighborhood of Bridgeport known as "the Patch." According to the *Tribune*, "a mob of three or four hundred infuriated Irish," including men, women, and children, "gathered together, and howling like demons, commenced an onslaught of the officers with bricks, stones, bottles and every missile they could find." Two officers were wounded in the assault before retreating.[70]

Despite the potentially deadly confrontation between Bridgeport's Irish and the police, it paled in comparison to the New York City draft riots. But why? Some historians have noted that Chicago's Irish owned more property relative to those in the Empire City, making them reluctant to destroy it. Others have suggested that Chicago's Irish were savvier about law and politics. Attacking the enrollment process, after all, impeded even the possibility of being drafted. Racial demographics may have been a factor as well, given that Chicago's African American population was much smaller than New York's.[71]

Yet another explanation, one recently put forth by historian Ryan Keating, clarifies further why Chicago's Irish resorted to violence far less than their eastern counterparts. Put simply, they were more ingrained in the community. They held more political power and owned more property. Despite fears over African American competition for low-wage jobs, and despite their opposition to a draft law that blatantly favored the wealthy, they did not harbor the same resentments as their New York counterparts. Chicago welcomed the Irish in ways that New York did not. One need look no further than the reaction of the Chicago German Workers' Club following the draft riots. In stark contrast to anti-Irish New York patricians such as George Templeton Strong, the club's president, Theodore Hielscher, called on "Germans, Americans, and Irish" to "stand together." Hielscher believed that he could count on "those Americans and Irish who have attained political independence," because they desired "neither mob rule nor sword rule." Chicago's Irish also wielded more authority than their eastern brethren. In 1864, they challenged the draft again, only this time through political channels. Alderman "Honest John" Comiskey, a promoter of both Mulligan's Western Brigade and the Irish Legion, spearheaded the opposition in the City Council. The measure failed, but Comiskey's effort revealed their power in municipal government—a power that only continued to grow.[72]

Most probably shared the sentiments of Peter Casey, an Irishman and Chicago police officer who wrote in the summer of 1863, "I am sick sore and downhearted. . . . I wish every dam abolitionist in Chicago felt as I do this morning they would be careful how they have rushed the country into war." Few had a thirst for the violence that had gripped the New York Irish. Race rioting in Chicago would have to wait for another century.[73]

Throughout the first half of the nineteenth century, the Irish of Illinois did not face the same kind of racial antipathy that their fellow countrymen and women did on the East Coast. In places such as Boston and New York, nativists increasingly based their disdain for Irish Catholics on "scientific" theories of racism. Unlike common prejudices that abounded prior to the famine, which regarded immigrants as unrefined but capable of learning American ways, many antiforeigners by the 1860s considered Ireland's exiles to be biologically inferior. During New York's draft riot, patrician George Templeton Strong described the Irish as "creatures that crawl and eat dirt and poison every community they infest." In the aftermath of the Civil War, *Harper's Weekly* cartoonists such as Thomas Nast represented the Irish with sloped brows and apelike or "simian" features.[74]

This was far less the case in Illinois. Even the *Chicago Tribune*, a noted anti-Catholic publication, described the Irish as a "brave, pugnacious race" in the mid-1860s. Military service helped make this possible. Illinois regiments, even the state's ethnic regiments, included both immigrant and native-born volunteers, something that further integrated the Irish into the state's social fabric. And they shared a common ideology. As historian Ryan Keating puts it, "Immigrant loyalty to and inclusion within the United States . . . stood as a reflection of a transatlantic republican identity . . . for the preservation of republicanism in America was vital to the spread of this ideology abroad." To be sure, the *Tribune* and other like newspapers continued to be suspicious of Irish Catholics into the late nineteenth century. The Irish in Illinois, however, like many of their fellow countrymen and women, fared better in the West.[75]

Toward Respectability

History has vindicated Thomas D'Arcy McGee. From statehood to the end of the Civil War, the Irish of Illinois acquired political power, found gainful employment, and established religious institutions. They mined the lead of Galena. They served in the Black Hawk War. Amid disease and miserable working conditions, they dug canals and built railroads. They served as maids, opened laundries, and ran boardinghouses. Thousands farmed the state's rich prairie soil. They flexed their political muscle, voting, running for office, and winning. Some, such as General James Shields, became national heroes and politicians. They advocated for a free Ireland, with many supporting O'Connell's repeal campaign as well as the Fenian Brotherhood. Most of them were Catholic, and they weathered insults and epithets—often from hostile newspapers. The Irish of Chicago briefly endured the tenure of a Know-Nothing mayor. But in comparison with their counterparts in the urban Northeast, the Irish of Illinois had it better. What is more, they knew it. In March 1867, the Irish of Chicago hosted, in the words of the *Tribune*, "one of the finest and most extensive displays ever seen here upon St. Patrick's Day." In an address to the Society of St. Patrick, President Roger J. Bross summed up the emotions of many an Irish man and woman in Illinois. "We," he proclaimed, "have exchanged our island home to become citizens of this free and glorious country, and in whatever situation we may be placed, there are none in this broad Republic who, while loving their native land as we do, are more loyal to this our adopted country." The audience roared in applause. The Irish had, after all, proved their mettle and sacrificed much during the American Civil War. New waves of immigrants were soon to arrive, allowing them to reach higher rungs up the social ladder. The Irish of Illinois were moving toward respectability.[76]

3

AT THE FOREFRONT OF THE MULTIETHNIC CITY: THE IRISH IN CHICAGO, 1865–1933

I know histhry isn't thrue, Hinnissy, because it ain't like what I see ivry day in Halsted Sthreet. If any wan comes along with a histhry iv Greece or Rome that'll show me th' people fightin,' gettin' dhrunk, makin' love, gettin' married, owin' the grocery man an' bein' without hard-coal, I'll believe they was a Greece or Rome, but not befure. Historians is like doctors. They are always lookin' f'r symptoms. Those iv them that writes about their own times examines th' tongue an' feels th' pulse an' makes a wrong dygnosis. Th' other kind iv histhry is a post-mortem examination. It tells ye what a counthry died iv. But I'd like to know what it lived iv.

—Finley Peter Dunne, *Observations by Mr. Dooley* (1902)

In the late nineteenth century, no fictional character captured the Irish experience in Chicago like Martin Dooley, a Bridgeport saloonkeeper and amateur philosopher who regularly commented on immigrant life on the city's South Side. Mr. Dooley was the invention of Finley Peter Dunne, son of Irish immigrants and a Chicago native whose promotion to editorial chairman for the *Evening Post* in 1893 gave new voice to the city's Irish community. Scrutinizing his own experiences and family history, Dunne created a character familiar to readers, one who pondered the city's milestones from a humble, immigrant perspective: the Chicago Fire of 1871, the murder of Dr. Patrick Cronin, the Columbian Exposition of 1893, and the Pullman Strike of 1894. Often humorous, but also thoughtful and occasionally cynical, Mr. Dooley opined about the institutions that had already become synonymous with the Irish Catholic experience: the Democratic Party, Irish nationalist associations, and the Catholic Church. He was beloved and hated by Americans of all backgrounds, including his fellow Irish.

Dunne left Chicago in 1899 to pursue his career further as a nationally syndicated author for outlets such as *Collier's Weekly* and the *American Magazine*. Yet it was the sentiments of Dunne's Bridgeport publican, the "provider of companionship and solace to bone-weary working people," as the pioneering scholar Charles Fanning later put it, who provided an invaluable glimpse into the lives of South Side immigrants. He captured the development of America's first ethnic group. In politics, religion, labor, race, and eventually suburbanization, the Irish blazed a path for new waves of immigrants to follow. In Chicago, the quintessential American city, the Irish came to dominate the urban frontier.[1]

A Booming Irish American City

Immigration turned Chicago from a desolate frontier post into a thriving multiethnic city. At the time of statehood in 1818, only a small army post named Fort Dearborn consisting of a few log cabins stood at the location. Upon the town's founding in 1833, barely 300 people, some of them Irish soldiers stationed at the fort, resided in the community. Yet over the next four years, easterners and foreign immigrants pursued economic opportunities westward. By the time the lakeside town was incorporated as a city in 1837, Chicago had, in the words of one historian, "a distinctly Irish coloration." By 1840, the population had grown to nearly 4,500, with an estimated 10 percent of that number Irish-born. Ten years later, the city had expanded to nearly 30,000, with some 20 percent having been born in Ireland. On the eve of the Civil War, the city's residents numbered just over 112,000, and by 1870, Chicago boasted a population of almost 299,000. The Irish constituted over 13 percent of the population—nearly 40,000 individuals. By the turn of the century, Chicago had become the second-largest city in the United States, with only New York and Philadelphia boasting more first- and second-generation Irish Americans.[2]

By the 1870s, Chicago had become "the Irish capital of the Midwest." Upon the completion of the Illinois and Michigan Canal in 1848, hundreds of workers and their families settled in the community of Bridgeport, often scraping by as laborers or seeking relief in the city's poorhouses. As late as 1868, the *Chicago Evening*

Post scoffed, "Scratch a convict or a pauper and the chances are that you tickle the skin of an Irish Catholic at the same time—an Irish Catholic made a criminal or a pauper by the priest and politicians who have deceived him and kept him in ignorance, in a word, a savage, as he was born." Yet such editorial statements also masked real concerns about Irish political power. They were already a formidable voting bloc, with typically Democratic politicians rewarding loyal patrons with jobs and municipal posts. In 1850, of the nine police officers on the city's payroll, six were Irish. Ten years later, Irishmen constituted nearly half of the department's 107 officers.[3]

The Irish also dominated the Catholic institutions of the city. Bishop Quarter's decision to organize parish lines according to language effectively positioned the Irish to control the city's Church hierarchy. Religious orders founded or staffed by Irish women, such as the Sisters of Mercy, the Sisters of the Blessed Virgin Mary, and the Sisters of the Good Shepherd, helped establish schools and hospitals. Female immigrants, increasingly more literate and economically self-reliant than their male counterparts, became laundresses, house maids, nuns, and teachers. Historian Lawrence McCaffrey describes Irish women as the "civilizers of Irish-America." The vast majority of males, nearly 60 percent by the 1870s, found work in the city's meatpacking or railroad industries. Others entered the priesthood, became proprietors of saloons, or served as firefighters. And many of these working-class immigrants continued to join Irish nationalist associations, such as the Clan na Gael, established in Bridgeport in 1869. By the 1870s, Chicago's Irish not only were a visible part of the city's social and economic fabric but also exerted a remarkable degree of influence over its political and religious institutions.[4]

The Great Chicago Fire

Rapid growth soon caught up with the burgeoning metropolis. On Sunday, October 8, 1871, at approximately 8:45 P.M., the barn of Irish immigrants Patrick and Catherine O'Leary caught fire. The flames spread rapidly through the city, burning for nearly three days. As many as three hundred people died, and an estimated one hundred thousand people were made homeless. More than three and one-third square miles of property, totaling $192 million in damages, was destroyed in the conflagration. The Great Chicago Fire of 1871 forever changed the city's landscape.[5]

Newspapers almost immediately blamed the destruction on Mrs. O'Leary, whose cow apparently had knocked over a lantern in the barn. The evidence is far from clear. A more likely story is that the fire was started by a neighbor of the O'Learys' by the name of Daniel "Peg Leg" Sullivan, who had received his sobriquet as a Civil War veteran and amputee. In his testimony before the city's Fire Inquiry, Sullivan claimed to have spotted the fire from across the street before he attempted to put it out and save the O'Learys' barn animals. The disabled Sullivan scarcely had time for such heroics, however, if he had been down the road from the O'Learys', as he testified. In some ways, Sullivan acted like someone who accidentally started the fire—attempting to extinguish it, and then saving the animals and alerting the neighborhood when it grew out of control. In retrospect, there is no way to know for sure how the fire began. Perhaps more important was the way that the antiforeign press latched onto the urban legend of Mrs. O'Leary's cow, which both reflected and reinforced stereotypes of Irish Catholic immigrants. Anti-Irish sentiment had tempered in the years that followed the American Civil War, but it had not disappeared entirely.[6]

For the city's Irish population, as for Chicagoans overall, the Great Fire of 1871 proved to be a paradoxical calamity. In the fire's aftermath, much of Irish Chicago lay in ruins. St Mary's Cathedral had burned to the ground, as had six smaller churches, rectories, convents, and schools in Chicago's commercial district. Holy Name Church had burned, along with St. Paul's and the Church of the Immaculate Conception. The Irish slum known as Conley's Patch was completely destroyed. And the dress shop of future labor organizer Mary Harris "Mother" Jones was also reduced to ashes.

The fire's devastation also created new opportunities. Irish laborers cleaned the rubble and rebuilt the infrastructure. They built the tens of thousands of dwellings and apartments needed to shelter the homeless. Irish clerics initiated a brick-and-mortar campaign aimed at replacing wooden churches with brick structures. Their efforts were so successful that by 1873, appraisers estimated the value of Catholic parishes at over $2 million. Newspaper editors throughout the city, some of whom feared the expansion of Catholic institutions, occasionally applauded the effort. Their construction, one editor commented, "improves and helps to fill up the surrounding neighborhood and swells and enhances the value of property." Simultaneously, a small middle-class Catholic community, often labeled the "lace-curtain Irish," began to emerge in the city—notably at the east end of St. John's Parish on Prairie Avenue. Eschewing banking and finance, most became lawyers and business owners. Yet for the Irish poor, derogatorily referred to as "shanty Irish," the fire had stripped them of their possessions. And the paradox was not lost on Mr. Dooley during the 1897 commemoration of the Great Chicago Fire: "Oh! A fine thing, f'r Chicago. It desthroyed old buildin's so that new wans cud be put up. But did ye iver think that th' ol' buildin's was homes

Holy Family Church. Courtesy of the Chicago and the Midwest Collections, Newberry Library.

Holy Family Church and the Great Chicago Fire of 1871

In 1871, Holy Family had become the largest parish in Chicago, boasting a congregation of almost twenty thousand people. Its complex, located near Twelfth and Halsted, contained a Gothic brick church, a convent academy, three schools, and the predecessor of Loyola University, St. Ignatius College. Legend has it that when the fire began spreading toward the church, Father Damen, who was away preaching in Brooklyn, promised to light seven candles in front of Our Lady's statue and invoked Our Lady of Perpetual Help to spare the complex. The winds shifted, and the church was saved. As promised, Father Damen lit the candles, and to this day seven electric lights burn at Our Lady's shrine in respect of the memory.[7]

f'r poor people? Ye hear iv th' men who be nerve an' interprise took advantage iv th' fire to build up fortunes. D'ye iver think if thim that had no nerve an' interprise afther th' fire to begin new again? Poor souls."[8]

Chicago's Catholics in the Wake of the Fire

Irish immigrants who came to Chicago after the Great Fire viewed religion differently than their predecessors did. This reflected a transformation of religious belief and practice in postfamine Ireland, a phenomenon that historian Emmet Larkin terms the "Devotional Revolution." Before the famine, Irish Catholics seldom interacted with the clergy, most receiving the sacrament but a few times per year. This was primarily due to the extremely low ratio of priests to parishioners in prefamine Ireland—an average of one priest per three thousand people. In the wake of the famine, however, mass death and emigration, along with a concerted effort by the Church to train a greater number of priests and nuns, changed that ratio. Priests expanded the Church's influence by speaking to the cultural dispositions of the peasantry. They emphasized miracles, healings, and the power of saints. But they also emphasized guilt and the power of sin, with drunkenness and sins of the flesh being worst of all. Moreover, rising literacy rates and respect for institutional practices not only bolstered the status of the Church but also led to an improvement in social behavior. "Not only were later immigrants less drunken and less prone to violence," Larkin notes, "they also had acquired basic educational skills and were actually less poor." Irish Catholic institutions trained hundreds of priests each decade to serve in North America and other outposts in the spiritual empire. When these clergymen arrived in Chicago during the final third of the nineteenth century, they found a real and pressing demand for their services.[9]

The Irish-led Catholic Church became a pillar of stability for the city's first- and second-generation immigrants. The parish of Annunciation, for example, grew rapidly during the 1870s. It built a new brick church that cost $50,000 and served some eight hundred families. The community's Total Abstinence Society discouraged excessive drinking, while the St. Vincent de Paul Society aided the poor. Parishioners distributed prayer books and magazines, such as *Ave Maria*, a publication of the University of Notre Dame. Women religious, such as the Sisters of Charity of the Blessed Virgin Mary, advanced parochial education in the parish. The Sisters also advocated service into the priesthood, an increasingly prestigious vocation for many Irish American families. The clergy of Annunciation performed the rituals and sacraments that had become so integral to Irish Catholic life: communion, baptism, and confession. They performed marriages as well, although Irish men and women typically married later in life than other immigrants. For those comparatively few Irish women who turned to prostitution, the community's House of Good Shepherd gave them shelter and helped them start their lives anew. To be clear, Irish Catholics in the 1870s were not necessarily more internally pious than their predecessors. Fewer than 50 percent attended mass on a weekly basis. Catholic social and religious institutions, however, increasingly satisfied the needs of an immigrant community growing in numbers and respectability.[10]

Strike!

The Irish had long developed a reputation for collective action in the workplace. This originated in Ireland, where clandestine associations collectively labeled the Ribbonmen enforced an informal system of retributive justice when employers maltreated or underpaid their workers. These groups occasionally issued threatening notices, destroyed property, and used violence to get what they wanted. In the United States, immigrant laborers resorted to similar actions when other avenues were closed. In June 1877, a band of Pennsylvania miners known as the Molly Maguires became the most famous of these groups when forty individuals were convicted—some wrongfully in a trial that has been described as a near "travesty of justice"—for the assassinations of six company men. Ten were hanged in a single day. Yet the memory of their tribulations lived on.[11]

Less than a month after the Molly Maguires went to the gallows, labor violence erupted across the United States. The Great Railroad Strike of 1877 began in Baltimore on July 16, when the B&O Railroad announced its decision, in the midst of a three-year economic depression, to reduce wages by 10 percent. The strike spread throughout the country to cities such as Philadelphia, New York, St. Louis, and San Francisco. Scores of protesters, including men, women, and children, were killed as state militias fired into crowds. Rioting in Pittsburgh ceased only after President Hayes ordered federal troops to quell the strike. In

Sister Mary Agatha Hurley (1826–1902)

Born in 1826 in Cloyne, County Cork, Sister Mary Agatha (Ellen) Hurley was an important figure in Catholic girls' education in late nineteenth-century Chicago. A member of the Sisters of Charity of the Blessed Virgin Mary (BVM), Hurley first came to Chicago in August 1867, answering the Reverend Arnold J. Damen's call for the expansion of girls' education in the city. She was one of nine nuns who traveled from Dubuque to Chicago to help establish St. Aloysius Convent and School for Girls on Maxwell Street in Holy Family parish. Hurley's leadership skills were tested almost immediately in the Great Chicago Fire of 1871, when she and other BVM sisters distributed food and other necessities to those in need. Sister Mary Agatha was the convent's first mother superior and presided over St. Aloysius's dramatic growth. By 1885, the school had one thousand students in regular attendance. Nine years later, church leaders, her fellow sisters, and hundreds of former students gathered at St. Aloysius to celebrate Sister Mary Agatha's fifty years of service. She passed away in 1902.[12]

Sister Mary Agatha Hurley. Used with permission of the Mount Carmel Archives of the Sisters of Charity of the Blessed Virgin Mary, Dubuque, Iowa.

Illinois, where Irish efforts to organize collectively had been rebuffed by the state during the 1860s, railroad employees walked off the job in Aurora, Springfield, Peoria, and Quincy. Coal miners in LaSalle and Carbondale waged sympathy strikes. Railroad traffic ceased entirely.[13]

Protests engulfed Chicago, as the city's working classes banded together. On July 23, the Workingmen's Party issued leaflets that accused "money lords" of voter repression and encouraged strikers to defend "the fruits of your labor." As many as thirty thousand individuals gathered in support. Trade unionists joined socialists and unskilled workers of all ethnicities across the city. Police officers, ordered to break up the demonstrations, fired into the crowds. The protestors fought back, attacking depots, laying waste to freight yards, and destroying roundhouses. Two U.S. Army regiments were called into the city, and Mayor Heath ordered up the militia. By the time the strike ended on July 27, nineteen people had been killed and more than one hundred injured. Yet the violence served to unify the city's working poor. As historian Richard Schneirov observes, "1877 seemed to whet the appetite of Chicago working people for new and more inclusive forms of solidarity and action."[14]

At the same time, the strike exposed fissures in the ethnic solidarity that appeared to bind together Chicago's Irish Catholics. Most presumably supported the strikes. As many as one-third of all railroad workers in the 1870s were Irish. The Irish Labor Guard, a militant ethnic wing of the labor movement, conspicuously fought the police and soldiers. Thousands of men, women, and children from Bridgeport, derided by the *Tribune* as "a generic term for smells, for riots, bad whiskey, and poor cigars," joined the strikes. And more than half of the casualties reported had Irish surnames. Yet Irish police officers and soldiers helped quell the rioting as well. A significant minority of the police force's three hundred officers were Irish, as was the entire 2nd Illinois Regiment, called up to support the police. Irish crowds booed and hissed the soldiers. According to one *Tribune* reporter, "The Second Regiment carried a flag which did not seem to meet with much favor by the mob, for shouts of 'Take home your rag,' and 'Down with the Irish flag' were heard on every side." Mayor Monroe Heath was careful to avoid blaming the Irish for the calamity. Rather, he accused "the large class of half-savage Bohemians . . . imbued with communistic ideas." At least temporarily, the Great Railroad Strike of 1877 revealed divisions within Chicago's Irish community.[15]

Following that watershed year, thousands of working people across the country joined a new organization called the Knights of Labor. Formerly a Philadelphia secret society, it was brought into the mainstream by Terence Powderly, a second-generation son of immigrants from County Meath. Under Powderly's leadership, the Knights' membership quickly soared to one hundred thousand, at least half of whom were Irish American. The association won an important strike over Jay Gould's Southwestern Railroad in 1885. The victory inspired James and Emily Talmadge to publish a celebratory collection of music titled "Labor Songs Dedicated to the Knights of Labor." Church leadership began backing the labor movement. In 1886, Archbishop James Gibbons of Baltimore announced to the Vatican, "Catholic prelates will to a man declare in favor of the organization of Labor."[16]

Chicago's Irish enthusiastically supported the Knights of Labor, which in turn reshaped their own conceptions of class. This transformation occurred in Chicago during the early 1880s, just as Irish nationalist organizations such as the Clan na Gael (formerly the Fenian Brotherhood) gained support. In 1879, in the United States and Ireland, advocates of violent revolution and advocates of constitutional reform attempted to set aside their differences. They agreed that "moral force" should replace physical force in the struggle for Irish independence. *Boycotts*, so named for an organized effort to undermine the despised County Mayo land agent Captain Charles Boycott, replaced violent strikes. As early as 1881, Irish nationalists in Bridgeport refused to do business with shops selling English goods. A year later, Chicago's Knights of Labor, now led by Irishmen, began advocating similar tactics. Boycotts and political action replaced strikes, which in turn made the Knights more appealing to skilled laborers and trade unionists. Reform replaced radicalism. And as the Knights grew in membership and political power, their influence in municipal politics grew as well. By the mid-1880s, as Schneirov puts it, the Knights had become not only "distinctly Irish in leadership and tone" but also "more in touch with Chicago's industrial working class . . . while retaining [their] prior commitment to labor reform." This transformation soon became manifest during the Haymarket Affair.[17]

On May 1, 1886, a mass movement consisting of various labor factions, including anarchists and radicals, attempted to organize a nationwide protest. From New York to Detroit to Milwaukee, thousands of workers demanded an "eight-hour day with no cut in pay." Yet to Powderly and the Knights' leadership, this went too far. Mass strikes, they argued, frequently led to violence that undermined efforts to improve working conditions and wages. Indeed, the demonstrations proved disastrous. Across the country, workers won small pay raises, but at the expense of public opinion. And in Chicago, protests again turned deadly.

Irish involvement in the Haymarket Affair was much less prominent than it was in the Great Railroad Strike of 1877. On May 3, members of the police force, most of whom were Irish, shot and killed four individuals while attempting to stop a fight between union men and strikebreakers. Few Irishmen, in fact, were among the demonstrators, as the Knights' opposition to mass demonstrations kept them at home. Irish support for a more cautious approach to labor politics stemmed from the belief that they had begun climbing up the city's ladder of relative respectability. Newly arrived Poles and Bohemians took a larger share of the lowest-paying jobs. Encouraged by Irish political success (and the patronage jobs that came with it) and the gradual emergence of an Irish middle class in Chicago, a growing number of Irish workers moved away from more confrontational tactics. Politics and patronage were critical. According to Sam Mitrani, "Irish influence on Chicago's politics . . . ultimately led many of Chicago's poorest workers away from the influence of anarchists and toward a reformist version of labor politics that included employment on the police department." The following evening, thousands of workers gathered at Haymarket Square to protest the police department's use of force. The meeting proceeded peacefully, until some two hundred police officers attempted to disperse the crowd. An unknown individual threw a bomb into their ranks. One officer was killed. The police opened fire on the crowd. Armed strikers returned fire. Four laborers and seven officers were killed in the melee. Nearly one hundred people were wounded: sixty police officers and thirty to forty strikers. Powderly condemned the bombing, but the press and the public generally lumped all labor organizations into the same pool as the protestors. The Knights fell into an irreversible decline.[18]

Haymarket revealed a transformation in Irish conceptions of working-class politics. The opportunities provided by municipal patronage, as well as generational shifts and the appeal of Irish nationalism, led many Irish workers to adopt a more cautious, bread-and-butter approach to labor issues. In Chicago, the working classes began to join forces with liberal reformers. "After 1886," Schneirov argues, "elite liberal reform thinking and practice began to be rethought. In the course of that process, organized labor, the labor question, and prolabor policies attained political credibility, electoral appeal, and legitimacy in respectable discourse." In this transformation, the Irish had led the way. Irish nationalism introduced the boycott to labor strategists. The Irish-led Knights, in turn, embraced the formal channels of politics in their cause. Even after the Knights declined, the Irish working classes influenced liberal reform through machine politics. Their alliance with Mayor Carter Harrison in 1886 ensured that the (predominantly Irish) police force would rarely be used to break strikes in the city. To be sure, Irish American radicals continued to play key roles in labor activism, notably Mother Jones, Sylvester Kelleher of the American Railroad Union, and John Fitzpatrick of the Chicago Federation of Labor. Irish socialists James Connolly and James Larkin developed national followings in the early twentieth century. Yet most of these leaders were immigrants, and their goals often differed from those second- and third-generation workers who sought what historian David N. Doyle calls "proudful Americanism." In Chicago, respectability appears to have trumped radicalism. "The Irish," as historian Eric Hirsch concludes, "were militant in their tactics, but reformist in their goals."[19] Or, as Mr. Dooley put it:

> I see by this pa-per . . . that anarchy's torch do be uplifted an' what th' 'ell it means, I dinnaw; but this here I know, Jawn, that all arnychists is inimies iv governmint, an' all iv thim ought to be hung f'r th' first offence an' bathed f'r th' second. Who are they annyhow, but foreigners an' what right have they to be holdin' torchlight procissions in this land iv th' free an' home iv th' brave? Did ye iver seen an American or an Irishman arnychist? No, an' ye niver will. Whin an Irishman thinks th' way iv thim la'ads, he goes on th' polis force an' dhraws his eighty three-thirty-three f'r throwin' lodgin' house bums into th' pathrol wagon. An' there ye a'are.[20]

Perhaps because of their disconnection from municipal politics, Irish women waxed more radical than their male counterparts. Whereas Powderly had denounced violence and abandoned the cause of the eight-hour workday, prominent female Irish labor leaders sanctioned both. One such individual was Elizabeth Rodgers. Often remembered as the first woman to join Chicago's Knights of Labor, Rodgers by 1886 had taken charge of the city's branch, overseeing some twenty-seven thousand members. Later that year, she led a failed strike at the stockyards. She left the Knights three years later, although she continued to fight for the rights of workers into the early twentieth century.

Even more famous, however, was Mary Harris "Mother" Jones, a labor activist and Chicago resident. In the wake of the Haymarket incident, at a time when "Chicago was a hotbed of labor radicalism," as historian Jay Dolan describes it, "Mary Jones, a struggling seamstress, was transformed into Mother Jones, the radical labor organizer." "The Johnny Appleseed of American activists," in the words of Elliott Gorn, organized mining

Mary Harris "Mother" Jones (1837–1930)

Born in 1837 in County Cork, Mary Harris escaped the famine along with her family in the 1840s. After growing up in Toronto, Harris moved in her twenties to Memphis, Tennessee, where she married George Jones and had four children. She tragically lost her entire family to yellow fever in 1867, after which she relocated to Chicago, only to watch her seamstress shop burn to the ground during the Great Fire of 1871. A transformed woman, Jones joined the Knights of Labor and became an ardent supporter of Eugene Debs's Socialist Party and the radical Industrial Workers of the World. Mother Jones, as she came to be known in the late 1890s, achieved fame and notoriety as a public speaker and union organizer. She continued to agitate on behalf of working people into her midseventies. Mary Jones Harris died at the age of ninety-three. She recently has been honored with a museum in Mount Olive, Illinois, the place of her death.[22]

Mary Harris Jones, also known as Mother Jones. Photograph by Bertha Howell; Library of Congress.

strikes in Pennsylvania, West Virginia, and Colorado. "The miners loved, worshipped, and adored her," one miner recalled. "And well they might, because there was no night too dark, no danger too great for her to face, if in her judgement 'her boys' needed her." Throughout the late nineteenth century and across the country, Mother Jones led strikes, served time in jail, and promoted socialism as the panacea for the nation's economic injustices.[21]

Chicago's Irish labor advocates, from Powderly's legions to Elizabeth Rodgers to Mother Jones, made an indelible mark on the movement during the 1870s and 1880s—and set it up for future successes during the Progressive Era.

The Origins of Machine Politics

If Chicago's Irish helped shape the city's labor movement, they made an even bigger impact in politics. Irish influence dated back to the 1830s, as saloonkeepers organized voting blocs and ran candidates. But it ramped up even more after the election of the antiforeign mayor Levi Boone in 1855. The following year, Irish and German electors, temporarily united in their opposition to Boone's nativist policies, swung the election to Thomas Dyer, a Democrat who served from 1856 to 1857. During the 1860s, Irish candidates gained ground in the city council, occupying fifteen of forty seats by the end of the decade. In the wake of the Chicago Fire of 1871, the business-backed Joseph Medill consolidated power behind the office of mayor. He reformed the fire department and the police force. By increasing the size and pay of the force, however, he also enhanced the political and economic leverage of working-class immigrants—particularly the Irish, who made up roughly half of the force. This had a snowball effect, as Irish cops and neighborhood bosses worked together to perpetuate their power.[23]

Chicago's Irish also recognized the value of maintaining interethnic coalitions. During the 1870s, this meant working with the city's German community. In 1873, Irish and German voters formed a separate People's Party to oust Medill's successor, Lester Legrant Bond, who foolishly ignored the foreign-born electorate during the campaign. They defeated the incumbent party in an astounding landslide, electing Harvey Doolittle Colvin, whose promise to prevent crime rather than punish it appealed to immigrants. Success begat success, as Irish candidates could increasingly count on German votes. By the mid-1870s, nearly half of all seats on the city council were Irish. Following the Great Railroad Strike, Irish laborers again joined with fellow German workers in support of the Socialist Labor Party, although its successes were short-lived. Nevertheless, interethnic cooperation had served Irish politicians well.[24]

By the 1880s, Chicago's political machines were up and running in Irish neighborhoods. And mayoral candidates took notice. In 1879, a new regime came into power—one eager to harness the city's numerous Irish machines. Carter Henry Harrison, a Democrat who served as mayor from 1879 to 1887, worked with bosses such as Mike McDonald, Irish-born saloonkeeper and "king" of the First Ward. Over the decade, McDonald built a veritable commercial and political empire in the heart of Chicago. His ward boasted mansions and department stores, but it also contained brothels and gambling houses, the most disreputable of which were located near Clark and Taylor Streets. McDonald rewarded police officers with kickbacks and politicians with votes, provided they turned a blind eye to the seedier methods of his business. The Irish voted early and often. As one of Mr. Dooley's regulars named John McKenna later recalled, "We cast twinty-wan hundherd votes f'r Duggan, an' they was on'y five hundherd votes in th' precinct. We'd cast more, but th' tickets give out."[25]

In retrospect, Irish political muscle is all the more impressive given the fact that during the 1880s, they constituted a majority in merely 11 of 303 census districts, while securing 23 of 68 aldermen. Irish bosses of this era became expert assemblers of ethnic political coalitions. They could never expect to maintain power if they nominated an excessive number of Irish candidates. While three-fourths of the city's Democratic committeemen were Irish during the 1880s, party bosses typically nominated no more than one of their countrymen to the four major citywide offices. What is more, Mayor Harrison advocated law enforcement reforms that benefited all working-class immigrants. He promoted Irish Americans, such as second-generation Austin Doyle, to the Board of Police and refused to order the police to break strikes, such as the McCormick Reaper Works Strike of 1885. Essentially, Harrison hired Irishmen and held back from strikebreaking to solidify a political alliance between the municipality and laborers. It worked. Businesses chafed at the apparent quid pro quo and hired private strikebreakers from the Pinkerton Agency to put down labor unrest. Detectives from the agency claimed to have infiltrated the force, which allegedly contained a sizable number of officers who were members of Irish nationalist organizations such as the Ancient Order of Hibernians. The practice of hiring members of different ethnic groups had the effect of providing the force with a renewed sense of authority, which eventually made it effective at strikebreaking, but it also bound the Irish even more tightly to the Democratic Party—an alliance that lasted well into the next century.[26]

Irish American Nationalism: Clan na Gael

Politics for first- and second-generation Irish Americans also meant supporting a free and independent Ireland. After the failed Fenian uprisings of the 1860s, a County Cork native and New York intellectual by the name of Jerome J. Collins founded a new revolutionary association called Clan na Gael. Unlike their Fenian predecessors, Clan members kept their inner workings secret—something than put them at odds with the Catholic Church. By the late 1870s, Clan na Gael claimed as many as ten thousand predominantly working-class members, although the organization also had middle-class leaders such as Terence Powderly. Espousing the motto "England's difficulty is Ireland's opportunity," the Clan called for the violent overthrow of British rule in Ireland, presumably during a future war with rival Germany.

It also advocated high-profile propaganda exercises like the Catalpa Incident, where exiled Fenians were rescued from an Australian prison in April 1876. Many members funded O'Donovan Rossa's "dynamite campaign," advertised in Patrick Ford's New

York *Irish World*, which promised to use explosives to terrorize Britain into negotiating Irish independence. Yet neither the Clan nor the dynamiters constituted the largest Irish nationalist association in America. That designation belonged to the Irish Catholic Benevolent Union, which had the support of the Catholic Church and boasted a membership easily twice the size of the Clan's. Many of these more moderate Irish American nationalists supported the growing movement for Irish Home Rule, which centered on a nonviolent and constitutional campaign for a semi-independent Irish parliament, similar to Daniel O'Connell's vision of repeal. The sheer range of Irish nationalist opinion in America provided some problems for supporters. As the prominent Minnesota Irish nationalist Dillon O'Brien put it in 1877, "We have in this country Fenians, nationalists, Home Rulers, and Repealers. All are good true men, but all are more or less like jealous peddlers, praising their own wares and decrying the wares of others."[27]

In Ireland, the fight was compounded by a series of poor harvests in the late 1870s. Many feared another famine, while politicians anticipated a national uprising. In 1879, the agrarian activist Michael Davitt founded the National Land League, which united the peasantry in the face of impending starvation and pressured landlords to relax rents in the face of boycotts. The crisis, however, effectively pulled together the more radical Irish and Irish American nationalists, such as Davitt and John Devoy, with the more politically minded constitutionalists, led by the Irish member of Parliament (MP) Charles Stewart Parnell. Both sides agreed to table their differences in favor of a united front against Britain. The *New York Herald* referred to this merger as the "New Departure," since the union of the two camps represented a novel approach to Irish independence. Between January and March 1880, Parnell whipped up support for the cause on an American tour. In Ireland, the movement came to a head in 1882, after members of Davitt's Land League renewed the use of agrarian violence and retributive justice, championed earlier by the Ribbonmen and Molly Maguires. During the crisis, Parnell was imprisoned. Britain's prime minister William Gladstone, recognizing that Ireland stood at the precipice of revolt, agreed to work with Parnell, who was soon released from prison. In 1886, Gladstone introduced the First Home Rule Bill to the House of Commons. The world, and Irish Americans in particular, watched to see what would become of Ireland.[28]

Chicago's Irish leaped at the new opportunities to support Irish independence. The working classes of Bridgeport founded a branch of the Clan na Gael in 1869. One year later, their membership included some forty thousand first- or second-generation Irish. By 1890, that number had soared to seventy thousand. A group of dynamiters led by Patrick Crowe, a man John Devoy later praised as the "real author" of the dynamite campaign, openly confessed to crafting "infernal machines," which they later detonated in Britain—even sharing a duplicate with a local newspaper. The Clan's leadership typically included members of the professional classes: doctors, lawyers, and politicians. Alexander Sullivan, a crafty politician and secretary of the Board of Public Works, headed the Chicago branch. Dr. Patrick H. Cronin, a noted physician with a "fine tenor voice," also became a senior member, as did John Finerty, editor of the *Chicago Citizen*. Some members of the city's Catholic clergy, unlike their northeastern counterparts, backed the Clan. Patrick A. Feehan, archbishop of the Chicago Diocese, openly supported Irish republicanism. Father Maurice Dorney, known locally as "the Stockyards Priest" for his role in founding St. Gabriel's Parish near the Union Stock Yard, was an enthusiastic Clan member, even hosting dinners and celebrations in the church. Many of the city's Irish women joined the Ladies' Land League. Perhaps the most notable of these was Margaret Buchanan Sullivan, wife of Alexander Sullivan and acclaimed editorialist of the *Chicago Tribune*, who presided over one branch of the League.[29]

Some local Irish priests supported the Clan as well. In the 1870s, the Reverend John Waldron publicly advocated for Irish independence. This went against Church policy, which specifically denounced secret societies and violent nationalist organizations. Yet the city's priests and parishioners had long shown their willingness to think and act independently. Waldron's popularity soared. During his twenty-seven-year tenure as pastor, he hosted numerous meetings of the Fenian Brotherhood, the Ancient Order of Hibernians, and the Clan na Gael. On such occasions, Waldron proudly displayed two pikes that he owned, relics of the failed Rebellion of 1798. His steadfast support for republicanism not only endeared him to Chicago's working classes, but it also continued to reinforce a distinctly Irish and American brand of Catholicism that had long existed in the city.[30]

Chicago's Irish took great pride in their support for an independent Ireland. As historian Thomas N. Brown has shown, involvement in nationalist associations helped bring respectability and intergenerational coherence to Irish-American communities. Michael Davitt put it another way. Speaking before a New York crowd, he stated, "You want to be honored among the elements that constitute this nation, as a people not coming from a paupered land . . . to remove the stain of degradation from your birth." Chicago's Irish certainly rallied to the cause. In August 1881, the city hosted a national convention of the Clan that attracted two thousand delegates and showed the world that, as Brown notes, "the center of Irish republicanism in America was in Chicago."[31]

Factionalism and political setbacks, however, doomed the Irish republican movement of the 1880s. As the Land War continued in Ireland, cracks began to appear in the alliance between physical force revolutionaries and the New Departure's semiconstitutional approach. The convention of 1881 saw increased support for the dynamite campaign. In March of the following year, bombers detonated explosives at a land agent's house in County Galway, marking the first of multiple attacks to come. Two months later, a secretive Irish society known as the Invincibles murdered Chief Secretary Lord Cavendish and Undersecretary Thomas Burke in Dublin's Phoenix Park. Alexander Sullivan of Chicago was elected president of the new Irish National League of America in April 1883, officially merging the constitutional methods of the American Land League with the revolutionary tactics of the Clan—but few doubted Sullivan's preference for violent measures. Between October 1883 and February 1885, dynamiters targeted London Bridge, Westminster, the House of Commons, and even the Tower of London. They spent thousands of dollars creating the explosives. Three people were killed and eighteen injured. The Dynamite War proved to be an unmitigated disaster for Irish republicans. It turned American public opinion against the revolutionaries, attitudes that only increased after the Haymarket bombing the following year.[32]

Simultaneously, political scandal plagued the cause. In June 1886, the First Home Rule Bill failed to pass the House of Commons. The Clan began to split further in August, when John Devoy accused Sullivan of refusing to provide financial support for the widow of one dynamiter. In 1888, Alexander Sullivan, Michael

Boland, and Denis Feely—known as the "Triangle"—privately stood trial in New York before a Clan commission for embezzlement, malfeasance, and a betrayal of trust. More important, if testimony revealed that moneys received for Parnell's constitutional efforts had been used to fund the dynamite campaign, it could ruin the Irish MP's career and sink further efforts to obtain Home Rule through parliamentary action. Sullivan was eventually acquitted, but Parnell lost his political future nevertheless. Late in 1889, newspapers reported that the popular MP had engaged in a ten-year affair with Captain William O'Shea's wife, Katherine, who had given birth to three of Parnell's children during the 1880s. The scandal ruined his career and sent him to an early grave in 1891. Home Rule died two years later, when Gladstone failed in his last attempt to push the measure through the British Parliament. Independence would not come to Ireland until the next century.[33]

The dramatic denouement of Chicago's Clan organization occurred in 1889. On Wednesday, May 22, three public works employees investigated a pungent odor emanating from a storm sewer in the community of Lake View, which was not incorporated into the rapidly expanding city until later that year. There they discovered the beaten and bloated corpse of Dr. Patrick Cronin, who had gone missing nearly three weeks earlier. Chicago's Irish suspected foul play. The respected physician had already received numerous death threats, and friends warned him to be careful. He had created powerful enemies in the Clan, who had expelled him four years prior. By the mid-1880s, Cronin had become, in the words of historian Gillian O'Brien, "Alexander Sullivan's most tenacious and vocal opponent." Throughout the summer, Chicago newspapers sensationalized the case, while foreign magazines depicted the city's Irish as bloodthirsty subhumans. In October, three suspects went to trial: Patrick O'Sullivan, Dan Coughlin, and Martin Burke, all former Clan members. Despite rumors of bribery and Illinois legal practices that effectively gave juries carte blanche, the three men were convicted and sentenced to life in prison. The verdict fractured the Irish American community in Chicago. Many native-born as well as Irish Americans, including John Devoy, howled for the death penalty. Still others argued the defendants' innocence. Either way, the incident splintered the city's Clan organization and broke Alexander Sullivan, who was repeatedly implicated in the murder but never charged.[34]

Alexander Sullivan. *Harper's Weekly*, June 2, 1883; Library of Congress.

Alexander Sullivan (1848–1913)

The son of an Irish officer in the British army, Alexander Sullivan was born in Amherstberg, Ontario, in 1848. Sometime before his twentieth birthday, he moved to Detroit and purchased a shoe store, which curiously burned to the ground. Despite allegations that Sullivan had started the fire, the testimony of a young woman named Margaret Buchanan saved him from jail. Following a brief stay in Santa Fe, Sullivan eventually settled in Chicago, where he worked intermittently for various newspapers. In 1874, he married Margaret Buchanan, whose journalistic talents so impressed the city's newspapermen that she served on four editorial boards, including that of the *Chicago Tribune*. Sullivan again escaped criminal conviction in 1876, this time for allegedly killing a man who had accused his wife of a scandalous relationship with the mayor. Two years later, he became a member of the Clan na Gael. Sullivan was elected chair of the Clan's executive committee in 1881. The following year, he traveled to Paris, where he acquired a donation of $100,000 from the Irish Land League, although records suggest that Sullivan pocketed the money for himself. In 1883, he was elected president of the Irish National League of America, a position he held until Patrick Cronin's murder trial in 1889. Widely believed to have been behind the killing, Sullivan was never charged but remained associated with the Cronin murder for the rest of his life. His wife, Margaret, died of a stroke in 1903. Alexander Sullivan died ten years later.[35]

Over the next four years, at least a dozen people associated with the case, including O'Sullivan and Burke, died mysterious deaths. In 1894, Coughlin was acquitted in a retrial that again divided Chicago's Irish. Mr. Dooley was aghast: "Acquitted him!" the barkeeper remarked. "'Tis a disgrace." His faithful customer John McKenna vehemently disagreed. Dooley chased him out of his bar. "Then he paused and let his hand drop. 'Jawn,' said he, 'ye're a British spoy.'" The case may have exposed rifts within the city's Irish community, but they came together for Patrick Cronin's funeral. On May 26, 1889, nearly forty thousand people gathered along Michigan Avenue to honor the deceased doctor in a grand funeral procession. The city was brought to a standstill, as a horse-drawn hearse transported his casket to Calvary Cemetery. Gillian O'Brien emphasizes the drama of the event: "Chicago hadn't seen its like since Abraham Lincoln's body had lain in state at the Cook County Courthouse in 1865." In burying the doctor's remains, the city's Irish buried with him their militant fervor for independence—bequeathing that struggle to the next generation.[36]

Bringing Art and Culture to the Urban Frontier

While dramatic events like the Cronin murder certainly dominated the headlines, most immigrants quietly continued the work of building stable communities. One such neighborhood was Holy Family Parish, located around the present-day intersection of Roosevelt and Racine. After the Great Fire of 1871, the community built a magnificent Gothic style church and St. Ignatius College. Both were decorated with imported European statues and ornate carvings. Architect J. P. Huber designed an impressive 226-foot tower for the church's facade. The working classes invested in the church as well. James T. Farrell, the acclaimed Irish American author, later recalled that his grandmother contributed 25 cents to a stained-glass window for the church: "She was proud of this all of her life." In 1876, the Little Sisters of the Poor purchased the Hull mansion on Halsted Street, the same venue later acquired by social workers Jane Addams and Ellen Gates Starr, where the nuns opened a home for the elderly until the space became overcrowded. They then spearheaded a fund-raising campaign from small donors to build a larger facility on Harrison Street. Into the 1880s, Mother Elizabeth Mary Sheridan and her fellow Sisters of the Religious of the Sacred Heart Convent ensured that children of the parish had proper schooling. Thomas S. Fitzgerald, a famine immigrant and County Tipperary native, grew up in the parish and later became a priest, devoting much of his energy to church beautification, which included Christmas decorations and a refurbished pipe organ. By the 1890s, although the parish covered less than a square mile, Chicago newspapers frequently applauded its St. Patrick's Day celebrations and Confirmation Day parades. Participants marched past the Sacred Heart Convent on Taylor Street, St. Joseph's Home for Working Girls, Sodality Hall, and St. Ignatius College before concluding at the church.[37]

When reformers Jane Addams and Ellen Gates Starr established the Hull House—a settlement dedicated to providing social, educational, and artistic services to disadvantaged communities—they virtually ignored the social and aesthetic contributions of the Irish at Holy Family. In her theoretical writings, Addams maintained that settlements thrived where one "finds a complete absence of art"—a bizarre claim, given that she had repeatedly walked past Holy Family Church on multiple occasions en route to Hull mansion. Addams's Protestant worldview perhaps blinded her to Irish Catholics' aesthetic contributions. Historians such as Sue Ellen Hoy have made the case that the city's Mercy Sisters performed social work earlier and on a larger scale than Addams, who nevertheless left the distinct impression that the Hull House was the neighborhood's lone source of culture and refinement. In any event, as historian Ellen Skerrett observes, "By building ornate churches and establishing schools, working-class Catholics created community and identity—and put their imprint on the urban landscape."[38]

Into the 1890s, Irish Chicagoans continued to build institutions dedicated to strengthening their communities. Women increasingly spearheaded such efforts. The Catholic Women's League founded day nurseries. Still novel for the era, they served multiethnic neighborhoods on the West Side (St. Anne's), the North Side (St. Elizabeth's), and the South Side (All Saints). They provided childcare for working mothers and were frequently staffed by working-class Irish women. Female volunteers of all social classes taught catechism, showed films, put on plays, and organized games. Meanwhile, a wealthy proprietor named Agnes Ward Amberg, a Chicago native of Irish descent, helped establish the Guardian Angel Mission in 1898. The mission was eventually transformed into a full-fledged settlement house, which served newly arrived Italians by providing alternatives to middlemen labor contractors known as padrones. Guardian Angel ultimately severed its ties to the parish, and the house was rebranded as a secular institution called the Madonna Center. In 1914, another settlement house, called the DePaul Center, was founded by members of St. Vincent's Parish, who later turned it over to the Daughters of Charity. It continues to serve the community today. History may remember the Hull House as the quintessential settlement house of the Progressive Era, but Chicago's Catholic settlements, and the Irish who built them, created an infrastructure that has persisted into the twenty-first century.[39]

The Columbian Exposition and Economic Depression

In 1893, Chicago was a city on the move. In the two decades following the Great Fire of 1871, Chicago's population had soared from 300,000 to 1.3 million. Its Irish-born population topped 70,000. The number of households with at least one Irish parent reached 180,000. The city was selected to host the Columbian Exposition of 1893, a world's fair that celebrated the four hundredth anniversary of Columbus's voyage to the Americas and touted the city's coming of age. Promoters were so enthusiastic about winning the bid that rival New Yorkers gave Chicago its enduring nickname, the "Windy City."[40]

The Irish helped make the Columbian Exposition a success. In April, former mayor Carter Henry Harrison, who had left office in 1887, reclaimed the position with the support of working-class immigrants by promising to be the "Fair Mayor." It did not hurt that Harrison quietly pledged to secure patronage jobs for the Irish living in "Bathhouse" John Coughlin's First Ward. Chicagoans worked feverishly to prepare for the event. The epicenter of the fair, a temporary village that covered more than six hundred acres and featured two hundred neoclassical buildings, stood in dramatic contrast to the permanent city. Visitors marveled at its public restrooms, clean water, sewage processing plant, and electric streetlights. At the center of the venue lay an enormous waterway, symbolizing Columbus's challenge in sailing to the New World. The exposition's hastily erected structures, particularly at the Court of Honor, were often covered in white stucco, thus earning the fair another moniker: the "White City." Guests often were astounded by novel modern inventions, including automatic dishwashers, Edison's Kinetoscope, the zipper, and even Aunt Jemima's pancake mix. Between May and October, nearly 26 million people attended the event.[41]

Yet 1893 was just as often remembered for a series of murders that swept the city. On Saturday, October 28, an exhausted Mayor Harrison, who had welcomed five thousand elected officials from across the country to the fair that day, came to his front door to greet an unexpected visitor. Patrick Prendergast, a mentally ill Irishman who had supported Harrison with the expectation of being promoted to the city's corporation counsel, fatally shot the mayor three times with a revolver. He was later hanged for the crime. Simultaneously, an apparent psychopath named Herman

Webster Mudgett, more commonly known as H. H. Holmes, was methodically luring victims into a hotel at the southwest corner of South Wallace and West Sixty-Third Street in Englewood—where he killed them by gassing them while they were asleep. In all, Holmes confessed to killing twenty-seven individuals, although the true number may never be known.[42]

Across the country, hard times lay ahead. By the close of the exposition, the worst national depression to date had beset the nation. Railroads declared bankruptcy. More than six hundred banks closed, as did some fifteen thousand businesses. Unemployment soared to 25 percent among unskilled urban laborers. Federal monetary policies, such as the repeal of the Sherman Silver Purchase Act, compounded matters by slashing the amount of money in circulation. In Chicago, George Pullman of the Pullman Palace Car Company laid off three thousand of his fifty-eight hundred employees and slashed wages up to 40 percent. On May 11, 1894, the Pullman laborers went on strike. Eugene Debs, founder of the American Railway Union and a close associate of Mother Jones, attempted to negotiate a deal. Pullman refused to budge. Mail services were stopped, and violence broke out between workers and strikebreakers. On July 3, President Grover Cleveland sent federal troops into Chicago. Three days later, two strikers were killed and several others wounded.[43]

At the outset, Mr. Dooley denounced the unrest: "That ain't no sthrike. A sthrike is where th' la-ads lave off wurruk an' bate Germans and thin go back to wurruk f'r rajooced wages an' thank hivin f'r it. This here is a rivolution again constitooted authority." "Th' counthry," he added, "do be goin' to wrack an' roon." Indeed, Mr. Dooley lamented, the strike had deprived his saloon of "limons an' ice." But when Debs finally called off the demonstrations in mid-July and the carmen returned to work, Pullman refused to change his policies. Amid the widespread deprivation and near-starvation that followed, Mr. Dooley turned his ire against George Pullman. "But what's it all to Pullman? Whin Gawd quarried his heart a happy man was made. He cares no more f'r thim little matthers iv life an' death thin I do f'r O'Connor's tab. 'Th' women an' childhren is dyin' iv hunger,' they says. 'Will ye not put out ye'er hand to help thim?' they says. 'Ah, what th' 'ell,' says George. 'What th' 'ell,' he says." Years later, Dunne remembered that the typesetters broke into applause when they put the story to print. It was, a colleague added, "one of the great thrills of his life."[44]

At the Forefront of the Multiethnic City

When immigrants from southern and eastern Europe came to Chicago during the early twentieth century, they expected to find America. As historian James Barrett has made clear, what they found instead was *Irish* America. Jewish author Harry Golden's New York City experience was typical: "We identified the Irishman not only with the English language but also with the image of what an American looked like. The Irish were the cops and the firemen and the ballplayers. Although the immigrant Jew and the Irish poor did not get along well, these Irish were still the figures Jewish immigrants wanted to emulate." For the thousands of Poles, Italians, and Jews who came to Chicago at the turn of the century, "Irish" meant "American."[45]

Of course, from the Irish perspective, this transition had not been easy. Since before the famine, their status as poor, exiled Catholics had set most apart from the American mainstream, although to a lesser degree in Chicago than on the East Coast. Even in the urban Midwest, however, they faced discrimination enough that they had to band together, effectively becoming the nation's first ethnic group. By 1900, the Irish dominated the city's neighborhoods, the Catholic Church, labor unions, entertainment, machine politics, and increasingly city government. They were the contractors, teachers, priests, nuns, saloon keepers, policemen, bureaucrats, and politicians. If one accounted for the city's first and second generations, more than 237,000 individuals, roughly 14 percent of Chicago's population, were Irish American. Between the 1890s and the 1930s, as Lawrence McCaffrey puts it, "they seemed to be everywhere."[46]

Street, Church, and Schoolyard

The Irish had long contributed to Chicago's street culture. During the late nineteenth century, immigrant residents divided the city's neighborhoods along specific boundaries, or "deadlines," a term coined by veterans of Civil War prisoner-of-war camps. In the decades that followed, gangs such as Ragen's Colts, Gimlets, and Shielders protected those neighborhoods, also known as their "turf," a native word for the peat common to the bogs of their homeland. The Irish coined other words common to the streets of Chicago: *slugger, dude, squealers,* and *phonies.* This vernacular language often underscored the rough-and-tumble lifestyle of the streets, where Irish gangs developed a reputation for employing violence. University of Chicago sociologist Frederic Thrasher later described fighting among the Irish as "a sort of national habit." As a result, other immigrant groups consciously avoided Irish neighborhoods, such as the deadline at Sixty-Ninth and Robey, lest the Gimlets or some other gang assail them.[47]

Most of these conflicts were fought over territory rather than for ethnic or racial reasons. During the early 1900s, the Shielders and the Dukies waged a neighborhood war for control of Bridgeport. Ragen's Colts protected Canaryville, although they later integrated other gangs into their own. Into the 1910s, the Colts boasted a membership of nearly three thousand, many of whom were police officers or gangsters. As members of the same gang or even the same families, they often assisted each other, with police officers turning a blind eye to crime and criminals providing the police with kickbacks. Not all Irish street culture was violent or corrupt, however. The Colts protected labor unions, backed candidates who promised assistance to the working classes, hosted Christmas parties for children, and earned a reputation for assisting the needy. Irish cops, such as Daniel J. Talbot on the city's West Side, knew the people on his beat personally and played the role of his community's unofficial social worker. He encouraged delinquents to avoid crime, intervened on behalf of minor offenders, and collected food and apparel for the needy. Irish street gangs eventually integrated with other white ethnic gangs, as they rarely amounted to a majority in their neighborhoods. But they did establish a rough-and-tumble culture that permitted them to exert power and influence in Chicago's streets. Those immigrant groups that followed effectively took their places.[48]

During the early twentieth century, the city's Catholic Church reached out to record numbers of parishioners. Irish clergy such as Archbishop Patrick A. Feehan and the Reverend Bernard P. Murray began expanding into the affluent neighborhood of Englewood, as the "lace curtain" contingent of Chicago's Irish reached larger proportions. Despite suspicions by the "old guard" Protestants of the community, the new parish grew to six hundred families in 1895, the same year it broke ground for a magnificent church with a marble edifice. Parishioners added a hospital ten years later. Archbishop Feehan, who served Chicago's Catholics during this impressive period of growth, further expanded Irish control by forming small parishes, some with as few as fifty families. More parishes, after all, meant more priests. In the first two decades of the twentieth century, some 80 percent of Chicago's priests, and over 60 percent of its bishops, were first- or second-generation Irish.[49]

Under Feehan's leadership, the Catholic Church in Chicago became even more American. His near-monopoly of power created friction with the city's Polish, Czech, and Italian Catholics. As Jay Dolan notes, "Other immigrant groups resented such Irish domination, and before long the Irish became the common enemy." Italian and particularly Sicilian immigrants tended neither to observe the formal practices common to Irish American Catholicism nor to train many members of their own clergy. Consequently, they were left at the mercy of Irish priests, who frequently found traditional Italian rituals "alien" and an "embarrassment" to their faith. Poles, by contrast, followed a more institutional brand of Catholicism, but they also revered Vatican authority more than the Irish. In short, Irish Catholics continued to support a more American version of their faith than most of their immigrant counterparts. To be sure, Irish American Catholicism enjoyed little hierarchical support from the Universal Church. In 1899, the Vatican had made that clear with Pope Leo XIII's condemnation and opposition of a distinct American Catholic Church. But it mattered little. In 1915, Archbishop George Mundelein, a New York native and the son of German immigrants, allied with Chicago's Irish bishopric to rebuff appeals by the city's Polish community that future bishops be appointed directly from Poland. Mundelein, only the second non-Irish archbishop since 1844, argued that such a move would embolden a dangerous "spirit of foreign nationalism." Chicago's Irish Catholics, and American Catholicism in general, had won an important victory.[50]

To ordinary Irish Catholics in the city, however, the daily ministry at schools and churches had a more tangible impact on their lives. By the 1890s, nearly thirty-three thousand students, roughly 25 percent of the city's public school enrollment, attended Catholic schools. The parishes of St. Patrick's, Sacred Heart, and Holy Name continued to attract the largest number of students, but new parishes were expanding as well. As second-generation Irish men and women, more upwardly mobile than their predecessors, established new parishes on the West Side, their schools helped ease the movement into the traditionally Protestant neighborhoods of the city. Through the late 1890s, the parishes of St. Malachy's,

St. Charles Borromeo, Blessed Sacrament, St. Matthew's, St. Agatha's, and Presentation built new educational facilities. By 1911, Visitation parish was educating more than thirteen hundred students annually. The parish later invested $150,000 in a new high school. Irish children who attended parochial schools through the 1930s often remained as separated from other ethnic Catholics as they did from children who attended public schools.[51]

Irish parents and educators also played important roles in developing the city's public school system. Since the mid-nineteenth century, a small but not insignificant number of Irish-born children attended public schools. According to historian Mimi Cowan, this number exceeded four thousand as early as the 1870s. Attendance at public schools gave immigrant boys and girls opportunities to network with Chicago's more affluent families. Irish women who pursued careers as teachers often received their education from the city's public schools. As Cowan explains, educators such as Mary Boughan and Lizzie McKeon escaped "the dictates of the Catholic clergy" and made middle-class livelihoods in the public system. Just as important, influential Irish Catholics served on the Chicago Board of Education during the late 1880s. Thomas Brenan, whose tenure lasted from 1878 until 1904, worked alongside Presbyterians, Jews, and Germans. He also served with the board's first female member, Ellen Mitchell. During the early 1890s, Brenan and his fellow colleagues loudly condemned Illinois legislation known as the Edwards Law, which ruled that classes be conducted entirely in English and placed severe restrictions on Catholic schools. During the elections of 1890 and 1892, Irish Democrats in Chicago helped secure the nomination of German candidates who opposed the law. In the 1892 contest, they ensured the victory of the state's first foreign-born governor, John Altgeld, who oversaw its repeal. Irish participation in the city's public school system is a reminder that at times "negotiation" rather than "oppression and hostility" characterized the narrative of the Chicago Irish.[52]

The Catholic Church also retained its historic independence in the new century. Amid a resurgence of anti-Catholicism in the 1910s, Irish priests began reaching out to immigrants of different nationalities. Most notably, the Reverend T. E. O'Shea of Visitation parish worked to soften the ethnic barriers that had divided Catholics in previous decades. He organized a social center for adolescents, one of the predecessors of the Catholic Youth

Organization. He founded a summer camp in Palos Hills. And he transformed the parish into a community that strove to meet the social, as well as the spiritual and educational, needs of the community. The Knights of Columbus, established by Catholic men to promote a more masculine image of self-improvement and resist the rising tide of nativism, gave common cause to individuals of different ethnicities. By the 1930s, the Irish had made their mark on Chicago's Catholic institutions—not by controlling them, but by helping new waves of immigrants adjust to life in the Windy City. As Ellen Skerrett puts it, "The Irish in Chicago formed parishes and schools that met their special needs as *American* Catholics." This parish model endures today.[53]

Labor Unions

Just as Irish priests and bishops paved the way for Chicago's Catholic institutions, Irish workers led the city's labor movement during the early twentieth century. Perhaps the most powerful of the city's associations was the Teamsters, whose membership included people of various races and ethnicities but was led by the Irish. The Teamsters were rooted in Irish street gangs and nationalist organizations, and they used political connections and social networks to secure power. But they also protected their working-class neighbors. In 1905, the Teamsters waged a series of sympathy strikes on behalf of female garment workers. During the work stoppage, they fought against fifty-eight hundred "scabs" who had been hired by employers to break the strike. Despite the association's diversity, the Irish targeted the much smaller number of black strikebreakers, a clash that added to the city's growing racial tensions. At least 21 people were killed and 416 injured. The Irish led other local unions as well: public school teachers, garbage workers, and meatpackers. Indeed, the Irish made up 57 percent of the meatpackers' union officers—but only 25 percent of its laborers.[54]

One of the most visible and influential organizers of the meatpackers' union was John Fitzpatrick. Born in County Westmeath in 1871, he immigrated to Chicago and found employment in the stockyards at age twelve. He rose quickly through union ranks and was elected president of the Chicago Federation of Labor (CFL) in 1902. Echoing the labor ideologies of Terence Powderly, Fitzpatrick believed that the city's union should welcome all workers, regardless of race, ethnicity, sex, or skill. His incorruptible reputation, devout Catholicism, and progressive political stances—including his support for women's suffrage—endeared him to Chicago's working classes. So did his successes. Fitzpatrick challenged the industry and won. His most significant accomplishment began with the organization of the Stockyards Labor Council, composed of workers and residents of the slum known as Packingtown, made famous in Upton Sinclair's *The Jungle.* On Easter Sunday, 1918, Fitzpatrick and the council celebrated a stunning victory over the city's top companies, known as the "Big Five," which agreed to increase wages significantly and provide workers with an eight-hour day. "It's a new day," Fitzpatrick addressed an ebullient crowd, "and out in God's sunshine you men and you women, black and white, have not only an eight-hour day but you are on an equality." Interracial cooperation, however, proved tenuous, as Irish gangs from Bridgeport turned on African American meatpackers the following year. Nevertheless, Fitzpatrick remained extremely popular. In 1919, he organized a national steel strike with fellow Irish American William Z. Foster. He won sixty thousand votes in his bid for mayor the same year. And he remained president of the CFL for life.[55]

Irish women established labor unions of their own. At the turn of the century, nearly one-fourth of Irish women worked in white-collar jobs (compared with 16 percent of Irish men). Mary Kenny O'Sullivan, a bookbinder, became the American Federation of Labor's first full-time female organizer. Mary McDermott led the Chicago's Scrubwomen's Union, Josephine Casey organized the Elevated Road Clerks, Margaret Duffy headed the city's Telephone and Switchboard Operators, and Elizabeth Maloney provided steadfast leadership in the Waitresses' Union. Margaret Haley founded the Chicago Federation of Teachers. In fact, by 1920, nearly half of all public school teachers were second-generation Irish women. To be sure, many remained poorer and less educated than many of their Protestant American counterparts. As one Irish Catholic teacher put it in the 1920s, "We are only half way up the ladder." Nevertheless, Irish American women won important concessions for working people in the early 1900s—and paved the way for more substantial gains during the mid-twentieth century.[56]

Athletes and Entertainers

Chicago's Irish also made their mark as athletes. South Siders participated in track and field events at Gaelic Park. Frank Ragen founded his Social Athletic Club in 1908. The association provided members with a clubhouse, equipment, and uniforms—although by 1919, their notoriety for violence led officials to describe them as "athletic only with their fists and brass knuckles and guns." For many of the working classes, life on the streets informed their concept of sport. Bare-knuckle boxing drew large crowds. Irish "pugs," such as John L. Sullivan, provided immigrant boys not only with dreams but also with distinctly Irish and American notions of masculinity. Similarly, aspiring Italian, Jewish, and Polish boxers frequently adopted Irish names before entering the ring. Racial hostilities, however, continued to divide black and white athletes. Boxing often became an outlet for racial tensions. In 1910, when the black champion Jack Johnson defeated Jim "Boilermaker" Jeffries, white people throughout Chicago neighborhoods hung the victor in effigy. Chicago's black population responded by referring to white gangs as "Mickies," regardless of their ethnicity. Other Irish athletes rose to greater heights. In 1896, James B. Connolly won the first Olympic gold medal for the United States in the triple jump. Irish boxers such as James J. Braddock continued to dominate the sport, until Joe Louis defeated him in Chicago in 1937. Some of the city's most prominent high school athletes went on to play football for the "Fighting Irish" of Notre Dame.[57]

In the realm of athletics, however, the city's Irish made their most enduring mark on baseball. Nationally, as many as one-third of all baseball players at the turn of the century were of Irish descent. In Chicago, team owners had long hired Irish athletes to attract Irish spectators. White Stockings (later White Sox) fans adored Michael "King" Kelly, a confident second-generation Irishman who batted .308, played outfield, and was arguably the game's first superstar. The faithful wept in 1886 when he was sold to Boston for an unprecedented $10,000. Yet the city's most notorious Irish baseball personality of the early twentieth century was undoubtedly Charles Comiskey. The son of an Irishman, Comiskey managed the St. Louis Browns before purchasing the White Sox in 1900. Ten years later, the self-aggrandizing owner built his organization a new park and characteristically named it after himself. Deserved or not, Comiskey went down in history for underappreciating his championship-caliber "Black Sox," who threw the World Series in 1918.[58]

Irish actors and musicians entertained Chicago's residents in new ways. Into the late nineteenth century, Irish minstrels had engaged white audiences by donning blackface in performances such as "Sambo" and "Mose." Patent racism and bigotry, evident in tunes such as Irving Jones's "St. Patrick's Day Is a Bad Day for Coons," were common into the 1890s. The city's growing diversity, however, along with the rise of vaudeville, led to the decline of such blatantly racist entertainment. At the same, anti-Catholicism reemerged at the turn of the century. Chicago's Irish increasingly contested the stage stereotypes of "Old Pat" and "Biddy." When predominantly white Protestants of Chicago's Hyde Park High School advertised the play *Mrs. Mulcahy*, Catholic newspapers protested. "Are you content that your mothers, daughters and sisters," the *New World* queried, "the ornament and glory of their sex, should be misrepresented in this gross, sensual, bestial manner?" Shows about Ireland and Irish nationhood grew in popularity. Actors such as Allen Doone and Andrew Mack performed in Irish plays like *Molly Bawn* and *Sergeant Devil McCare*. The popular Irish actor-singer Fisk O'Hara entertained enthusiastic audiences into the late 1910s. Captain Francis O'Neill, chief of police in Chicago from 1901 to 1905, preserved traditional Irish music. During

Captain Francis O'Neill (1848–1936)
Born in 1848 in County Cork, Francis O'Neill served as a cabin boy on an English merchant ship before immigrating to the United States. He later married Anna Rogers in Bloomington, Illinois, and from there the couple moved to Chicago. O'Neill joined the Chicago police force in 1873 and rose through its ranks to become chief of police in 1901. Yet he was most renowned as a talented musician who played the flute, pipes, and fiddle. Possessing a remarkable memory and musical ear, O'Neill frequently recruited officers and patrolmen to play for the city's prestigious Irish Music Club. Throughout his adult years, he assembled the largest collection of traditional Irish music ever published. He died in 1936 at his home in Chicago. In 2000, Francis O'Neill's hometown of Tralibane in County Cork unveiled a life-size monument of the Irish Chicagoan playing a flute.[59]

Captain Francis O'Neill. Francis O'Neill, *Irish Folk Music: A Fascinating Hobby . . . and Touhey's Hints to Amateur Pipers* (Chicago: Regan Printing House, 1910), front matter.

the Irish War of Independence (1919–21), audiences clamored for Emmett Moore's "Ireland a Nation." These entertainers paved the way for national icons of the 1930s—Jimmy Cagney, Pat O'Brien, Frank McHugh, Spencer Tracy, and Bing Crosby, Irish Americans whose work transcended those older negative stereotypes that had plagued Irish Catholics for a century.[60]

Politicians

Chicago's Irish left their most indelible mark in the realm of municipal politics. "No symbol," as James Barrett aptly puts it, "is more central to Irish American mythology than the big-city political boss." Two types of Irish bosses derived their power from the streets of Chicago. Neighborhood politicians, such as Johnny Powers and Edward Cullerton, maintained powerful social and economic connections, often illegally but also through sponsoring community parades and holiday celebrations. These "neighborhooders" enhanced their power by helping new arrivals find work and shelter. In return, immigrant patrons gave them their votes. "Levee and Lodinghouser" bosses, on the other hand, built emerging political machines by mediating between the worlds of municipal politics and crime. For men such as Michael "Hinky Dink" Kenna and John "Bathhouse" Coughlin, these connections went all the way up to the mayor. In either case, street gangs, the arm of local politicians, enforced a rough-and-tumble style of electioneering, should anyone attempt to countermand the boss. Some reputedly stuffed ballots and intimidated voters.[61]

By the 1890s, ward bosses had developed even more sophisticated methods of politicking and further increased their influence. Irish-controlled political machines played key roles or even governed half of the nation's twenty largest cities. In Chicago, as elsewhere, this was primarily due to their disproportionate participation in electoral politics and their urban mobility. The Irish, whom the *Chicago Tribune* referred to as "the governing race," voted in far greater numbers than their immigrant counterparts while simultaneously living in fewer ethnic enclaves. Although they made up only 17 percent of the city's population in 1890, they held fourteen of eighteen seats on the Democratic Central Committee and more than a third of the city council positions. Of the city's twenty-eight wards, twenty-four were under Irish control. John "de Pow" Powers of the city's Nineteenth Ward held office from 1888 to 1927—a remarkable sixteen terms in all.[62]

Admittedly, these politicians were often corrupt. Irish aldermen notoriously traded public infrastructure contracts for cash payoffs. They profited from a form of graft called "boodling," wherein elected officials sold city franchises to business owners. To be sure, the Irish were not alone in such practices. Politics could be a dirty business, as Mr. Dooley humorously observed: "'Hogan was just in here an' he was ta-alkin' about his little kid. . . .' 'There's priests an' lawyers enough," I says, 'to sind two worlds to hell,' I says, 'an' get thim out again,' I says. 'Make him an aldherman,' I says. An' thin what d'ye think th' big fool asks me? 'Where can I find a school,' he says, 'to sind him to?' School, mind ye, Jawn. 'School,' says I. 'Faith, Hogan, if ye don't sind him to school at all, at all, he's sure,' I says, 'to be wan.'"[63]

Between 1893 and 1915, Chicago's Irish political machines grew in power and influence. In 1893, following the assassination of Carter Henry Harrison, the Windy City elected its first Irish Catholic mayor, John Patrick Hopkins. With the support of Irish businessman Roger Sullivan, Hopkins orchestrated a massive boodling scheme, granting electric and gas companies utility franchises and making a handsome profit all the while. Although such practices were not technically illegal, they did hurt Hopkins's image, and he chose not to run again in 1895. Two years later, the city's Irish threw their support behind Democrat Carter Henry Harrison II, son of the former "Fair Mayor." The younger Harrison, who had graduated from St. Ignatius College, shared the spoils of his victory with neighborhood bosses such as the Stockyards' Tom Carey and the First Ward's "Bathhouse" Coughlin and "Hinky Dink" Kenna.

Sensing new political opportunities, ward bosses and the Sullivan-Hopkins faction nominated the Democratic reformer Judge Edward F. Dunne as mayoral candidate in 1905. Elected the city's second Irish Catholic mayor, Dunne promoted reforms that did not interfere with the city's machines: increased corporate real estate taxes, improved salaries for municipal employees, and city ownership of transportation systems. Some of Dunne's reforms may have concerned Chicago's Irish bosses, but they terrified its "goo-goos"—a derogatory term for Republican good-government reformers, who had no desire to see private transportation businesses fall under the city's control. In 1907, Dunne was defeated by the Republican Fred Busse, the city's first German mayor. Dunne rallied the following year, however, and was elected governor of

Illinois, the only Irish Catholic to hold the office until Patrick Quinn (2009–14). Carter Henry Harrison returned for a final term as mayor in 1911, which lasted until 1915, a year that witnessed significant changes in Chicago politics. Republicans retook the mayorship, a position they held until 1923. The Democratic Party, meanwhile, under Roger Sullivan and later George Brennan, began to unite the bosses.[64]

World War I and the Easter Rising

In 1914, Americans looked on in horror at the prospect of a distant yet terrible war. The world's most powerful empires—Britain, France, Russia, Germany, Austria-Hungary, and the Ottoman Empire—stumbled into a global conflict that wrought unimaginable devastation. By the end of World War I in 1918, somewhere between 15 and 20 million people lay dead. The world would never be the same.

This was certainly true in Ireland. On the eve of the Great War, John Redmond, the leader of the nationalist Irish Parliamentary Party, seemingly had won Home Rule for Ireland, the primary goal of constitutional nationalists since the 1880s. Aided by the Parliament Act of 1911, a coalition of British liberals and Irish nationalists had passed the measure through Parliament, but the law was suspended for the duration of the war. Supported by the vast majority of nationalists in Ireland and across the diaspora, Home Rule was divisive at home, where hundreds of thousands of Protestant Unionists mobilized against the prospect of a Dublin parliament. Determined to prevent Home Rule, militant unionists formed the Ulster Volunteer Force in 1913. Nationalists followed suit with the Irish Volunteers later that year. Civil war seemed imminent, but this too was suspended by the outbreak of World War I.

More than two hundred thousand Irish men fought for the British army during the Great War, many of them volunteers in the first weeks. Redmond and other nationalist leaders initially encouraged military service, hopeful that it would heal relationships between nationalists and unionists and lend credence to the idea that Ireland deserved legislative independence. Always a dangerous position for an Irish nationalist, Redmond's stance became increasingly controversial as the war continued. And this had real consequences for Irish politics. Unable to support the notion that Irishmen should serve in the British army no matter where it fought, a minority split from the Irish Volunteers in late September 1914 to create the Irish National Volunteers. It was these men and women that would plan the Easter Rising of 1916. Meanwhile, the war's death toll continued to rise, eventually claiming more than seven hundred thousand British soldiers, including nearly fifty thousand Irishmen.

The political stalemate created by war provided an opportunity for Irish revolutionaries. Nearly two thousand members of the Irish Citizen Army, the Irish National Volunteers, and the Irish Republican Brotherhood occupied a number of sites across Dublin on Easter Monday 1916. Standing in front of the General Post Office in central Dublin, Patrick Pearse read the Proclamation of the Republic, declaring Ireland's independence and detailing the rights of the Irish people. Although they initially took the British by surprise, the rebels had to surrender after a week, overwhelmed by the British military's superior resources. The British crackdown that followed the rising snatched defeat from the jaws of victory, moving an increasing number of Irish men and women toward more advanced nationalist positions. During a two-week period in May, army firing squads executed fifteen leaders of the rising, including Thomas Clarke, James Connolly, and Patrick Pearse. Scores more were sentenced to death, and thousands, far exceeding the actual number of participants, were incarcerated without charges. Three years later, in 1919, gunmen of the newly formed Irish Republican Army (IRA) waged a guerilla-style war that featured a crescendo of atrocities committed by both IRA volunteers and their British foes. Irish diplomats eventually brokered a treaty with Britain in 1922 that created the Irish Free State, a twenty-six-county state with dominion status like Canada or Australia. Controversially, the treaty left the six counties of Northern Ireland under British rule, and British negotiators insisted that the new state retain some of the symbols of British sovereignty. Disagreement over the terms of the treaty led to the Irish Civil War (1922–23), a relatively small-scale conflict that left deep and lasting legacies in the new state. Protreaty forces prevailed, and Ireland had won its independence, but many wondered about the cost.[65]

In Chicago, as throughout much of the rest of the United States, most Irish Americans anxiously supported the rising and the war for independence that followed. A few questioned the wisdom and timing of the revolt. Charles Ffrench, the president of the Irish Fellowship Club of Chicago, argued that it was "utter madness for the Irish people to be so followed as to rise against the English power." Most were more supportive. Hugh O'Neill, a Chicago attorney, described John Redmond as "Ireland's Benedict Arnold" and called for full-fledged support for the republicans. Nationally, John Devoy and other nationalists continued to raise funds and maintain transatlantic connections with revolutionaries in Ireland. Two of the men who signed the Proclamation of the Republic, Thomas Clarke and James Connolly, lived in the United States before returning home, and much of the money used to prosecute the failed insurrection came from Devoy's revived Clan.[66]

When news of the rising reached Chicago, many noticed that the Easter Proclamation identified only one country besides Ireland by name—crediting "her exiled children in America." Yet information regarding the insurrection reached Chicago slowly, as the British government carefully censored any material leaving Ireland. On April 25, the day after the rising began, the *Tribune* informed its readers, "REVOLT IN DUBLIN, RUMOR." As more and more stories of the rebellion reached Chicago, newspapers featured them prominently. Between April 24 and May 12, when the executions finally ceased, the *Tribune* ran eleven front-page stories on the Easter Rising. Its coverage also began to reflect the growing sympathy for the revolutionaries. On May 5, three days after Clarke and Pearse had been executed and thousands of Irish men and women were thrown in jail, the *Tribune* described the crackdown as "Unnecessary and Inexpedient." In the wake of the rising, Chicago's Irish renewed their financial support for the cause of independence. Many joined John Devoy's new organization, called the Friends of Irish Freedom, although others broke away and supported Eamon de Valera's American Association for the Recognition of the Irish Republic in 1920. During the civil war that followed in 1922, Chicago's Irish also split along the lines that had splintered their fellow country men and women. Yet when the Irish Civil War finally stopped in 1923, so too did the interfactionalism that had long divided the city's Irish nationalists. Not until the 1940s did they again pay much attention to the national politics of their homeland.[67]

The Chicago Irish, like other immigrant communities across the country, regarded the First World War not only as England's difficulty but also as an opportunity to prove their loyalty to the

United States. This had not always been the case, however, since America did not enter the war until April 1917. Prior to American involvement, neither the Irish nor the Germans, the nation's two largest immigrant groups, supported the war. German Americans held little animosity toward their relatives, in some cases brothers or cousins, and Irish Americans expressed hostility toward a British Empire that continued to rule over their homeland. Even Americans of other ancestries opposed U.S. entry into the conflict, popularizing songs such as "I Didn't Raise My Boy to Be a Soldier" and reelecting President Wilson in 1916 with the motto "He kept us out of war." Yet when the fighting commenced, Chicago's Irish answered the call. The city's forty-nine councils of the Knights of Columbus, boasting over twenty-five thousand members, played a disproportionate role. At least 25 percent of its membership, whom James Barrett describes as "second- and third-generation Irish men who were anxious to prove just how Catholic and American they had become" joined the armed forces. The "Caseys," as the Knights were often called, publicly dedicated themselves to the U.S. Constitution, to law and order, and to practicing their faith "openly and consistently, but without ostentation." Those Knights who remained stateside volunteered their time and donated money to the creation of parochial schools and youth organizations. World War I, like the American Civil War, provided the Irish of Chicago with opportunities, albeit deadly, to demonstrate yet again their support and appreciation for their adopted homeland.[68]

Race Riot

Veterans of the war returned to find Chicago beset by racial, ethnic, and religious tensions. The summer of 1919, which also featured widespread labor strikes and anxieties about communism, quickly became known as "Red Summer" for the number of violent race riots that occurred across the United States. A resurgent Ku Klux Klan began espousing an ideology of "one hundred percent Americanism," declaring marginalized groups to be enemies of the nation: immigrants, Catholics, Jews, and especially African Americans. Chicago's Irish soldiers returning from the war expected a hero's welcome. Instead, they were greeted by nativism and unemployment. During the war years, to fill the factory and warehouse jobs left vacant by the men headed off to war, businesses recruited African Americans from southern states. Tens of thousands answered the call. Although the sacrifices of black Chicagoans helped win the war, returning Irish American soldiers resented the fact that their sacrifices in Europe did not translate into job security when they came home.

Yet African Americans had also served overseas, and they returned to find a lack of housing and increased racial animosities. Red Summer was hot both metaphorically and literally. On July 27, tragedy struck when a teenage African American boy named Eugene Williams went swimming in Lake Michigan. He crossed a deadline between the city's white and black beaches, upon which several white men threw stones at Williams, who drowned. The police refused to arrest the alleged perpetrators in spite of the appeals of black eyewitnesses. Angry crowds began to assemble. Rumors spread rapidly throughout the city. Violence ensued, as members of Irish American athletic clubs in Bridgeport and Canaryville attacked African Americans. In one instance, Ragen's Colts blackened their faces and set fire to a Polish and Lithuanian neighborhood in an effort to trick the communities into joining in the fray. The police were again slow to make arrests. According to the *Chicago Defender*, the city's influential black newspaper, the Colts were "allowed to operate free from police interference." Many African Americans, recognizing their vulnerability, fought back. After four days of rioting, the state of Illinois ordered in the militia, although the fighting continued for another four days. In all, the riot took the lives of at least fifteen white people and twenty-three black people. More than five hundred people were injured. Arson attacks left as many as one thousand African American families homeless. The Chicago Commission on Race Relations eventually blamed the rioting on job competition and overcrowding, among other things. But it also singled out Irish American athletic clubs as the key perpetrators. "But for them," the commission argued, "it is doubtful if the riot would have gone beyond the first clash."[69]

From an Irish American perspective, the Chicago Race Riot of 1919 contrasted sharply with the city's relatively nonviolent draft protests of 1863. For one thing, Chicago's African American population had grown considerably, more than doubling between the turn of the century and the end of the First World War. An influx of black residents, coupled with the return of thousands of veterans, presented city officials with new problems related to overcrowding and unemployment that were not issues during the Civil War. But there was more. Black residents across

Illinois represented a new political threat in the twentieth century. And across the nation, the complicated relationship between Irish and African Americans had grown worse. Editorializing about President Theodore Roosevelt's dinner with civil rights activist Booker T. Washington in 1901, Mr. Dooley expressed the prejudice, anxieties, and contradictions felt perhaps by many of the Chicago Irish: "Th' black has manny fine qualities. He is joyous, light-hearted, an' aisily lynched. But as a fellow bong vivant, not by anny means. . . . 'Tis not me that speaks, Hinnissy, 'tis th' job. Dooley th' plain citizen says, 'Come in, Rastus.' Dooley's job says: 'If ye come, th' r-rest will stay away.'"[70]

The Race Riot of 1919 marked another turning point in the history of Chicago's Irish: the move toward suburbanization. Fire and violence had destroyed large sections of the city. Housing was already in short supply. Many white homeowners feared that rebuilding would be a poor investment and contemplated leaving the city. Significantly, Irish and German residents had been faced with a similar choice in the wake of the Great Fire. When the city attempted to rezone downtown Chicago in 1872, both immigrant groups protested. Both intended to rebuild their homes inside the city. Not so in 1919. The increased presence of African Americans in Chicago, along with racial bigotry and the belief that property would bring prosperity, led the South Side Irish to look elsewhere. The establishment of public housing in the 1920s only accelerated the trend. And that trend set a pattern for other American cities throughout the twentieth century.[71]

Prohibition: Al Capone and Dean O'Banion

The year 1919 also saw the ratification of the Eighteenth Amendment. Prohibition, as the amendment was more commonly known, banned the production, transportation, and sale of alcohol across the country. Despite the relative ease with which the amendment and consequent legislation were passed, neither the federal nor state governments took the enforcement of Prohibition seriously. At its peak, the U.S. government employed a paltry 1,520 agents to monitor 18,700 miles of coastline and countless miles of forest, harbors, and riverfronts. State governments spent more money on regulating hunting and fishing than they did policing alcohol. Agents were often underpaid and hence vulnerable to bribes.[72]

In Chicago, multiple criminal organizations vied for control of the city's liquor supply. The most renowned were Dean O'Banion's

North Side Gang and Johnny Torrio's Chicago Outfit, later run by the infamous Al Capone. The former was predominantly Irish and the latter predominantly Italian. Both competed for shares in a business made lucrative by high demand and low supply. At the peak of Capone's success, the notorious bootlegger made over $100 million in 1927 alone—roughly $1.3 billion in today's money. He and other mob leaders consequently could afford to bribe and cajole local law enforcement. By 1923, Capone's organization employed over seven hundred men and owned 161 illegal bars, and the mob boss maintained a personal headquarters at the Hawthorne Hotel in the Chicago suburb of Cicero, from which he effectively controlled the office of the mayor and the town council.

The rival gangs fought a bloody war over control of the liquor supply. In a daring move in 1924, Capone put out a hit on Dean O'Banion, who was shot to death in the back room of his flower shop. The Chicago Outfit sent a bouquet to the funeral with a card that read, "from Al." The remaining members of the North Side Gang vowed revenge. In September 1926, a caravan of eight vehicles approached the Hawthorne Hotel in Cicero, where an unsuspecting Al Capone was eating lunch in the lobby. The lead car fired a series of blanks, which effectively dispersed innocent bystanders and brought Capone and his men to the windows. Gangsters in the remaining seven cars emptied the chambers of their Thompson machine guns into the building, shattering windows and forcing Capone to the ground. Remarkably, despite the element of surprise and the sheer number of bullets discharged, Capone survived. In February 1929, he struck back at O'Banion's former gang on St. Valentine's Day, virtually eliminating it as a threat. Gang violence and Prohibition continued into the 1930s, until the Twenty-First Amendment repealed the failed measure in 1933.[73]

Prohibition made life more difficult for all of Chicago's residents. Throughout the era, gangsters committed over five hundred murders. The violence employed by Chicago's organized crime syndicate reinforced the negative stereotypes about ethnic Catholics espoused by nativists and the Klan. These attitudes spilled over into municipal politics as well. Republicans employed antiforeign and anti-Catholic rhetoric to great effect. With the exception of a single term, the GOP's William "Big Bill" Thompson—a skilled politician who could simultaneously court the votes of Catholics and anti-Catholics—served as the city's mayor from 1915 to 1931.[74]

Irish Women and Suffrage

Along with their female counterparts throughout the country, Chicago's Irish women won the right to vote in 1920 with the ratification of the Nineteenth Amendment. Prominent immigrant women had long advocated for suffrage rights. As early as 1894, Mr. Dooley commented on Miss Molly Donahue's attempt to vote in the city's school trustee election, the only type of election where Illinois women were able to cast ballots. "She's been to raygisther an' be hivins she swears she'll vote," Dooley declared. Molly Donahue was not too far ahead of her time, however. In the early twentieth century, Elizabeth Maloney, a union activist in Chicago, organized the city's Self-Supporting Women's Equal Suffrage Association. Garment worker Leonora O'Reilly and bootmaker Emma Steghagen promoted the Wage Earner's Suffrage League. In 1904 and 1906, Irish woman Kenney O'Sullivan persuaded the American Federation of Labor to endorse women's suffrage. In 1909, glove maker Agnes Nestor lobbied the Illinois legislature on behalf of the cause. Beginning in the 1920s, the votes of Irish women further strengthened the rise of Chicago's Democratic machine.[75]

A Citywide Political Machine

If Irish municipal power appeared to decline in the 1920s, the city's Democratic politicians were quietly building one of the most potent electoral machines in U.S. history. On the surface, the Republican Party continued running roughshod over Democrats. Not only did William Thompson hold the mayorship for thirteen of sixteen years, but all three presidents elected to the oval office in the 1920s belonged to the GOP. In Chicago, the lone exception to the Republican succession occurred with the election of William E. Dever, an Irish Catholic reformer with a reputation as a public servant. In 1923, he defeated the poorly organized Arthur C. Lueder, who ran in place of the corrupt and briefly unpopular Thompson. During his tenure, however, Dever lost the support of key Irish bosses by enforcing Prohibition—even ordering the city's police to raid breweries, speakeasies, and private residences. When Thompson ran again in 1927, he faced a severely weakened Dever, whose allies desperately resorted to racist rhetoric in their campaign. George Brennan, the Irish American chairman of the county Democratic Party, publicly referred to Thompson's political machine as the "Black Belt," since he enjoyed the support of the city's African American electorate. South Side Irish boss Michael Igoe asked crowds, "Shall the white people continue to rule Chicago?" Democrats hung racist posters throughout the city and drove through African American neighborhoods in trucks playing the song "Bye Bye Blackbird." Their tactics backfired. Dever garnered barely 43 percent of the vote, losing Italian and Jewish support in the process.[76]

Behind the scenes, however, the city's competing Irish machines had been reorganizing into a much-needed broader ethnic coalition. In 1920, over one-third of the city's population had been born in eastern or southern Europe, and many clamored for a political voice. Democratic Party leader George Brennan complied. As early as 1918, 15 percent of the party's candidates were new immigrants. Four years later, a young and talented Bohemian politician named Anton Cermak won the nomination for the Cook County Board of Commissioners over incumbent Dan Ryan. In 1924, the percentage of new-stock candidates had slightly dipped, while two-thirds of Chicago's committeemen remained Irish. By 1928, primarily under Brennan's influence, 21 percent of the party's candidates came from eastern or southern Europe.

Throughout the 1920s, despite the appearance of a Republican hold on politics, the Democrats quietly retained control of the city council. Meanwhile, Brennan died in 1928, and the resourceful Cermak, with the assistance of his powerful West Side Irish ally Patrick Nash, took over as party chair. Cermak not only adopted Brennan's strategy of building a multiethnic coalition but raised it to a new level. He abandoned the racist rhetoric of his predecessors and appealed to immigrant communities by championing the repeal of Prohibition and blue laws. Yet as one historian noted, "If Cermak was the architect of the new machine, Pat Nash was its engineer." Nash worked tirelessly behind the scenes to encourage the city's second- and third-generation Irish to support a bigger Democratic tent. Following the market crash of 1929 and the severe economic downturn that followed, Nash and Cermak expertly built a panethnic coalition of energized Democrats, many of whom had been hit hard by the Depression. During the mayoral election of 1931, Cermak tested the strength of the new, citywide coalition by challenging the incumbent. Thompson inadvertently played into the hands of his opponents by appealing to a mainstay of the Republican Party: 100 percent Americanism. Belittling Cermak as "Pushcart Tony" and insulting other Slavic names on the ticket, Thompson seemingly hoped to convert older-stock Democrats to his side. The tactic backfired. The Cermak-designed and Nash-built coalition gained 671,189 votes compared with the incumbent's tally of 476,922. Two years later, while visiting president-elect Franklin Delano Roosevelt in Florida, Cermak was mortally wounded by an Italian immigrant attempting to assassinate Roosevelt. Patrick Nash handpicked his successor, Edward J. Kelly—the first mayor in the most impressive Irish municipal dynasty in U.S. history.[77]

The Chicago Irish came a long way between 1865 and 1933. More literate and better prepared for modern, urban life than their predecessors, Irish Catholics achieved new levels of social and economic security. Following the Great Chicago Fire of 1871, the Irish continued their rise to prominence in shaping the city's neighborhood street culture, leading its Catholic institutions, building the labor movement, and acquiring power in municipal government. By supporting nationalist organizations, they helped win independence for Ireland—and respectability for themselves as exiles of a free nation. They often did so, however, at the expense of African Americans. And their greatest advances still lay ahead of them. At the national level, WASPs continued to dominate the most powerful political and economic institutions. Widespread nativism and distrust of Catholics continued through the 1920s. The first Catholic nominee to the office of the presidency, Al Smith, the son of County Westmeath immigrants, found it impossible to overcome the religious bigotry that had infected the electorate in 1928. Even for the city's "lace-curtain" Irish, as Kerby Miller describes it, discrimination "embittered the Irish middle class and kept old, inherited wounds fresh." Respectability for the Chicago Irish had to wait for another era, one marked by economic depression, a second world war, and a powerful political machine. The Irish nevertheless had played key roles in building the most American of cities. To the new immigrants who settled there in the late nineteenth and early twentieth centuries, Irish America *was* America. Urban pioneers in their own right, the Chicago Irish helped bridge older generations with the new—eventually providing a model, and hope, for future waves of American immigrants.[78]

4

BEYOND THE SOUTH SIDE: THE IRISH OF DOWNSTATE ILLINOIS, 1865–1960

> What Irishman awakes and sniffs the balmy breezes of his home in Illinois, and fills his lungs with the pure air of the prairies and the ozone of freedom, but looks back with love to the land of the shamrock, the primrose, the yellow-blossoming "whin" and the daisy? The greater Ireland of America has not forgotten the emerald that sparkles on the bosom of the wild Atlantic. The greater Ireland of today—perhaps the greatest element of the fifty millions of our people—love the United States so much and the old Ireland so much that they with all their hearts wish that Ireland were a state of our union. St. Patrick's Day and the Fourth of July divide equally the honors with the Irish-American.
>
> —*Daily Pantagraph*, Bloomington, Illinois, March 18, 1886

In the century that followed the Civil War, the Irish made their mark on the Prairie State. Although Irish immigration to the United States declined dramatically after 1920, the number of Irish Americans in Illinois continued to increase across this period. By 1900, communities such as Ottawa and Bloomington boasted Irish populations of 18 and 25 percent, respectively. Two decades later, nearly three-quarters of the individuals who described themselves as Irish also claimed to be at least third-generation American. By 1960, only German Americans had a larger ethnic base in Illinois than the Irish. Most Irish immigrants during this period were women. Most were young and unmarried. Whether male or female, the vast majority were Catholic. And most of these came from the southern and western parts of Ireland.

The Irish of downstate Illinois played pivotal roles in many of the same areas as their Chicago peers: labor, politics, religion, and urban development. In many ways, Irish Americans who lived outside the state's metropolis tended to advance more quickly, becoming part of the early twentieth-century civic establishment in cities such as Bloomington, Joliet, Ottawa, and Rockford. Tragically, they were also central participants in the era's racial violence, most notably in infamous race riots in Springfield in 1908, East St. Louis in 1917, and Chicago in 1919. Irish Americans across the state suffered through the Great Depression, a catastrophe tempered by federal and state efforts to provide relief. It was the advent of World War II that ended the Depression, with massive increases in government spending and efforts to mobilize the American public to fight in a global contest. The war also had a dramatic impact on the Irish American experience. The patriotic celebration of war heroes such as Audie Murphy and Edward "Butch" O'Hare finally broke down long-held stereotypes about the Irish in America, a process reinforced after 1945 by the popularity of films that celebrated a new, more inclusive vision of American identity. Irish Americans were now quintessentially American. This sense was only strengthened by the postwar emergence of a new sense of American Catholic identity, one set up in part by Irish domination of the Catholic Church in the United States. This did not reflect a dilution of the connection between Irish Americans and the Emerald Isle, something expressed in both the growth of transatlantic tourism after the 1950s and the dramatic increase in the number of Irish festivals across the state. Irishness would remain firmly in the hearts of millions of Illinois residents.[1]

A Modernizing Economy

Following the Civil War, Illinois residents were clearly concerned that their state's system of government was ill suited for the demands of a modernizing economy. In 1865, cities such as Chicago, Decatur, Peoria, and Jacksonville petitioned the general assembly to have the capital moved to their communities. The bids failed, but they were leading indicators of other changes. In 1870, legislators convened in Springfield to create a new constitution. This document, ratified on July 2, was massive in scope. It expanded executive powers. It permitted the reelection of governors and required a two-thirds majority to override a gubernatorial veto. It also extended universal suffrage to all males over twenty-one years of age who had resided in Illinois for at least one year, regardless of skin color. Delegates such as Lake County's Elijah M. Haines even pressed for women's suffrage, but that measure fell to defeat. The assembly did manage to establish the nation's first system of state regulations, designed to curtail excessive railroad fees. In 1877, the U.S. Supreme Court upheld the regulatory provisions of the Illinois charter, which soon was a model for other states. For the next one hundred years, the Constitution of 1870 served the Prairie State well.[2]

The new constitution, along with an influx of immigrants, helped propel the state's economic development. Throughout the remainder of the century, Illinois became a leader in both population growth and industrial output. In 1870, Illinois's population ranked fourth in the nation. By 1890, it had moved to third, with over 3.8 million residents. Of these, nearly 22 percent were foreign-born, with Irish immigrants totaling 124,498. Communities such as Bloomington, Springfield, Joliet, and Rockford grew into thriving cities with significant Irish populations. The state's industrial capacity surged as well, providing its burgeoning population with jobs in coal mining, steel production, and railroads—jobs taken by Irish and Irish American immigrants. From the 1870s, they worked in the mills of the Joliet Steel Company, producing sheet metal, barbed wire, and steel rails. Others cut stone and mined quarries. Into the 1890s, Irishmen mined coal throughout counties such as Bureau, Macoupin, Montgomery, Will, and St. Clair. Mining operations also attracted Irish Catholics to Gallatin County, eventually making it the second-most "Irish" county in Illinois.[3]

Organized Labor

Industrialization led to labor strife in many mining communities, where Irish politicians and business leaders frequently supported workers. One such community was Braidwood, fifty-three miles southwest of Chicago, which quickly developed into one of the state's most important centers of bituminous coal production. In 1874, Braidwood miners struck for better pay and benefits. The Chicago, Wilmington, and Vermillion Coal Company (CW&V) attempted to break the strike with scabs and eventually hired Allan Pinkerton's infamous detective agency. Pinkerton quickly recognized the folly of his endeavor. When the women and children of Braidwood (many of whom were Irish) assaulted Pinkerton's son and pelted pit bosses with stones, Deputy Sheriff Cornelius O'Donnell refused to intervene. According to Pinkerton, the town's mayor and local judge William Mooney not only dismissed his pleas but were outright "in sympathy with the women" who had attacked them. O'Donnell, also a former miner and the town's most prominent saloonkeeper, told Pinkerton that "the women had a right to do just what they did." Pinkerton eventually left town convinced that as long as O'Donnell could count on "a good many votes from the Braidwood section," the CW&V would have a hard time. The miners eventually won the strike but lost a key ally when O'Donnell died in 1879.[4]

Political connections also helped Irish union leaders in East St. Louis. During the Great Railroad Strike of 1877, brakemen in East St. Louis walked off the job, as did laborers in Aurora, Carbondale, Peoria, and Effingham. In Chicago, the strikes grew particularly violent, as they had throughout the country. Yet due in part to the leadership of Jack McCarthy of the Vandalia Railroad, the protests remained nonviolent in East St. Louis. Strikers permitted passenger and rail trains through their picket lines, and McCarthy's political alliance with German-born mayor John Bowman led to a successful arbitration. "Their peaceable intentions," as historian Charles Lumpkins puts it, "won praise from the business community and laid the foundation for labor's future participation in government in East St. Louis."[5]

The Irish also helped unionize workers in Joliet, a community built on steel, stone, and railroads. During the 1880s, Irishmen of all skill levels banded together with Welsh, Scottish, and English laborers in the Amalgamated Association of Iron and Steel Workers. Most were first- or second-generation Irish Americans. Most were Catholic. And most, as historian Stephen Freeman argues, "were particularly adept at combining union affiliations with common membership in the Ancient Order of Hibernians and the Irish Land League." Indeed, between 1879 and 1881, Joliet unions protested Ireland's "infamous land system," maintaining that all citizens must stand in opposition of the "rich trying to crush out the poor" whenever and wherever it was happening. In 1884, the Amalgamated Association and prominent businessmen successfully lobbied against the use of convict labor from the state penitentiary. By the turn of the century, however, Joliet unions faced disunity as new waves of eastern European workers took jobs in the community. A reluctant and ultimately failed strike against

U.S. Steel left the Amalgamated Association impotent in 1901. The union disbanded until 1919, when, as Freeman concludes, "union organizers realized that Joliet workers, particularly first-generation immigrants, had a strong commitment to democratic ideals." Ireland's struggle for democratic Home Rule eventually translated to the Great War era, when union leaders organized political movements around the appeal to "Make Joliet Safe for Democracy."[6]

One of the most famous strikes in American labor history involved Irish coal miners at Virden in 1898. During the previous two decades, Irish, Scots, Welsh, and English immigrants had found work in the bustling mines of Macoupin County. Into the 1890s, Italian and Slavic laborers increasingly joined their ranks.

Patrick H. Morrissey (1862–1916)

Born in 1862 to a section foreman on the Chicago and Alton Railroad, Patrick Morrissey grew up in Bloomington and worked his way through high school as a railroad "call boy." On graduating, he became a brakeman, a job so dangerous that few in the position could acquire life insurance. In 1885, he joined a labor organization for railroad employees that eventually became the Brotherhood of Railroad Trainmen (BRT). He took a job as a clerk in the union office and was elected first vice grand master of the BRT in 1889. After the failure of the Pullman Strike in 1894, which had left the BRT $105,000 in debt, Morrissey was elected to the unenviable position of grand master. He shrewdly reorganized the union into three regions, thereby forcing railroad companies to negotiate over smaller territories. Morrissey simultaneously stressed institutional unity, pooling the union's financial resources. By the time he left the BRT in 1909, the union claimed 120,000 members and boasted insurance and strike funds of $2 million and $1.5 million, respectively. He later worked for the American Association of Railway Employees and Investors, as well as the Chicago, Burlington, and Quincy Railroad, for which he served as president. Patrick Morrissey died in 1916 and was buried in the Galesburg St. Joseph Cemetery, where the BRT later placed a monument over his grave.[7]

Patrick H. Morrissey. Courtesy of the McLean County Museum of History, Bloomington, Illinois.

Between 1890 and 1899 the number of non-English-speaking miners grew from 7 to 25 percent. Wages fell, and union membership surged. Meanwhile, the Chicago-Virden Coal Company (CVCC), had grown to become the largest producer in the state. By many accounts, however, the CVCC remained a "feudal" operation, whereby owners exercised control over practically all aspects of their laborers' lives: wages, rents, and goods at company-owned stores. Nearly all the coalfields in Illinois and the United States operated in the same way. Nevertheless, in January 1898, the United Mine Workers of America (UMWA) negotiated a settlement with the CVCC for eight-hour days, six-day weeks, and a one-third increase in pay to 40 cents per ton. By October, however, the CVCC reneged. And when strikers occupied the mines at Virden, company president J. C. Loucks and his manager F. W. Lukens ordered in African American strikebreakers from Alabama and guards from St. Louis. On October 12, the union faced off against the guards in a ten-minute pitched battle, as laborers attempted to prevent the train of strikebreakers from unloading. The guards, who had built a stockade on the grounds of the mines, fired into the strikers. Armed members of the UMWA returned fire. Seven miners and five guards were killed. At least thirty miners and four guards were injured.[8]

In the wake of the violence, Irish miners and union leaders helped ensure that the sacrifices at Virden were not in vain. Even before the dust of the battle had settled, many of the strikers argued that they should storm the stockade before National Guardsmen arrived. Irishman Edward Cahill, president of the local UMWA, urged them to refrain. Cahill suspected that such an attack not only would prove futile but also would turn public opinion against the strikers. He was right. In a maneuver calculated to win votes, Republican governor John R. Tanner denied the CVCC's request for National Guardsmen. Tanner hoped to follow in the footsteps of Democratic governor John Altgeld, who had won public approval by pardoning the Haymarket convicts. After all, many Illinoisans, including Irish voters, were sympathetic to the strikers. Governor Tanner's rejection of the CVCC marked the first time a governor refused to use state troops to defend "feudal" mining operations. Ultimately, the union prevailed. Success at Virden also led to the election of Braidwood native and second-generation Irish American John Mitchell to the presidency of the UMWA. Virden retained a distinctly Irish hue. Following her death in 1930, former Chicago resident and Irishwoman Mother Jones was buried at Mount Olive alongside the bodies of miners killed at Virden. "Generations of Illinois laborers," as historian David Markwell puts it, "looked to the occurrence in Virden as the reason why they lived better and freer lives."[9]

Farming

A growing minority of the Irish in Illinois settled in farming communities. An agricultural revolution was afoot, as scientific advances made commercial farming even more lucrative. During the late nineteenth century, the number of Irish men and women living in rural counties increased from 33 to 36.1 percent—even as three-quarters of the state's overall foreign-born population lived in cities. An increasing number of farms were operated by tenants rather than owners, up from 31 to 34 percent during the 1880s. Absenteeism grew, and with it came some of the problems that had plagued Irish tenants in their homeland.[10]

Nineteenth-century Illinois's most infamous absentee landlord was undoubtedly William Scully. The Irish-born aristocrat's reputation for heavy-handed "rack rents" and evictions originated in Ireland. Legend has it that Scully wore a bullet-proof coat under his vest and had been shot several times by angry tenants on his County Tipperary estate. He purchased his first Illinois farms in 1850, allegedly by underpaying desperate veterans of the Mexican-American War for land scrip. In 1868, he was forced to resettle in London. During the following decade, he acquired some 200,000 acres of farmland in Illinois, Nebraska, and Kansas. At least 110,000 of these acres were located in Illinois, primarily in Logan, Grundy, and Sangamon counties. News outlets despised Scully. In an 1886 article titled "Irish Landlordism in America," the *Farm, Field, and Stockman* claimed that he exacted $400,000 from his U.S. properties each year, with an estimated $150,000 from Logan County alone. The majority of his tenants, the article continued, were "unnaturalized foreigners . . . usually poor and kept poor by his systematic exactions." The "monstrous land tyrant," as many newspapers remembered him, died in 1906 at eighty-four years of age. His descendants settled in Logan County and continued to rent the land, at more reasonable rates, into the twenty-first century.[11]

The high-profile case of William Scully notwithstanding, most Irish farmers in Illinois worked their own land. Representative of many rural immigrants were Lawrence and Cornelius Curtin of Christian County, Illinois. Born in West Limerick during the 1840s, both boys grew up during the Great Famine, along with their sister, Margaret. All three helped raise crops on "conacre land" (rented land less than an acre in size, usually with a small cottage). All were Catholic. While records are sketchy, at least Lawrence seems to have attended the Courtenay School in County Limerick. During the mid-1860s, the older brother, Lawrence, packed his trunk and left for America. After a brief stint working for the U.S. government at the end of the Civil War, he moved to Illinois. In 1866, Cornelius joined his brother in the Prairie State. Both became farmers and U.S. citizens. In 1872, Lawrence and Anna Stacia O'Neill married at the Church of Immaculate Conception in Springfield. Cornelius and Sarah M. Molohon married two years later in the same church. Lawrence and Anna had three children and moved their family to Morrisville, where by 1880, Lawrence had acquired 170 acres of land. Cornelius and Sarah had ten children and settled at Bear Creek, where by 1887, Cornelius had purchased 120 acres. When their father wrote a letter in 1888 describing the condition of Ireland as nothing "but Landlords and Tenants fiting evicting them every day throwing themselves and their families out of their land," it must have given them pause. Both Lawrence and Cornelius Curtin farmed into the early twentieth century, when they passed along their lands to their sons. Their descendants still farm in Christian County.[12]

While historians long have argued that the history of Irish America is largely urban, questions remain about the significant minority of Irish men and women who farmed the prairie. Assertions that a larger Irish identity was formed through a common urban American experience may not pertain to the downstate Irish. What did expressions of Irish identity look like outside of Chicago? Certainly, St. Patrick's Day celebrations were common in smaller Illinois communities. What percentage of rural county populations was Irish? Did the Irish cluster into farming communities? How long did they farm? And to what ends? How important were religion and church institutions? What were their politics? Answers to these and other relevant questions can be found in census data, newspapers, church records, and local histories. Research along these lines not only would benefit Irish histories in Illinois and the Midwest but also would connect to a growing body of literature exploring similar questions around the world.[13]

Urban Development

Despite a modest increase in the number of Irish farmers, it was urban growth that drove the modernization of the late nineteenth-century Illinois economy. The industrial revolution had come to the Prairie State, and with it came jobs, increases in real wages, and rapid growth—as well as the accompanying insecurities of unemployment and social change common to the urban frontier. Towns such as Springfield, Bloomington, East St. Louis, Joliet, and Rockford blossomed into cities. Between 1860 and 1900, Bloomington's population more than doubled. During the same period, Springfield's population more than tripled. Joliet more than quadrupled in size, and East St. Louis and Rockford more than quintupled. Irish men and women stood in the vanguard of urban development in late nineteenth-century Illinois.[14]

Irish women made important contributions to growing communities such as Bloomington. Indeed, the majority of emigrants from Ireland by the late 1870s were female. Most sought work as laundresses, nurses, and seamstresses. Others became teachers, hotelkeepers, and milliners. In Bloomington, which boasted a population of 14,590 at the beginning of the decade, Irish women often found employment in domestic service. Yet unlike their counterparts in eastern cities, Irish women enjoyed relatively more freedom and better pay in Illinois. They tended to escape the "Bridget" stereotype, common back east, which depicted Irish maids as clumsy and bad cooks. According to historian Cynthia L. Baer, shortages of qualified housemaids gave them "leverage in setting the terms of their employment and the wages." Others started businesses that provided jobs. In 1894, the O'Briens of Danville founded the Model Star Laundry, which employed forty women and claimed to be the first steam service west of the Alleghenies.[15]

Most Irish women eventually married and worked inside the home. They gardened, cooked, and canned food. They knitted and sewed. They helped manage the family finances. And they cared for their children. By the 1880s, a majority of Irish-born women in Bloomington were over forty years of age, and nearly two-thirds of these had three or more children. Helen Ross Hall gave birth to fourteen children, the last of which came when she was forty-nine years old. She later described the experience as "unbelievable" and one that caused her "consternation." As business

Helen Ross Hall (1846–1928)

Helen Ross was born into an Irish Protestant family in the village of Kenogh, County Longford, in 1846. At the age of twenty-one, she met a young man named Samuel Hall. After two years of courtship, he proposed that the couple marry and immigrate to the United States. Helen consented. In 1870, after a brief stay in Brooklyn, she and her husband began a new phase of their lives in Bloomington, Illinois. Samuel initially found employment with the Chicago and Alton Railroad, although he later found more stable permanent work with the Bloomington City Police Department. Helen, meanwhile, tended to their fourteen children and managed the home. She also worked tirelessly to bring relatives from Ireland to Bloomington—eleven in all. Like Irishmen in Chicago, Samuel and his sons benefited from political connections, securing municipal jobs. The Halls' daughters found work as teachers and seamstresses. Samuel died in 1923, and Helen died in 1928. Their married life, as Samuel's obituary states, "was one of unusual happiness." Like their Catholic counterparts in other American cities, Helen Ross Hall and her husband, Samuel, not only carved out lives for themselves and their children but also actively encouraged their fellow Irish men and women to join them in their adopted land.[16]

Helen Ross Hall. Courtesy of the McLean County Museum of History, Bloomington, Illinois.

owners, employees, mothers, and wives, Irish women spurred the development of cities and towns in Illinois.[17]

Irish men worked the urban frontier as laborers, entrepreneurs, politicians, husbands, and fathers. In communities such as Joliet, Bloomington, Ottawa, and Rockford, they worked as police officers and fire fighters. They built roads and bridges. They worked in quarries, mills, and factories. Admittedly, economic and social advancement came slowly. Into the 1870s, 65 percent of laborers and 42 percent of unskilled workers in Ottawa were Irish, although the wealthiest man in town was also reportedly Irish. In Bloomington, they drove streetcars and worked for the railroad. Others became teamsters and machinists. Daniel O'Neill ran a grocery. Alonzo Dolan worked as a foreman at the *Weekly Pantagraph.* Irish police officers such as Samuel Hall walked the beat. By the 1880s, the Irish were building influential political machines in Joliet and Rockford. And Irish men ranked among Bloomington's most prominent citizens, including Mayor John W. Trotter (1881–83).[18]

The Catholic Church

As the state's population surged, the Catholic Church continued to grow under Irish leadership. Parishes founded across Illinois during the first half of the nineteenth century began to thrive. In 1875, the Church created the Diocese of Peoria, which oversaw some forty thousand Catholics in across twenty-two counties in northern Illinois. In 1908, the Church fashioned the Diocese of Rockford, which included eleven counties of the Peoria Diocese. The Joliet Diocese was not created until 1948. Across northern Illinois, new churches were built to accommodate expansion. In 1877, for instance, the Irish of Lockport built St. Dennis Catholic Church, which featured a 170-foot steeple and honored the parish founder, Father Dennis Ryan. Peoria's faithful founded schools and built cemeteries, such as St. Mary's. In Bloomington, an estimated one-third of the city's population was Catholic by the year 1900.[19]

The most distinguished prelate and defender of the Catholic Church was Bishop John Lancaster Spalding of Peoria. A distant relative of Irish immigrants, Spalding had, in the words of Eileen McMahon, "an affinity for the Irish." "No other people could have done for the Catholic faith in the United States," Spalding once declared, "what the Irish people have done." Sympathetic to the cause of Irish independence, the bishop often defended the Irish against nativism. He supported the Irish Catholic Colonization Association, which funded and promoted the resettlement of East Coast Irish to midwestern farms. Spalding played a key role in 1887 in founding the Catholic University of America in Washington, D.C. Careless with money and marred by scandal, the bishop was quietly denied promotion in his later years. He is nevertheless remembered for the many schools, churches, and convents that he chartered in Illinois.[20]

Catholic institutions, meanwhile, served communities' social as well as spiritual needs. Beginning in 1871, the Catholics of Bloomington organized an annual fair at Holy Trinity Church, which functioned as the epicenter of Catholic life in Bloomington. When Bishop Spalding appointed Father Michael Weldon to St.

Patrick's Parish in 1879, Weldon set about stabilizing finances by promoting the fair, although female parishioners organized and ran the event. Most of these women came from prominent families, and their husbands often participated in nationalist clubs and political parties. It was a truly *Irish* affair, featuring family names like Egan, Finley, Langdon, McCarthy, O'Brien, O'Day, Quinn, Sweeney, and Walsh. Patterned after town fairs in Ireland, the event was held in the fall and attracted one thousand to fifteen hundred guests each year. Attendees visited booths of local businesses, tasted local treats, and competed for prizes. As historian Mark T. Dunn observes, the fairs at Holy Trinity provided "substantial financial support to the parish, a milieu for social interaction, and a link to the participants' Irish homeland."[21]

Irish American Nationalism and Illinois Land Leagues

Irish nationalist organizations also thrived in downstate Illinois. During the early 1880s, Irish Land Leagues emerged throughout the state. In 1881, the Cairo Land League met in the basement of St. Patrick's Catholic Church. In March of the following year, the Ottawa Land League organized a St. Patrick's Day gala under the banner "Ireland for the Irish!" Throughout the decade, Irishmen sponsored Hibernian Rifle corps in Bloomington, Joliet, Aurora, and Ottawa. Some Illinoisans advocated the use of deadly force in liberating Ireland. In Peoria, dynamiter Patrick Crowe recruited fifty-two new members to the Skirmishing Fund, nearly twice as many as in Boston at the time. Their dues financed the production of dynamite machines, which Crowe built in his Peoria workshop and were later deployed in London bombing campaigns.[22]

Most Irish organizations, however, promoted less violent methods. In September 1885, a dry goods merchant from Bloomington named Patrick Kealy founded the city's Parnell Division of the Irish American Land League. The association listed twenty-five charter members from various professions: grocers, saloonkeepers, lawyers, shoemakers, painters, railroad workers, and at least one hardware store owner. Most were Republicans, although the organization also attracted prominent Democrats such as Alderman William Condon Sr. At its peak, Bloomington's Parnell Division boasted over one hundred members. Although no record exists of their total financial collections, the organization did contribute to the Chicago funds of 1886, which totaled $100,000 and ultimately helped finance land agitation back in Ireland.[23]

In all, Irish nationalist organizations in Bloomington accomplished many of the same things they did in other parts of the state: they brought respectability and further opportunities to network with "connected" members of their communities. In Joliet, they connected the business classes with labor. In Chicago, they linked labor reform with municipal politics. In Bloomington, the Parnell Division of the Irish American Land League brought together Irishmen of both political parties. As Mark T. Dunn notes, "Democratic support for a predominantly Republican organization would serve as a template for an Irish-American political machine that developed in Bloomington throughout most of the 1890s."[24]

Irish Politics

The Irish made their most distinctive mark in downstate politics. Irish Illinoisans could be found in virtually every elected post, as they had been since the state's founding. Governors Reynolds, Carlin, and Ford paved the way for future Irish politicians of the Prairie State. Between 1865 and 1960, at least five governors traced their ancestry back to Ireland. These included Charles S. Deneen (1905–13), former Chicago mayor and Irish nationalist Edward Fitzsimmons Dunne (1913–17), and two-time presidential nominee Adlai Stevenson II (1949–53). Lieutenant governors included John Dougherty (1869–73) and Thomas Donovan (1933–37). Senator James Shields forged the path for John A. Logan, Charles S. Deneen, and James M. Slattery, all U.S. senators of Irish ancestry. Throughout the state, others won office as mayors and city council members and also held other municipal posts.[25]

The Irish were political naturals. Outside of Chicago, they rarely had sufficient numbers to create political machines to control municipal governments. The exception to this rule was in Joliet, where, according to Daniel Elazar, "enough of them settled to ultimately come to dominate local politics." The Irish were active in other Illinois cities, using politics as an avenue of social advancement. They came to dominate one or two wards in Rockford and played key roles in Champaign, Decatur, Springfield, and the Quad Cities. They typically voted in blocs, but despite oft-repeated shibboleths to the contrary, the Irish of Illinois did not support the Democratic Party without question. No party could blithely count on their votes. In Cairo, much to the chagrin of Democrats, an embittered Irish electorate withheld their votes in

1868. Republicans won the contest, and Democrats learned to appreciate the Irish. A similar thing happened in Chicago during the 1880s, just as the Irish began to dominate the labor movement. As Richard Schnierov notes, "There was a large group of South Side Irish who could not be taken for granted by the Chicago Democratic party." In Bloomington, the Irish featured prominently in the city's Republican Party. During the 1884 presidential election, they founded the Blaine and Logan Club. James Gillespie Blaine, the Republican candidate for president that year, claimed Irish ancestry and advocated religious tolerance at a time when anti-Catholicism was on the rise. Some twenty-five thousand Bloomington residents welcomed him to the community on his whistle-stop tour later that year. Blaine lost the election in 1884, along with the state of Illinois. But in Bloomington, he won the Irish Republican vote along with the rest of the city.[26]

Into the twentieth century, the Irish of downstate Illinois exercised their political skills at the state and local levels, something contemporaries valued but historians have yet to explore. Moving forward, researchers should examine how the Irish practiced politics outside of Chicago. Did they win power through demographic consolidation, as they had in Joliet? Or did they obtain the reins of power through networking and alliances, as they had in Chicago? How important were Irish nationalist organizations to their success? What did their support for political parties look like? Were they reliably Democratic or Republican? Answers to questions like these—in cities such as East St. Louis, Carbondale, Springfield, Rockford, and the Quad Cities—will help create a clearer image of the history of the Irish in Illinois.

New Nativism: The American Protective Association

During the 1890s, Irish successes in municipal politics, along with an influx of new immigrants from southeastern Europe, led to a new wave of xenophobia. Around the country, secret anti-immigrant and anti-Catholic societies cropped up. The most significant of these was the American Protective Association (APA), founded in 1887 in Clinton, Iowa. The APA derived much of its support from midwesterners. The Haymarket and Pullman strikes revealed to many native-born Americans a new kind of danger posed by immigrant laborers. International crises over Cuba and Venezuela interjected a spirit of jingoism into the national dialogue. Historian John Higham summarized the spirit of the newfound nativism best: "To reformers, the immigrants were the source of municipal squalor and corruption, to workingmen a drag on wages, to militant Protestants the tools of Rome; and to nearly all their critics the newcomers were agents of discord and strife."[27]

The APA made significant headway in downstate Illinois. Branches appeared in cities such as Champaign, Rock Island, and Macomb. For more than ten years, however, it was Bloomington that stood at the epicenter of Illinois nativism. In 1884, the *Daily Pantagraph* ran an article with the headline "No Irish Need Apply—And No Catholic Ladies Wanted in the Qui Vive Club." The following year, a fiery Presbyterian preacher named John Guthrie White started a riot in nearby Lincoln. In the early 1890s, the Illinois APA state convention was hosted in Bloomington, which boasted multiple charters and a women's auxiliary. Prominent families opened their homes to the visitors.[28]

The success of the APA across the nation proved to be fleeting. In 1896, the national economy began to improve, and William McKinley won election. The following year, President Cleveland vetoed a bill in the lame-duck session of Congress that would have required immigrants to pass a literacy test before entering the country. In 1898, American armed forces defeated Spain in a four-month war. Confidence returned, and in Illinois, the APA declined rapidly. By the year 1900, newspapers across the state declared the association a "lost cause."[29]

Into the Twentieth Century

By the turn of the century, the Irish had made a lasting and largely positive impact on the Prairie State. Despite the meteoric rise and fall of the American Protective Association, Illinoisans generally commended the Irish for their contributions to the state's economic progress. One early twentieth-century Will County historian, William Wallace Stevens, praised local farmer James Baskerville for his "perseverance and industry *so characteristic of the Irish race.*" In 1901, the *Rock Island Argus* lauded the Irish for their steadfast support for Irish independence. "England has sought to subjugate Ireland for centuries," the newspaper observed. But the "Irish are not conquered today. The spark of liberty is still there. It will be rekindled whenever the chance to throw off the oppressor's yoke presents itself." As for those second- and third-generation Irish Illinoisans, most would have agreed. An article from the *Illinois State Register* titled "The Irish American" perhaps put it best:

Columbia the free is the land of my birth,
And my paths have been all on American earth;
But my blood is as Irish as any can be,
And my heart is with Erin afar o'er the sea.[30]

As Irish people from across Illinois looked toward the twentieth century, many had plenty to celebrate. They had blazed trails in the realms of labor, religion, and politics. Many had overcome prejudice and nativism. Illinois continued to offer some of the best opportunities for Irish men and women in the United States.

Reform Movements

Most progressive-era reformers saw the "Irish way" of politicking and socializing as corrupt and unethical. In Chicago, graft and bribery were indeed common in machine politics. City officials accepted payments to look the other way in the face of sanitation and infrastructure violations. In 1902, third-generation Irish American Alice Hamilton revealed links between city corruption and a typhoid epidemic in the Windy City. In 1910, she was appointed to the state's Occupational Disease Commission, where she exposed the risks of lead poisoning in industrial work. The state also sought to provide safety nets for vulnerable residents. In 1913, the Illinois General Assembly passed the Aid to Mothers and Children Act, which provided pensions for widowed mothers. But in coal-mining counties with immigrant populations, pensions also held widows to expectations of chastity, feminine morality, fiscal restraint, and child-rearing. Indeed, reformers were often middle-class Protestants who clashed with immigrants and ethnic minorities. Into the twentieth century, reformers lobbied hard to restrict liquor consumption. Evanston's Woman's Christian Temperance Union attracted a substantial following in small communities across the state. Throughout the early twentieth century, reform enjoyed far more support in rural areas than it did in urban communities.[31]

More often than not, Irish immigrants chafed at efforts to reform the state's drinking laws. Dating back to the Beer Hall Riot of 1855, Irish and German residents had resisted temperance legislation in Chicago. Immigrant "drinking rituals," as Steven Barleen notes, "formed the foundation of their community life." Saloons and saloonkeepers remained integral to places where Irish Illinoisans worked and lived. When Braidwood's Cornelius O'Donnell was tragically killed while attempting to break up a fight in 1879, his obituary noted that the stalwart sheriff and saloonkeeper "held a warm place in the hearts of nearly all who knew him." His widow, Margaret, continued to run the tavern after his death. In 1883, predominantly Republican legislators passed the Harper Law, which significantly increased the cost of a liquor license. Saloonkeepers from across the state responded by forming the Illinois Liquor Dealers Protective Association. Irish delegates such as Chicago's B. F. Maloney and Sycamore's James Brenan served as executives. Into the early twentieth century, working-class Irish patrons throughout the state frequented saloons, which increasingly served as veritable food pantries and unemployment offices for marginalized immigrants.[32]

In some corners of the state, however, Irish Illinoisans supported liquor reforms. Opposition to formal legislation, after all, did not necessarily mean opposition to *voluntary* temperance. In 1875, following a rousing sermon by the Reverend R. McGuire, Will County residents founded the Catholic Total Abstinence and Benevolent Society. That same year, residents established another temperance society: the Braidwood Lodge of Good Templars, known also as the "Miners' Friends Lodge." The state's key enforcer of the Harper Law, Attorney General James McCartney, was an Ulster native. And into the twentieth century, prohibitionists such as Irish temperance proponent Michael J. Fanning spoke before enthusiastic audiences throughout central Illinois. If most of the state's Irish Catholic population appear to have rejected the complete abstinence of liquor, at least some supported voluntary temperance.[33]

Middle-class Irish women also participated in organizations dedicated to the empowerment of working-class women. In rural counties, volunteers included professionals, teachers, and librarians. During the 1920s in Vermillion County, Danville native Irma O'Connell Giese joined other second- and third-generation immigrants at the local YMCA to coach sports, teach home economics, and instruct disadvantaged girls about health and nutrition. Raised in an Irish Catholic family and the sister of local elementary teacher Vera O'Connell Janes, Irma was regarded by her peers as a "marvelous athlete." Years later, Janes described her sister as a coach and a leader, "always willing to lend a hand to working women."[34]

As with downstate politics, more local research is needed to understand the relationship between Irish Illinoisans and these reform movements. How different were they downstate from those in Chicago? How important was religion? Generation? Gender? How did these relate to power and politics? Daniel Patrick Moynihan once argued that Irish Catholics levied their talents and energies to acquire power yet "never thought of politics as an instrument of social change." Others have since revised his thesis. The debate is far from settled, particularly outside of America's great urban centers. As Lawrence McCaffrey argues, questions of this nature "can only be found in examining Irish American Catholic politics in action." Illinois history, and the history of Irish America, awaits new answers to these old questions.[35]

Racial Strife

As African Americans moved north to the Prairie State for better work and better lives, they faced discrimination from white residents. In communities with significant Irish populations, increased economic and political competition led to violence that often was directed at black people. In the first two decades of the twentieth century, nationally publicized race riots broke out in two downstate cities: Springfield and East St. Louis. Irish Americans were active in both clashes. But this was hardly the whole story. In other Illinois communities, African and Irish Americans lived together in relative peace, if not harmony.[36]

Racial conflict came to Springfield in 1908. Late in the afternoon of Friday, August 14, an angry lynch party assembled outside the county jail. Rumors had spread that a black man from Springfield had raped a white woman and that the police were en route with the suspect. When it became apparent that the authorities had escorted their prisoner to

"Wild Mike" Casey

Urban life continued to be unkind to some Irishmen, particularly unemployed veterans of the American Civil War. There are few sources for most of these individuals, but "Wild Mike" Casey of Bloomington stands as an exception. Born in County Tipperary in the early 1840s, he immigrated to New York during the war. He found work as a wharfman before enlisting in the Union army. Somewhere during the postwar years, Casey became addicted to alcohol and developed a reputation as one of Bloomington's town drunks. Nevertheless, as the *Daily Bulletin* reported, "People liked 'Wild Mike' . . . in a tolerant, head-shaking sort of way. The police knew him best, and, many of them being Irish themselves, had sympathy for the weakness of a 'drunken man.'" But Michael Casey never overcame his addiction. In June 1899, the McLean County Courts declared him legally insane. Michael Casey spent the remainder of his years at the state asylum in Jacksonville.[37]

another jail, the crowd became angry. Turning their frustrations on the city's black neighborhoods, they burned buildings, looted stores, and lynched two innocent men. One Chicago newspaper described the scene as "a night of riot, arson, and slaughter." Many black residents fought back. Over the course of two days, at least sixteen people were killed. Scores were injured. Only after the arrival of thousands of Illinois National Guardsmen did the violence abate. A stunned American public looked on in horror. As historian Roberta Senechal describes it, "Not since New York's draft riot of 1863 had the white public been so forcibly reminded of the vehemence of anti-black hostility in the North." Tragically, a great historical irony underscored the incident. The "race war," as Illinois newspapers quickly labeled it, had occurred in "the capital city of Illinois, the home of Abraham Lincoln."[38]

Springfield's Irish population played a conspicuous role in the violence. Strong and enduring prejudice toward African Americans, along with local political conflict that typically pitted Irish Democrats against black Republicans, drove a disproportionate number of Springfield's Irish into the fray. While making up some 4.6 percent of the city's overall population, an estimated 9.6 percent of all American-born rioters were of Irish descent. Significantly, a mere 1.7 percent of all rioters had been born in Ireland—less than the percentage of the city's overall Irish-born population (2.1 percent) and of Italian- or English-born participants. In short, Springfield's race riot of 1908 was, if only partly, a distinctly Irish *American* affair.[39]

In at least some Illinois communities, however, relations between Irish and African Americans appear to have been more amicable. In Bloomington, for example, the city's Catholic institutions welcomed any and all residents. When the Sisters of St. Francis opened St. Joseph's Hospital in 1880, they announced, "Patients will be admitted without distinction of religion, nationality, or color." Irish and African Americans also resided in the same neighborhoods. According to historians Mark Wyman and John W. Muirhead, at least some black residents lived among the Irish in a part of town called the "Forty Acres." As early as 1897, the *Weekly Pantagraph* described the community as both "an Irish settlement" and "as representative as that of any other part of the city." But black residents remained a tiny proportion of the city. Bloomington's population stood at roughly twenty-three thousand at the turn of the century, of which only six hundred were African

Americans. With an Irish American population of 25 percent, it is significant that the city escaped the racial violence that plagued so many others throughout the state.[40]

Looking ahead, scholars need to examine relationships between downstate black and Irish residents. When and where were they more cordial? Why? Politics appears to have been a factor. In Cairo and Springfield, where Irish and African Americans affiliated with different political parties, bloodshed followed. As Roberta Senechal notes, "Many local elections in the capital were decided by slender margins, and the Democratic Irish-Americans may have perceived competition from power and patronage from the largely Republican blacks." In Bloomington, however, where significant numbers of Irish and African Americans belonged to the Republican Party, violence never reached the level it did in the state's capital. Population and religion were also important variables, as was the proportion of foreign-born Irish in communities. Historians have improved our understanding of racial violence in Springfield and East St. Louis. Irish American studies would benefit from similar explorations in other Illinois communities.[41]

World War I and the Prairie State

World War I dramatically altered the political, economic, and social landscapes of Illinois. Most residents supported President Woodrow Wilson's call to arms, although a noteworthy percentage of the state's German and Austrian populations initially backed the Central Powers. Rumors also circulated that Germany was actively attempting to sway Irish public opinion across the United States. In a public call to arms, Republican Governor Frank O. Lowden demanded that residents set aside their Old-World loyalties: "Either we are for the government or we are against it." Few Illinoisans volunteered to fight, however, and the U.S. government eventually compelled service through the Selective Service Act of 1917, which authorized the draft. In May, the Illinois General Assembly created the State Council of Defense (SCD), authorized to coordinate the state's transportation, industrial, and labor sectors. It also established a women's committee of the SCD, which promoted the sale of liberty bonds and the conservation of food and clothing. As jobs in defense industries opened up, tens of thousands of African Americans relocated to downstate Illinois, along with 50,000 more in Chicago. Black and white soldiers of the Prairie State fought in World War I. By the end of the conflict, over 315,000 Illinoisans had served in the armed forces.[42]

Irish Illinoisans' support for the war was uneven. In the coal-mining counties of Macoupin, Madison, and St. Clair, immigrant laborers struggled to balance patriotism with their own economic interests. When American Neutrality League publicity manager Eugene Vogt visited St. Clair County, his speech was met with applause. "England is not my mother country nor does she stand in relation to a majority of Americans," he thundered. "To our citizens of Irish extraction she enacts the role, rather, of cruel step-mother." Nevertheless, union leaders and members supported the war. President Frank Farrington of the Illinois UMWA argued that labor would receive postwar rewards for cooperating with the Wilson administration. An estimated one in four Illinois miners volunteered or were drafted. Similarly, the Catholic Church pressured miners to support their country, resist socialism, and embrace American patriotism.[43]

Such patriotism did not prevent violence and labor disputes. In October 1917, coal companies and the SCD failed to deliver on promised wage increases. Miners in Illinois and across the Midwest, a substantial number of whom were Irish, soon walked off the job. To the delight of the miners, the strike ended quickly. In the wake of their success, an "epidemic of forced flag-kissing, flag-saluting, and physical attacks on suspected disloyalists," as Carl Weinberg describes it, "swept through the region." The following year, a mob from the mining town of Collinsville lynched a German immigrant and suspected spy named Robert Paul Prager. The perpetrators escaped justice, but the local union split between pro- and antiwar factions. Public support for labor unions plummeted. When dissenting elements of the UMWA went on strike in 1919, Woodrow Wilson denounced the organization and called out federal troops. The strike ended in 1920, an abject failure. Some workers radicalized. As a visiting *Chicago Daily News* reporter put it, "The miners around these parts have lost their respect for the government. They no longer consider it a virtuous or square institution." Looking back, it remains unclear how many Irish Illinoisans would have agreed.[44]

Apart from the coal miners, wartime labor protests were rarely radical affairs. Most second- and third-generation Irish had managed to climb the social ladder by the eve of the Great War. Many had obtained high school degrees and found better-paying jobs.

During the wage strikes of autumn 1917, the most conspicuous "Irish" support for labor came from five female telephone operators in Collinsville. Pressing for better wages, Lola Higgs, Mary Killian, Lillian Walker, one Miss Higgins, and a Miss Baehler walked off the job. The management at Bell Telephone had been harassing these women for attempting to establish a local branch of the International Brotherhood of Electrical Workers. Yet these women and their allies employed traditional Irish methods of labor protest. They tapped into social and political networks. They organized a boycott of Bell Telephone. By January, they had won the public support of fifty local merchants, the UMWA, and other sympathetic unions. Following a month of negotiations, the women returned to their work victorious.[45]

For too many Irish and African Americans, the most visible form of wartime conflict continued to be racial. Barely one month after the United States formally entered the war, relations between black and white residents in East St. Louis began to deteriorate. In May, the city's Central Trades Labor Union voted to strike for increased wages against the Aluminum Ore Company. Hearing rumors of black strike breakers, and fearing job competition from black workers, over twelve hundred white men and women gathered at city hall on May 28 to press for a local ban on black migration. Union leaders lost control of the meeting, as nonunion speakers advocated vigilantism. And after word spread that a black man had shot a white resident, the crowd poured into the streets. Well into the following day, white mobs smashed windows, plundered buildings, and attacked establishments known to serve as headquarters for black politicians. No one was killed, although seventy black residents were arrested, along with a much smaller number of white people.[46]

The unrest of May 28 paled in comparison to the rioting that followed. During the early morning hours of July 2, 1917, white agitators led by local real estate magnates Thomas Canavan and Locke Tarlton began driving through black neighborhoods, firing gunshots into random houses along the way. Rumors that black residents had begun to arm themselves, along with simmering memories of May's unrest, transformed the assaults into a full-fledged riot. Hundreds of white people descended on the city's downtown, where they set fire to black businesses and homes. They attacked, beat, and hanged African American men, women, and children. "Black skin," the *St. Louis Republic* reported, served as "a death warrant." White police officers and National Guardsmen abandoned their posts and joined in the fray. The "white mobs," as historian Malcolm McLaughlin puts it, "were unrestrained." Officially, nine white men and thirty-nine black men, women, and children were killed. Unofficially, the count was far higher.[47]

As in the Springfield race riot, Irish Americans were active participants in the violence in East St. Louis. Making up an estimated 4.1 percent of the city's population, men and women of Irish descent ranked second only to German Americans in the city. And while it remains unclear how many Irish participated in the rioting, most had climbed the East St. Louis social ladder by 1917. Many had become skilled laborers, and most were Catholic. One of the central causes of the riot, the belief that black migrants were encroaching on white neighborhoods, was particularly evident in the Irish neighborhood of Canaryville. According to real estate icon Thomas Canavan, this marked "the prime cause of hatred of the negroes." Many of the city's white residents also regarded the arrival of black migrants as an invasion of public space. Albert B. McQuillan, the staff physician of the Aluminum Ore Company, complained that African Americans disregarded polite conventions on streetcars. Black passengers, he asserted, made "a great deal of noise" and sat "down on white women's laps."[48]

Perhaps most important, Irish Americans ranked among the city's most influential politicians, particularly those responsible for the rioting. Like their Springfield compatriots, the East St. Louis Irish typically voted Democratic, while black residents largely supported the Republican Party. As Charles Lumpkins argues, politics underscored the violence—what effectively became a "pogrom" in East St. Louis. By 1917, local African Americans had begun to build political machines to assert power. July's violence, according to Lumpkins, "represented a political solution planned by certain white real estate men, politicians, and businessmen." The testimony of Thomas Canavan, a real estate man and a Democratic political boss, clearly emphasized the same point. "Something has got to be done," Canavan stated, "or the damned niggers will take [over] the town." Racial violence again correlated with communities where Irish-American Democratic machines predominated.[49]

As racial conflict plagued the state, the Irish of Illinois continued to press for the independence of their homeland. In 1919, just as the Irish War of Independence broke out, President Eamon de Valera of the de facto Irish Republic toured the United States. From New York to San Francisco, he spoke before enormous crowds and raised $5 million in pledges. De Valera confessed to the mayor of San Francisco his true aim: "The main thing I want to get in this country is recognition of the Irish Republic." If it were up to Illinoisans, he would have had it immediately. In July, twenty-five thousand Chicagoans gathered to hear de Valera speak at Cubs National League Park (later renamed Wrigley Field), where he labeled his mission a "holy cause." In October, Springfield and Bloomington residents welcomed de Valera to their communities. In Springfield, he visited Lincoln's home and spoke before an enthusiastic crowd at the Leland Hotel. According to the *Illinois State Journal*, de Valera came "to plead the cause of an oppressed nation and to pay tribute to Abraham Lincoln, whose name has been the inspiration of the Irish people in their struggle for liberty." De Paul University and St. Ignatius College presented de Valera with honorary doctorates. In his immediate goal to create an Irish republic, de Valera failed. Ireland did not win Free State status until 1922, and it only became an independent republic in 1949. Nonetheless, Irish Illinoisans from across the state once again showed their support for Irish independence.[50]

The Twenties and Prohibition

After the fierce battles of 1919, the postwar economy revived across much of Illinois. When delegates met in 1920 to revise the state constitution to allocate more representation to rural counties, voters balked. The twenties were going to be an urban decade. Banks capitalized new business ventures. Utility companies laced the state with power lines. The Illinois General Assembly funded new roads to accommodate the spike in automobile traffic. The Chicago skyline expanded, as did the downtowns of bustling communities across the Prairie State. Wages and salaries soared. As historian Roger Biles notes, "Illinoisans in the 1920s earned more dollars, worked fewer hours, and made enough money to purchase a greater number and wider variety of goods than ever before."[51]

Amid the prosperity, gangsters vied for control of illicit and profitable enterprises in the age of Prohibition. Gambling and bootlegging thrived downstate just as they did in Capone's Chicago. In the Quad Cities, unscrupulous businessmen and women profited from gambling, automobile theft, and prostitution. The

Vera O'Connell Janes

Despite the urban life enshrined in novels of the Jazz Age, many Illinoisans preferred to remain in rural counties. One such individual was Vera O'Connell Janes. Born to an Irish Catholic family in Grape Creek, she attended Danville High School and graduated in 1920. Her first job was teaching at a school northwest of Danville, where she was hired "for the fabulous salary of $85.00 a month for eight months," she later reminisced. Her first year, Janes taught thirty-nine children ranging in age from five to fifteen. Facing equipment shortages and the responsibility of managing individual lesson plans, she multitasked as well as any big-city stock trader. "I felt as if I were on a merry-go-round trying to get a daily schedule outlined and then getting every lesson assignment covered every day," she recalled. Vera O'Connell Janes preserved these and other memories in an unpublished autobiography for her family.[52]

New York Tribune labeled Davenport the "worst town in America, bar none." At least one prohibitionist went even further, remarking, "If Davenport is hell, Rock Island is the chimney." A local saloonkeeper later claimed that the Quad Cities were so corrupt, they "made Chicago look like an old-people's home." In central and southern Illinois, the Birger and Shelton gangs competed violently for territory. During the latter half of the 1920s, they went to war over the control of Williamson and Franklin Counties. Two mayors, a state police officer, and eleven other individuals were killed in the hostilities.[53]

Outside of Chicago, the state's most notorious Irish gangster was undoubtedly Rock Island's John Looney. At the height of his power, Looney's criminal empire included a midwestern bootlegging operation, protection for Helen Van Dale's infamous brothel ring, and a stolen-car syndicate that ranged from Rock Island to Minneapolis to Philadelphia to New Mexico. In 1922, a former police officer and fellow bootlegger named William Gabel threatened to bring down Looney's empire by cooperating with federal prosecutors. Gabel had had a falling out with Looney's son Connor, who apparently had failed to compensate his business partners adequately. On July 31, 1922, three of Looney's henchmen gunned down the former policeman in broad daylight. Gabel's murder went unpunished.

But the *Rock Island Argus* refused to let the issue die, running a series of editorials implicating Looney's operation in the crime. Looney's own newspaper, the *Rock Island News*, accused the *Argus* of attempting to "Incite Bloody Riot." Rival gangs, meanwhile,

John P. Looney. Courtesy of the Rock Island Historical Society.

John P. Looney (1865–1942)

Born in Ottawa in 1865, John Looney (pronounced "Lowney") lived a remarkable life. Trained as an attorney, he quickly became a successful lawyer in Rock Island, a position the ambitious Looney used to establish a range of profitable business and real estate ventures in a town later described as the "Citadel of Sin." For several years, Looney managed to keep a respectable public face. In 1892, he married Nora O'Connor, and for a few years, the couple lived quietly in their stately Queen Anne home, raising two daughters, Kathleen and Ursula, and a son, Connor. Nora died of cancer in 1903. Looney tried his hand at politics, running an unsuccessful campaign for the Illinois legislature in 1900. Allegations of corruption and fraud dogged Looney throughout his public career. The most dramatic instance occurred in February 1909, when, after months of bitter and public feuding, Looney challenged a former business partner, W. William Wilmerton, to a duel on the streets of downtown Rock Island. Neither was seriously injured, and Looney left town in 1912.

He returned to the city in 1921, ready to profit from Prohibition. Many of his business ties were still intact, and the Tri Cities (Davenport, Moline, and Rock Island) were as hospitable to the vice industries as ever. Looney quickly built a new empire—at least, until the 1922 murders detailed above. Convicted in December 1925, John Looney eventually spent eight years in prison. He died in 1942 in southern Texas. Yet even today, as his biographers note, "there is still a feeling in Rock Island about John Looney. He will never be forgiven; nor will he be forgotten." Looney was the model for John Rooney, a character portrayed by Paul Newman in the award-winning film *Road to Perdition* (2002).[54]

had declared war on Looney. On Friday, October 6, 1922, just as hundreds of fans had gathered in Market Square to watch the World Series scoreboard, two carloads of gangsters ambushed Connor Looney. John fled to Ottawa and eventually New Mexico, as the state of Illinois indicted him on charges of murder, larceny, and fraud. In November 1924, Looney was apprehended when a deaf man by the name of L. C. Oliver recognized his face from a Wanted poster. One year later, a Rock Island jury found Looney guilty of murder. He was incarcerated at Stateville Prison in Joliet until 1934. He spent the remaining years of his life with his daughter Ursula's family in Texas. Looney died in 1942, but his legacy lived on. As Richard Hamer and Roger Ruthhart put it: "He was a crime boss long before Al Capone and others made it fashionable and glamorous. He devised an organized system, dividing his business into separate units, and used his newspaper as a 'hammer' over his enemies and detractors. Eventually, Chicago, Detroit, New York and other large metropolitan areas adopted his 'organized' crime technique."[55]

The Great Depression in Downstate Illinois

Although the Great Depression made life difficult in downstate communities, poverty was certainly nothing new to rural Illinois. In his 1965 memoir, the Dixon native Ronald Reagan made it clear that money was tight in the farm belt long before the 1930s. His mother, Nelle, he recalled, extended the family budget by making a kind of oatmeal stew, a dish he generously recalled as "the most wonderful thing I've ever eaten." The 1929 stock market crash that triggered the Depression certainly had a more immediate impact on the East Coast, but it reached the Midwest soon enough. By October 1931, government officials estimated that 1.1 million people were unemployed in Illinois; by January 1933, that number had reached 1.5 million. Between 1925 and 1932, factory payrolls fell 53 percent in Peoria, 54 percent in East Saint Louis, 58 percent in Aurora, 63 percent in Decatur, 70 percent in Quincy, 73 percent in Danville, 76 percent in Rockford, 80 percent in Rock Island, 86 percent in Joliet, and 93 percent in Moline. These cuts had devastating impacts on families and communities across the state. When the local cement plant closed in Dixon, a thousand people lost their jobs. Jack Reagan, the future president's father and a proud Irish American, was fired from his position managing a shoe store in Springfield on Christmas Eve in 1931. After reading the blue slip that had arrived in the mail, Reagan muttered that it "was a hell of a Christmas present." Most Illinois residents doubtless would have sympathized.[56]

Ronald Reagan (1911–2004)
Born in 1911 in Tampico, Illinois, Ronald Reagan was one of the most influential political leaders of the twentieth-century United States. The son of an Irish American father and Scots-English mother, Reagan and his family moved around northern Illinois before settling in Dixon in 1920. He went to nearby Eureka College before moving to California in 1937 to become a successful actor and president of the Screen Actors Guild. Reagan shifted to politics in the 1960s, becoming the Republican governor of California (1967–75) and later president of the United States (1981–89). He treasured his Irish roots (he was fourth-generation Irish American on his father's side), visiting his ancestral home in Ballyporeen, County Tipperary, in 1984, a trip he recalled as one of the highlights of his presidency. He died in 2004.

Communities across the state battled for survival throughout the 1930s. The Depression hit the mining industry particularly hard, pushing thousands of men out of work in central and southern Illinois as more and more mines closed across the region. With the industry in steep decline, unions battled both employers and each other over how to protect jobs and wages. This set the stage for the Coal Miner Union Wars of the 1930s, wide-ranging and often deadly clashes that involved competing unions, mining companies, and the state.

The UMWA had long been the dominant union organization in American mining, but after union president John L. Lewis negotiated a 1932 labor contract with significantly reduced wages, many southern Illinois miners left in disgust to form a more radical union, the Progressive Mine Workers of America (PMA). Within a few years, the PMA probably had secured a larger membership, particularly in its core area in Macoupin County. As the two unions struggled for workers' loyalties in 1933 and 1934, fights between members became more commonplace, and partisans of the two unions bombed coal-carrying railroads, blew up mine shafts, and burned down union halls and houses. Tragically, property was not the only target, as National Guardsmen, policemen, and union members attacked and killed their opponents across the region. The Irish no longer worked in substantial numbers in the mines, but they could not escape the fight. In a 1980 interview, J. R. Fitzpatrick, a Springfield businessman, recalled the ugly partisanship of the era: "My friendship, of course, was with the United Mine Workers and not with the Progressive Mine Workers, and by reason of that my name was mud with all the guys on the other side because they knew what was going on."

The wars did not end until 1937, when a federal grand jury found thirty-six PMA leaders guilty of conspiracy and interference with interstate commerce.[57]

The initial federal and state government response to the Depression was timid and ineffective. Private philanthropy increased in Illinois in both 1930 and 1931, but it failed to provide nearly enough resources to mitigate a crisis of this scale. The political dynamics of relief changed in November 1932, when Democrats Franklin Delano Roosevelt and Henry Horner were elected to the White House and the Governor's Mansion in Springfield respectively. The ensuing initiatives of the New Deal provided a sense of hope and tangible measures of relief for millions of Americans. Some were more effective than others. The Illinois Emergency Relief Administration dispensed much-needed relief to the unemployed, while the Civil Works Association and then the Civil Conservation Corps provided jobs. The Rural Electrification Administration transformed rural life, increasing the number of Illinois farms with electricity from 16 to 43 percent.

It was the 1935 creation of the Social Security Act and the Works Progress Administration (WPA) that brought real relief to Illinois. Better funded than previous aid programs, the WPA offered higher wages to significantly more people across the country. The program provided jobs for nearly two hundred thousand people at any given time in Illinois, work that dramatically improved the state's infrastructure. This made a real difference for many families. After Jack Reagan lost his job selling shoes, the lifelong Democrat got a position with the WPA in largely Republican Dixon, quickly rising to become the director of relief in town. According to his son, Reagan threw himself into the work, distributing food and the government scrip that families used to pay for groceries, as well as providing odd jobs for people the Reagans had known for years. If the New Deal failed to pull Illinois all the way out of the Depression, it prevented things from getting much worse.[58]

World War II and the Irish in Illinois

It was World War II that ended the Great Depression in the United States. Initial support for the war in Illinois was ambivalent at best, with Colonel Robert McCormick's *Chicago Tribune* championing the isolationist cause and some Irish-American nationalists hesitant to aid the British Empire in its war against Nazi Germany and its allies. Public opinion began to shift after the fall of France in June 1940 and was transformed by the Japanese attack on Pearl Harbor in December 1941. Governor Dwight H. Green and Chicago mayor Edward J. Kelly led delegations to Washington, D.C., to secure federal contracts for Illinois industries. They were quite successful, and manufacturers across the state converted factories for wartime production. Illinois ordnance plants in Rock Island, Illiopolis, Green River, East Alton, Elwood, and Kankakee produced more ammunition than any other state in the nation. The Dodge factory in Chicago employed thirty thousand men and women assembling the B-29 Superfortress bomber, while factories in Seneca in LaSalle County built amphibious landing craft and floated them down the Illinois and Mississippi Rivers to the Gulf of Mexico. Women were essential to this effort; the number of women in the state workforce rose from 854,276 in 1940 to 1,281,000 in 1944. At the Rock Island Arsenal, women made up 32.2 percent of the workforce in 1944.[59]

World War II solidified Irish Americans' place within the American cultural landscape. Military service clearly was central to this process. American Catholics constituted between 30 and 40 percent of the armed forces, and Irish Americans were among the war's most celebrated heroes, including Illinois's own Joseph J. McCarthy and Edward "Butch" O'Hare, both of whom were awarded the Medal of Honor, the nation's highest military decoration.[60]

The new image of the Irish-American war hero was both reflected and strengthened in film. Audie Murphy, one of the war's most decorated combat veterans, went on to a storied Hollywood career, playing himself in the 1955 *To Hell and Back*, before starring in a number of westerns. More generally, these years saw the emergence of a new movie genre: the World War II combat film, where the film's hero leads an ethnically mixed group of soldiers toward a military objective. A classic example is the 1949 *The Sands of Iwo Jima*, where John Wayne's Sgt. John M. Stryker leads a squad with characters named Conway, Dunne, Flynn, Harris, McHugh, Soames, and Stein, among others. This genre has had remarkable staying power with American audiences, as evidenced in films ranging from *Bataan* (1943) to *Saving Private Ryan* (1998). If Hollywood was any indication, World War II had made Irish Americans into Americans.[61]

Edward "Butch" O'Hare (1914–43)

Edward O'Hare was born in 1914 in South St. Louis, the son of the prominent Chicago attorney of the same name and his wife, Selma. His father provided key evidence in the Capone trials of 1931 and 1932 and was assassinated by gunmen in 1939. Lieutenant "Butch" O'Hare was the navy's first flying ace of World War II, shooting down several Japanese bombers set to attack the USS *Lexington* on February 20, 1942. He received the Medal of Honor from President Franklin Delano Roosevelt in a ceremony two months later. In November 1943, he was killed in action, shot down while defending the USS *Enterprise* in the Pacific. Six years later, at the suggestion of Colonel Robert R. McCormick, Orchard Field Airport was renamed O'Hare International Airport to honor his memory. A replica of his Grumman F-4 Wildcat is on display in the airport's Terminal 2.[62]

Lieutenant Edward "Butch" O'Hare.
Courtesy of the U.S. Naval History and Heritage Command.

American Catholicism and Irish Identity in Postwar Illinois

Movies were not the only factor in the redefinition of Irish American identity that occurred in the late 1940s and 1950s. Broader international and national political, religious, and social forces were also at play. In his pioneering study of midwestern cities, Daniel Elazar argues that Irish and Irish American domination of the Roman Catholic Church meant that Irish Americans living in midsize cities such as Champaign-Urbana, Peoria, Rockford, and Springfield did not have to form as many explicitly ethnic associations as in other communities. This was reinforced by the advent of the Cold War and the exodus from Chicago to more homogenous suburbs. At the same time, it is critical to understand that the postwar emergence of a stronger sense of a panethnic American Catholic identity did not reflect diminished ties to Ireland. The postwar revival of St. Patrick's Day celebrations and the post-1960 vitality of Irish academic and cultural associations speak to Ireland's continuing appeal for the people of Illinois.[63]

Irish and Irish American clergymen long had played a disproportionately influential role in the Catholic Church in the United States. Historian Lawrence McCaffrey has argued that English-language skills, numbers, and political talents made the Irish well suited to lead a multiethnic church. That continued to be true in Illinois well into the 1950s. One example of this can be seen in the Diocese of Rockford, which from 1943 to 1953 was led by Bishop James J. Boylan, the son of Lawrence and Bridget Morrisey Boylan of New York City. Consecrated by the powerful Irish American archbishop of Chicago, Samuel A. Stritch, Boylan championed Catholic education and youth programs in the diocese, putting a particular focus on the creation of Catholic Youth Organizations at the parish level. Irish American involvement in the northern Illinois diocese is impossible to miss. Bishop Boylan's first class of ordained priests included Father John J. Kilduff, Father James F. McGuire, and Father Arthur J. O'Neill (who later became the seventh bishop of Rockford). In 1950, Boylan appointed Father Michael Shanahan as director of Catholic Charities, replacing Father Francis P. McNally, who became pastor of St. Patrick's Parish that year. In Rockford, at least, the Irish clearly had not handed over the reins of the church just yet.[64]

If Irish leadership in the postwar Catholic Church provided a comfortable sense of continuity for Irish American parishioners in Illinois cities and suburbs alike, it also contributed to a largely successful effort to redefine both Irish and Catholic America in the early years of the Cold War. Throughout the late 1940s and early 1950s, American intellectuals attempted to forge a new national ideology that combined a robust patriotism with a more inclusive celebration of the United States as a nation of (white) immigrants. For many Catholic ethnics, communism replaced the Protestant establishment as the primary foe in the American firmament. Well established in political and religious leadership roles, and with newly minted records of military service, Irish Americans were well positioned to lead this charge. Historian Matthew O'Brien has shown how postwar scientific and history textbooks increasingly depicted Irish Americans as representative Americans. The leading Irish American nationalist organization, the Ancient Order of Hibernians, repeatedly stressed that they were an American organization dedicated to battling intolerance.

When Senator John F. Kennedy spoke before the Irish Fellowship Club of Chicago at its annual St. Patrick's Day Dinner in 1956, he gave a rousing lecture urging the United States to "speak out boldly for freedom for all people—whether they are denied that freedom by an iron curtain of tyranny, or by a paper curtain of colonial ties and constitutional manipulations," a clear reference to Northern Ireland. The celebration was chaired by Cardinal Stritch and the new mayor of Chicago, Richard J. Daley.[65]

Irish Americans' new assertion of a distinctly American identity did not reflect weakened ties with the Emerald Isle. In some ways, Irish Americans were closer to Ireland than ever before. Most transatlantic flights to Europe stopped at Shannon Airport in the 1950s, and Aer Lingus, the Irish national airline, began flights to the United States in 1958. Irish American tourism to Ireland increased dramatically from the 1950s onward, quickly becoming an important component of the Irish economy.

Irish Americans did not have to leave Illinois to celebrate their Irishness. Organizations like the Ancient Order of Hibernians and the Irish Fellowship Club of Chicago continued to work to maintain and strengthen Catholic education and other causes central to Irish American communities. And, of course, there was St. Patrick's Day. The rebirth and success of Chicago's official and South Side parades in the 1950s was perhaps the most visible sign of the continuing appeal of Irishness in Illinois. But such celebrations were hardly confined to the Windy City, or to Irish Americans. St. Patrick's Day was now a day for all to celebrate. In Sycamore, both the Elks Club and the local Turner Brass Foundry hosted annual St. Patrick's Day parties, often featuring well-advertised costume contests, dances, and a luncheon. At the University of Illinois in Urbana-Champaign, a range of organizations put on St. Patrick's Day events every year. These included a party in 1947 for twenty-five children of the Cunningham Orphanage, where students entertained the children with an informal dance called the "Killarney Stomp." When the new Moran Athletic Club opened in Joliet in March 1950, it did so with a St. Patrick's Day dance and party. Irish Americans were now firmly Americans. Nowhere was this more evident than in the city of Chicago.[66]

5

A SOUTH SIDE EMPIRE? THE IRISH IN CHICAGO, 1933–83

In 1932, James T. Farrell published *Young Lonigan*, the first in a remarkable series of novels that chronicle the Irish American experience in early twentieth-century Chicago. There is a strongly autobiographical dimension to Farrell's early work. He grew up in an Irish Catholic working-class family in the South Side neighborhood of Washington Park, and his early novels portray that rapidly changing world with searing power and humane sympathy. Farrell's most famous books, the *Studs Lonigan* trilogy, follow the travails of the Lonigans, an Irish American family proud of their achievement and place in a respectable working-class neighborhood dominated by the celebrated cornerstones of Irish American life: church, family, politics, and home.

The trilogy's narrative trajectory runs downward, however. Feeling threatened by black in-migration into their neighborhood, the Lonigans leave Washington Park for the South Shore, another displaced family dominated by a keen sense of loss. Standing in the empty parlor of their old home, Patrick Lonigan wistfully describes this feeling to his son Studs: "This neighborhood was kind of like home. We sort of felt about it the same way I feel about Ireland, where I was born." Studs dies of pneumonia at twenty-nine, shattered by alcoholism and a hard and violent life on the streets. Farrell's later novels strike a more optimistic tone, featuring a host of larger-than-life characters whose lives centered on St. Patrick's Church (St. Anselm's in real life), the local pool hall, and the fortunes of the Chicago White Sox. These books chart the ascent of Danny O'Neill, an intelligent and artistically inclined young man who escapes the limits of this world to become a writer. Taken as a whole, Farrell's Washington Park novels depict both the richness and vulnerability of Irish American urban life.[1]

In April 1933, just a year after the publication of Farrell's first book, Edward J. Kelly became mayor of Chicago. It was hardly the most auspicious of beginnings; the city council picked Kelly after Mayor Anton Cermak was killed by accident in a failed assassination attempt on President Franklin Delano Roosevelt. Kelly's nomination, however, proved to be of enduring significance: he was the first of five Irish American mayors who dominated Chicago and Illinois politics well into the twentieth-first century: Kelly, Martin Kennelly, Richard J. Daley, Jane Byrne, and Richard M. Daley. Four of these figures hailed from Bridgeport, the Irish American enclave on the near South Side made famous by Finley Peter Dunne's Mr. Dooley.

In many ways, Kelly seems like a character straight out of one of James Farrell's novels. One of nine children of a Galway-born policeman and his German wife, he dropped out of school at twelve, working a series of messenger jobs before landing a post with the Chicago Sanitary District. A hard worker with a taste for patronage and politics, Kelly rose through the ranks to become chief engineer, somehow avoiding prosecution in the corruption scandals that wracked both the district and Chicago politics in the late 1920s and early 1930s. He became president of the South Park Board, where he oversaw the creation of the city's modern lakefront, helping secure the private donations of the Shedd Aquarium, Adler Planetarium, and Buckingham Fountain for Grant Park. Kelly also presided over the construction of Soldier Field, an $8.5 million project that reflected his penchant for corruption—the stadium's cost overruns were ascribed in part to inflated contracts and kickbacks to the park board president. Kelly was well positioned in the Democratic contest that followed Cermak's death in 1933. Allied with Patrick Nash, the veteran chairman of the Cook County Democratic Party, he was mayor for fourteen years, creating an Irish-led machine that dominated municipal politics until 1983. Kelly was a complex figure. A man notoriously associated with personal and political scandals, he was one of FDR's key allies in New Deal politics and showed a real (if ultimately limited) commitment to civil rights and racial integration. As his leading biographer, Roger Biles, makes clear, Ed Kelly personified the strengths and weaknesses of Chicago's Irish-led political machine.[2]

It was the machine that united these seemingly disparate worlds, tying Washington Park and other city neighborhoods to the mayor's office through an elaborate hierarchy of ward committeemen and precinct captains. These were the men who delivered the goods, and they expected favors and votes in return. Irish Chicago was a substantial community. According the 1930 U.S. Census, nearly two hundred thousand of Chicago's 3.3 million people were of Irish stock, men and women who were born in Ireland or whose parents had been born there.

This was an increasingly Irish American world, a product of lower rates of Irish immigration to the United States between 1900 and 1950. Only 2 percent of the Chicago population was Irish-born in 1920, compared with 18 percent in 1860 and 6 percent in 1890. Most of these men and women were working class or lower middle class—the people who populated James Farrell's novels: laborers, firemen, nurses, policemen, social workers, teachers, and typists. These were the men and women who had used the opportunities provided by the Catholic Church, the Democratic Party, labor unions, and nationalist organizations like the Ancient Order of Hibernians to make lives for themselves in the Windy City. As historians like Eileen McMahon, John McGreevy, and Ellen Skerrett have all made clear, these were communities anchored in the local parish, territories that were divided among Catholic Chicago's many different ethnic and language groups. In the 1920s and 1930s, for example, the famous Back of the Yards district had eleven Roman Catholic churches in a square-mile space: two Irish, two Polish, two German, one Bohemian, one Croatian, one German, and one Italian. While Irish men and women lived in neighborhoods across the entire city, it was these parishes on the South and West Sides that formed the heartlands of Irish Chicago.[3]

These parish worlds existed on increasingly contested ground. Like the fictional Lonigans and the O'Neills, the Chicago Irish were proud of how far they had come and of the newfound respectability they believed they had earned over the previous generation. Both the Great Depression and increased African American migration challenged these precepts, forcing families to adapt or reconfigure their notions of community. Thousands chose to move to different parts of the city and its fast-growing suburbs. Four hundred thousand white people left Chicago between 1940 and 1960, many of them Irish Americans, who also moved within the city from areas like Englewood and East Garfield Park to neighborhoods like Beverly. Ironically, these changes occurred just

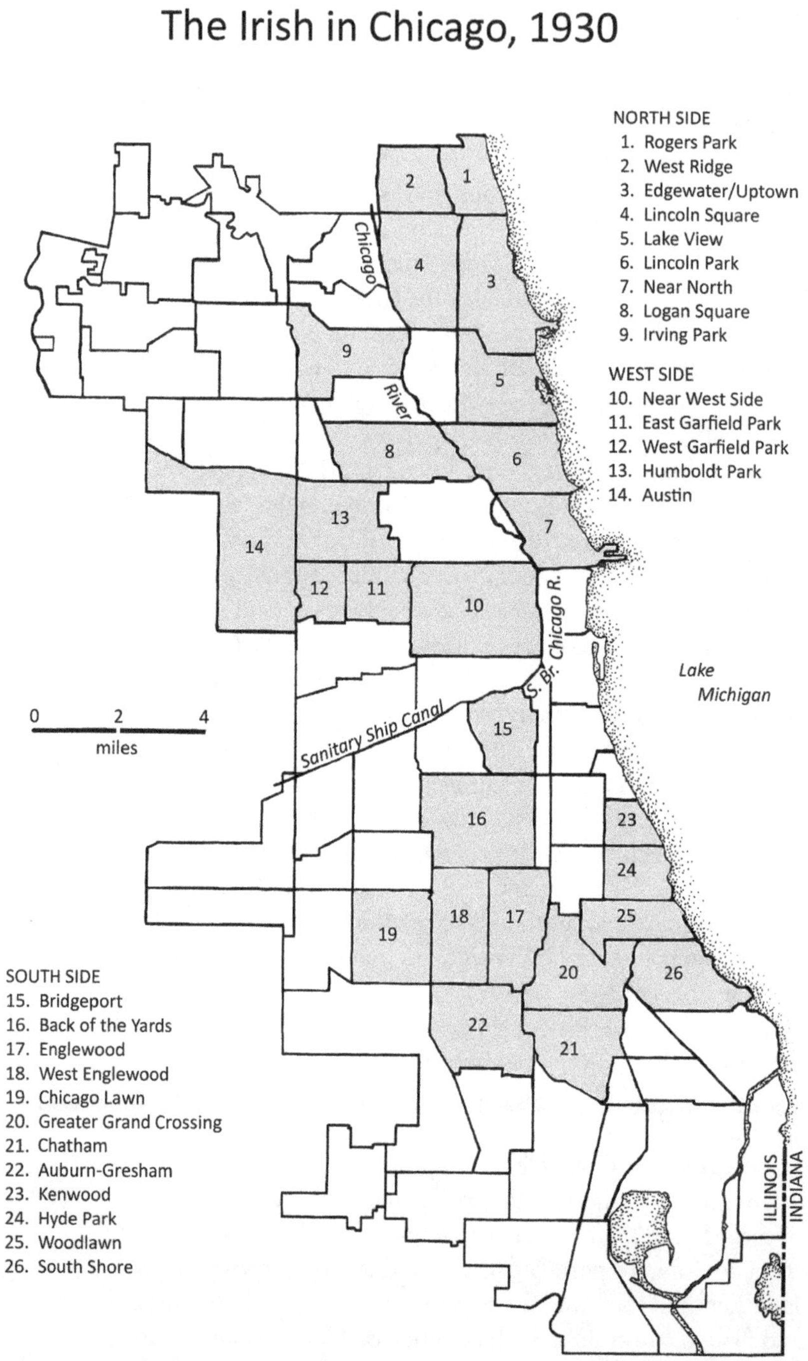

Map of Irish population in Chicago, 1930. Adapted from "Chicago's Irish Stock population, 1930," in McCaffrey et al., *The Irish in Chicago* (Urbana: University of Illinois Press, 1989).

as their Irish American political tribunes came into positions of regional and national authority at the head of the most powerful and enduring political machine in the twentieth-century United States. For all their influence, Chicago's powerbrokers, its politicians and its priests, could not wholly shield their communities from change.[4]

The Rise of the Machine: Irish Chicago and the Crisis of the 1930s

Like most communities across the United States, Chicago was in a state of crisis in the early 1930s. Because of its heavy reliance on manufacturing, the city was hit particularly hard by the onset of the Great Depression. Only 50 percent of the people who had jobs in manufacturing in 1927 remained in those same jobs in 1933.

James T. Farrell (1904–79)

James T. Farrell. Library of Congress.

Born into an Irish Catholic working-class family in Chicago in 1904, James T. Farrell became the leading chronicler of the twentieth-century Irish American experience. He attended St. Cyril (now Mount Carmel) High School and the University of Chicago. Farrell's most famous work is his *Studs Lonigan* trilogy (1932–35), which charts the travails of the Lonigans, an Irish American family that lives in Washington Park, the same South Side neighborhood where Farrell grew up. The books also document the fraught relationship between the emerging African American communities and the Chicago Irish, who fled their South Side parishes in increasing numbers for the edges of the city and the suburbs. The novels are an excellent example of Farrell's urban realism, as he charts Studs Lonigan's descent from newly forged working-class respectability to alcoholic bitterness and death. Made into both a movie and a television series, *Studs Lonigan* has been named one of the twentieth century's greatest novels and was cited by Norman Mailer as a major influence. Farrell's politics echoed his fiction: he was an active participant in various socialist political parties, publishing a number of political treatises advocating for labor rights. He died in 1979 and was inducted into the Chicago Literary Hall of Fame in 2012.[5]

While not hit as hard as the city's African American and Mexican workers, whose unemployment soared to reach 40 to 50 percent in 1932, Chicago's Irish communities nevertheless faced severe hardships, particularly in working-class districts that depended on the building trades or meatpacking. James Farrell chronicled this impact in *Judgment Day*, the finale of his Studs Lonigan trilogy, in which Patrick Lonigan's painting business fails and the bank threatens to repossess their home.[6]

The impact of the Depression in Chicago was made all the more severe by a local financial and political crisis triggered by a 1927 property reassessment that many viewed as inflated and corrupt. By 1930, the issue had mushroomed into a massive and long-lasting tax protest that exhausted the city's financial reserves, a situation that threatened lower-middle-class workers such as Chicago's public school teachers, who were still owed eight months' back pay in February 1933. Banks predictably called for retrenchment, forcing Mayor Anton Cermak to cut the city workforce by 10 percent and salaries by 20 percent. Disproportionately dependent on public employment, Chicago's Irish population was hit hard by these cuts. Cermak's successor would have a difficult job.

By all accounts, it was the veteran alderman Patrick Nash who set the stage for the Irish ascent to political dominance in Chicago. Appointed Cook County Democratic chairman by Cermak in 1931, Nash worked with other Democratic leaders, most notably Jacob Arvey, the powerful alderman from the Twenty-Fourth

Patrick Nash (1863–1943)
Patrick Nash was a successful businessman, politician, and one of the primary architects of the Chicago political machine. Born on Rush Street in Chicago in 1863, Nash grew up on the West Side, becoming a ward committeeman under Roger Sullivan, the influential Irish political boss. With his brother Richard, Nash formed a company specializing in sewer construction that received profitable contracts from the Sanitary District. By the late 1920s, Nash's business and political ties made him a rich man; he had one of the highest incomes in Chicago. A close ally of Anton Cermak, Nash was named Cook County Democratic chairman in 1931. After Cermak's death, Nash helped broker the selection of Edward Kelly as Chicago's mayor in April 1933. He worked closely with Kelly to build an organization that dominated Chicago politics into the late 1970s. Nash died in 1943. His family home at 3234 West Washington Boulevard in East Garfield Park was designated a Chicago landmark in February 1988.[7]

Ward, to get his friend Edward Kelly into City Hall. A master of behind-the-scenes negotiations, the seventy-year-old Nash wanted a mayor who would be willing to distribute contracts and patronage jobs effectively, a talent that Kelly had shown throughout his time at the Sanitary District and South Park Board (enriching both himself and Nash in the process). In this regard, Kelly would more than reward Nash's faith. Nash and his Democratic allies worked in Springfield and Chicago to make Kelly's selection a reality, and he was duly named mayor in April 1933. Edward J. Kelly was the first Irish mayor of Chicago since Edward Fitzsimons Dunne (1906–7). He would not be the last.[8]

Between 1933 and 1943, Edward Kelly and Patrick Nash built the most successful urban political machine in the twentieth-century United States. They were a good combination. As mayor, Kelly was the duo's charismatic public face, an ambitious dealmaker whose penchant for publicity and extravagance was evidenced at the Chicago World's Fairs of 1933 and 1934, which featured Major League Baseball's first All-Star Game. The festivities also included two Irish and Irish American exhibits: an official Irish Free State site, which emphasized modern Ireland's achievements in business, science, and the arts, and a commercially oriented Irish Village, which sparked sharp disagreements between Irish Americans and image-conscious Irish officials. The mayor managed to steer clear of the controversy, taking credit for the largely successful events. Kelly had an independent streak, shaped by the fact that he had not come up through the ranks of the Democratic Party in Chicago. Patrick Nash was more comfortable behind the scenes, using his position in the party to manage patronage and secure votes.[9]

Edward J. Kelly. Library of Congress.

While the Irish had long been influential in city politics, the Kelly-Nash machine was something new to Chicago, a product of Anton Cermak's effort to "build a house for all peoples" in the Democratic Party of the 1920s. Chicago's new multiethnic machine differed from the Irish-dominated political organizations in cities such as New York, Kansas City, and New Orleans, all of which fractured and disappeared in the 1930s. Kelly and Nash forged a delicate but largely successful balance in the city, rewarding both their traditional Irish constituents and other ethnic and racial communities essential to maintaining Democratic rule. Ironically, the mayor's primary opposition within Chicago politics came from Thomas Nash, a distant cousin of Patrick's and one of the city's leading criminal defense attorneys (he was one of the lawyers who defended Al Capone). Thomas Nash was the leader of a group of aldermen that Chicago newspapers labeled the Southwest Side Irish bloc. The continuing existence of these factions underlines the fact that the political machine of the 1930s and 1940s had multiple centers of patronage and power, a far cry from the more centralized organization headed by Richard J. Daley in the late 1950s and 1960s. An adroit political operator, Kelly managed to remain in power for thirteen years, largely because of the support of the city's growing African American population.[10]

Black support for Kelly and the Democratic Party was neither unanimous nor a given. African American voters traditionally had supported the Republican Party, a legacy of Lincoln's advocacy and the Democratic Party's own poisonous racial politics. This changed with the advent of the New Deal in the mid-1930s, a shift that happened dramatically on a national level in 1936. Things changed more gradually in the Windy City. The complexity of black political realignment is symbolized by the career of William Dawson, one of the key figures in midcentury Chicago politics. An ambitious and able man who began his career in politics as a Republican in 1928, Dawson switched parties in the late 1930s, a move encouraged by Mayor Kelly. "Boss" Dawson gave Kelly critical support in Chicago's black wards in the 1940s, first as a party committee man and then as congressman for the First District of Illinois (1943–70). Both Dawson and Kelly had close ties to the city's lively gambling industries, which brought much needed revenue and votes to the Democratic machine. But it was not just a matter of quid pro quo. Unlike so many of his Irish American constituents, Kelly had relatively liberal views on race relations. When controversy erupted in October 1934 over efforts to keep Morgan Park school district segregated, Kelly intervened to support African American parents, ordering the school district to readmit black students to Morgan Park High School and threatening police action against aggrieved white parents.[11]

This was always a difficult balancing act, and the Irish political bosses of the mid-twentieth century had to manage the city's shifting political alliances with deftness and tact. Some (Kelly and Daley) did it more effectively than others (Kennelly), but there can be no doubt that the Irish-led political machine rose and fell with Chicago's African American electorate. It may be, as historian James Barrett argues, that Chicago's ethnic and racial diversity forced the Irish to increase their political skill. To be successful, however, political machines need to do more than simply dole out patronage and manage votes; they also need access to resources. In the 1930s, that meant that Kelly and Nash needed the support of the federal government and its New Deal policies.[12]

In 1933, Chicago was not well placed to secure federal resources. Like many Catholic politicians across the country, Anton Cermak had been an avid supporter of FDR's opponent in the 1932 primary, Al Smith, and the new Democratic administration in Washington seemed inclined to work with the liberal governor of Illinois, Henry Horner, rather than the Chicago politicians. Kelly's administration had some notable successes in his first year, hosting the two world's fairs, paying the city's teachers most of the money owed them, and collecting some of the taxes owed the city since 1928. The crisis remained, however, and Kelly sought to control costs in the city's public school system, reducing teacher salaries by 23.5 percent and firing over thirteen hundred teachers, a move that fell disproportionately on Irish women. It was only in 1935 that Kelly and Nash were able to turn things around.[13]

The Irish political bosses understood that only the federal government had the resources to allow them to rebuild and strengthen Chicago. To gain access, Kelly and Nash successfully courted Harry Hopkins, FDR's key advisor. Of the various New Deal programs, the Works Progress Administration (WPA) was particularly attractive, a $7.8 billion program to provide jobs on small-scale, locally controlled public works projects. For all their hard work in Washington, D.C., however, it was Kelly and Nash's success on the ground in Chicago that transformed their relationship with the Democratic administration. In the 1936 election, Kelly and Nash showed FDR the full power of the Chicago political machine, defeating Republicans by a record 630,000 votes, an effort that reportedly required the mobilization of the living and the dead. One of the precinct captains active in securing votes was one Richard J. Daley, a Bridgeport native who had risen through the ranks under the patronage of ward boss "Big Joe" McDonough.

Always a pragmatist, FDR ceded control of the state WPA to Kelly and Nash after the election, a patronage windfall for the Chicago bosses. Numbers clearly illustrate the impact of this New Deal program. In 1936, Chicago had 29,500 city workers and 68,400 WPA workers. Characteristically, Kelly and Nash used the WPA to garner votes as well as jobs, adding party workers to the WPA payroll to help with elections. And these jobs could make a real difference on the ground. In St. Sabina's parish in Auburn-Gresham, members celebrated their political patrons' ability to get them WPA ("We Poke Along") jobs that sustained their families through hard times. As parishioner Terence O'Rourke remembered, "People who never were in politics, took political jobs when they lost out. They were glad to get those political jobs. They had steady income. . . . [The parish] didn't have any soup kitchens set up." While O'Rourke's comment doubtless reflects the human tendency to minimize the extent of one's own poverty and suffering, there can be no doubt that the resources provided by the New Deal allowed the Kelly administration to shield constituents from the full impact of the Great Depression.[14]

Not everyone was so lucky. The heightened unemployment of the late 1920s and 1930s also brought disease and destitution to the working-class Irish in Chicago. Nowhere is this depicted more clearly than in the novels and short stories of James T. Farrell. Poverty and death are everywhere in *Studs Lonigan*. Riding back to Chicago from a funeral with his remaining friends, Studs lists his friends who have died, "Paulie and Shrimp, Arnold Sheehan, Slug Mason, Tommy Doyle, Hink Weber," making "all the world seem to Studs like a graveyard." In similar fashion, Farrell's short story "Jim O'Neill" (1932) features a tired working-class father with hopes that his son is strong enough to escape the drudgery and poverty of his own life. Politics could only do so much.[15]

The Kelly administration was certainly no friend to organized labor. Throughout the late 1930s, Chicago policemen, disproportionately Irish American, regularly broke up picket lines and attacked men and women on strike. The mayor refused to apologize for his hardline tactics, arguing that "the people of Chicago want law and order, and insist that the laws be obeyed by everyone regardless of who he is." The worst incident was the 1937 Memorial Day Massacre, when police fired into a crowd of striking protestors outside the South Chicago Republic Steel plant on the Southeast Side. Although a Cook County investigation exonerated the police, a U.S. Senate subcommittee chaired by Wisconsin senator Robert M. LaFollette Jr. found that the police had used excessive force. While Kelly refused to discipline the police, he and other Democrats quickly moved to improve their relationships with organized labor, meeting with Congress of Industrial Organizations (CIO) officials soon after the inquiry. Promised an exemption from police intervention in the future, the CIO supported the machine in both the 1938 elections and the mayoral contest of 1939.[16]

If FDR's New Deal policies provided a measure of relief for hundreds of thousands of Illinois residents, it was World War II that brought the United States out of the Depression. Edward Kelly was an effective and national political figure throughout the war, supporting the president's internationalism and mobilizing resources behind the war effort. Under his energetic leadership, Chicago bought more war bonds than any other American city. His local popularity flagged after 1943, a decline dominated by a series of scandals in the Chicago Police Department, deteriorating city services, and increasing racial tensions over nascent efforts to integrate public housing and schools. The aging Irish tribune defended his administration against charges of corruption, arguing, "There will be a measure of larceny in our state and urban politics, just as there is in business. Show me an administration that is one hundred percent pure and I will show you a new species of human being."[17]

It is no coincidence that Kelly's effectiveness and reputation declined after the 1943 death of Patrick Nash, whose cautious counsel had always acted as an effective brake on the less disciplined mayor. But it was more than the loss of Nash's political skills and sage advice. Racial integration was a particularly challenging issue in postwar Chicago, as demobilized soldiers returned to cities that were in economic transition. Housing shortages were acute, and Kelly's relatively liberal views on racial integration alienated constituents who felt threatened by African American in-migration into traditionally Irish parish communities. Kelly backed the Chicago Housing Authority's hesitant efforts to integrate public housing projects such as Airport Homes in West Lawn on the Southwest Side, sending police to defend black families from white demonstrators. He also sponsored the Conference for the Elimination of Restrictive Covenants, part of a broader public relations campaign to end housing segregation led by the liberal Catholic bishop Bernard J. Sheil. Both efforts failed. As historian William Grimshaw puts it, "Chicago was not ready for racial progress, even in small increments." Kelly was forced out of office in 1947, but the Irish machine he had done so much to build would adapt and live on for another generation.[18]

The first of Bridgeport's Irish mayors died of congestive heart failure on October 20, 1950, at seventy-four years old. Kelly was buried in Calvary Cemetery in Chicago at a funeral presided over by Cardinal Samuel Stritch and attended by political elites such as Governor Adlai Stevenson, Senator Paul Douglas, and U.S. Attorney General J. Howard McGrath, who represented President Harry S. Truman. Characteristically, Kelly's estate was soon wrapped in controversy, as his widow, Margaret, and the estate's executor, Michael Mulcahey, squabbled over how much money remained, a mystery that has never been solved. In recent years, historians have reassessed Kelly's reputation, balancing the corruption of the machine against his political effectiveness and his liberal (if limited) efforts to integrate a racially divided city. Unfortunately, his hesitant steps in that direction would not be nearly enough to save the city from tragedy.[19]

The Search for Respectability: The Irish Fellowship Club of Chicago

Irish American political success reflected the growing status and respectability of Chicago's Irish middle and professional classes. In many ways, Irish political and social advancement were mutually constitutive. Nothing exhibits this symbiotic relationship better than the twentieth-century growth of the Irish Fellowship Club of Chicago (IFC). Founded in 1901 as the Red Branch Knights, the organization was designed to both reflect and cultivate a sense of Irish American respectability, a deliberate effort to counter powerful anti-Irish stereotypes. According to lifelong member Roger Faherty, the Irish Fellowship Club, as the organization was renamed shortly after its foundation, had been created "to take the Irish off the streets." This was an exclusive association for the Chicago Irish elite. Its first president was Edward F. Dunne, the future mayor and governor, and the group's initial membership was dominated by prominent businessmen, journalists, and judges. Chicago's Irish political leaders played key roles in the organization: Edward Kelly, Richard J. Daley, and Richard M. Daley were all presidents of the Irish Fellowship Club of Chicago. The association's focal point was an annual banquet on St. Patrick's Day. These dinners quickly grew to be impressive affairs; by 1910, President William Howard Taft was the guest speaker at the IFC's banquet at the LaSalle Hotel. The Chicago Irish, or at least some of them, had come a long way.[20]

The organization grew dramatically in stature and membership in the 1920s and 1930s, a reflection of the rising influence of Irish Americans in the city. In June 1926, the IFC hosted two thousand guests for a banquet at Palmer House in honor of Cardinal Patrick O'Donnell, the Catholic archbishop of Armagh. The organization's high point, however, came two years later, when the association hosted a luncheon and dinner for William T. Cosgrave, the prime minister of the Irish Free State. The visit, a stop on Cosgrave's first official tour of the United States, was initiated by Kevin Kelly, secretary of the IFC, who had invited the Irish leader to speak at the club's 1928 St. Patrick's Day dinner. While Cosgrave's schedule did not permit that to occur, he arrived at LaSalle Station in Chicago on January 21, 1928. Speaking to a crowd of forty-five thousand people at the Stevens Hotel, Cosgrave emphasized the modernity and stability of the Irish Free State, urging Irish Americans to come to Ireland so that they could judge for themselves how Irish men and women were using their newfound freedom. The prime minister's North American tour proved to be a ringing success, strengthening both the legitimacy of the Irish Free State and its ties to the United States and Canada. On a private level, the visit initiated lifelong friendships between IFC members such as Roger Faherty and Cosgrave and other Irish government officials. Other prominent Irish figures followed in the 1930s and 1940s, including notable authors George William Russell (AE) in 1928 and Padraic Colum in 1941.[21]

Most of the speakers at IFC events were more local, ranging from Chicago-based academics interested in Irish historical and literary matters to prominent public figures such as Senator Robert LaFollette and Cardinal Samuel Stritch, the Catholic archbishop of Chicago. In March 1945, the IFC, with Mayor Kelly's help, managed to get Vice President Harry Truman to speak at its St. Patrick's Day luncheon (during World War II, the celebration was moved from dinner to lunch). Merely a month before he became president, Truman wowed a crowd that included forty-five wounded Irish Americans, describing St. Patrick as "the good saint who condemned slavery, fought racial discrimination, and sought to end the tragic isolation of Ireland from the civilization and culture of the outside world." Truman's version of Ireland's patron saint sounded more like a New Democrat than a medieval Irish monk, but the vice president's appearance was a clear marker of Irish American respectability.[22]

The Irish Fellowship Club of Chicago continued to thrive after the war. An IFC membership list for 1950 includes over four hundred paid members, a substantial increase over earlier years. Northern Ireland and partition became an increasingly important topic of discussion for the organization. On April 18, 1949, Seán MacBride, the forceful Irish minister for external affairs, spoke to the IFC the same day the newly declared Republic of Ireland left the British Commonwealth. When the organization published its official history in 1963, its leaders listed "actively seeking an end to partition" as one of its four primary goals. The onset of the Troubles in the late 1960s only increased the spirit and volume of discussion about Northern Ireland across the Irish diaspora.[23]

Finally, the IFC tried to foster increased cultural ties between the United States and Ireland. This was not just a matter of increasing trade and travel to Ireland; the IFC also attempted to raise the profile of Irish studies at local universities and supported exchange and study abroad programs for Irish and American students alike. This became increasingly important in the 1950s and beyond, as transatlantic flights made travel between Illinois and Ireland easier. By the late 1950s, with Mayor Daley running the city and rising Irish American prominence and prosperity for all to see, there was little doubt that the Chicago Irish had made it.

Moving Up? Irish American Women and Education in Chicago

The businessmen, lawyers, and politicians who made up the IFC were hardly representative of the Irish in Chicago. The majority of Irish Americans in the early twentieth-century city were working-class men and women who had to struggle to make ends meet and improve their circumstances. For the most part, they did. Between 1880 and 1920, families like the fictional Lonigans or the real-life Daleys or Kellys had moved from unskilled jobs on the canals and in domestic service and slaughterhouses to better-paid and more stable positions as city workers, firemen, policemen, and schoolteachers. These changes in social class were reflected in the city's shifting ethnic and racial geography, as Irish families moved from the Back of the Yards to neighborhoods like Washington Park and eventually on to places on the edge of the city like Beverly and the South Shore. The paths these families charted were neither straight nor easy. Nowhere was the halting Irish American struggle and rise to respectability more evident than in Chicago's schools, where Irish women worked in disproportionate numbers. In 1920, George Mundelein, the archbishop of Chicago, an admittedly biased source, estimated that an extraordinary 70 percent of the city's teachers were Irish American women. While the accuracy of these numbers is debatable, Irish predominance in Chicago's schools was not, a trend that generated repeated efforts to limit the number of Irish Catholic teachers in the city. In 1903, 1906, and 1915, the Chicago school board attempted to create quota systems to curtail the number of Catholic high school graduates teaching in the city's schools. As Mundelein's report suggests, their efforts failed.[24]

If the movement of Irish women from domestic service into education was a dramatic success story, it was not an easy one. In her study of the history of Irish American teachers in New York, San Francisco, and Chicago, historian Janet Nolan illustrates this journey through the life and career of Amelia Dunne Hookway, the oldest sister of writer Finley Peter Dunne. Born in St. Patrick's Parish in Chicago in 1858, Amelia Dunne joined the faculty at Scannon School in 1880, a position that allowed her family to move to a better house. Her ascent within the city school system was rapid: she became head assistant at Central Park School before she was named principal of George Howland School on the city's west side in 1895, a position she held until her death in November 1914. In her eulogy, Ella Flagg Young, the first female superintendent of schools in Chicago and Hookway's friend and mentor, celebrated the ways that "Mrs. Hookway achieved marvelous results in arousing a sense of personal dignity and responsibility in [her pupils] through literature and drama." While Amelia Dunne Hookway's career may not have been representative, the path she made in teaching and administration reflected the efforts of a generation of Irish American women in Chicago.[25]

In many ways, these opportunities were a product of Chicago's dramatic population growth, which rose from 500,000 in 1880 to 3.3 million in 1930. This transformed the city's educational landscape. Between 1890 and 1920, the number of students in public elementary schools rose from 130,000 to 260,000, and the number of teachers in these schools nearly tripled, from 2,600 to 7,400. Similar growth occurred in Catholic schools in many parishes across the city. In St. Sabina's parish on the South Side, for example, the number of enrolled students more than quadrupled between 1917 and 1929. Both the city's public school system and the Catholic Church expanded their educational outreach to meet the increased demand, creating greater possibilities for women like Amelia Dunne Hookway and her Irish American compatriots.[26]

Although most teaching jobs were a dramatic improvement for working-class women, they should not be romanticized. In late nineteenth- and early twentieth-century Illinois, female teachers were heavily concentrated in low-pay positions in elementary schools, and it is telling that almost all the school administrators were male. To combat this situation, two Irish American women, Margaret A. Haley and Catherine Goggin, helped found the Chicago Teachers Federation (CTF) in March 1897. Both were the daughters of Irish immigrants and had extensive teaching experience at schools on the near South Side. In 1881, Goggin moved to Jones School in the city's First Ward, teaching to the city's largest enrollment of African American and Chinese children in some of the worst conditions in Chicago. Goggin and Haley brought this practical work experience to the CTF. Unlike the National Educational Association (NEA) and other teachers' unions, the CTF barred administrators from membership and participation. The organization was designed to raise the public profile of the teaching profession by securing the conditions, pay, and support needed for effective teaching and learning. Goggin was particularly concerned with women's economic independence, arguing that a good teacher "learns to govern and not be governed" and that such teachers provided young women with good role models.[27]

But it was not just a matter of economics; the CTF pushed for educational independence, arguing that top-down centralized models of schooling undermined educational achievement. Haley in particular treasured her Irishness, celebrating the fighting Irish and identifying with "the Tones and the Emmets and the Parnells" of the Irish nationalist tradition. At the same time, she rejected the Irish tendency toward ethnic clannishness, arguing that she would "be damned" if she would "stand with any Catholic, Irish or Dutch or anything else, who'd defend" a bad law. With the fiery Haley's support, Goggin became president of the CTF in 1900, an organization whose membership had grown to three thousand after the turn of the century, almost exclusively women. To increase its political leverage, the CTF voted in 1902 to affiliate with the Chicago Federation of Labor, a relationship strengthened by Haley's friendship with another Irishman, John Fitzpatrick, the association's organizer and future president.[28]

It was Haley who led the way in what became the CTF's greatest victory: the Tax Fight of 1900–1904 to increase funding for

Margaret A. Haley (1861–1939)
Born in 1861 to an Irish immigrant family in Joliet, Margaret Haley was a teacher and pioneering union activist. Haley received a progressive education at normal schools across Illinois before moving to Chicago in 1882 to begin her teaching career. After teaching at Hendricks School in the stockyard district for two decades, she left the classroom to become the paid business secretary and vice president of the fledgling Chicago Teachers Federation (CTF) in 1900. For the next "forty fighting years," Haley worked to raise teacher salaries, professional status, and educational independence in Chicago and Illinois schools. She was a strong advocate of democratization in education, fighting against what she saw as linked bureaucratic and corporate interests. After some initial successes in Chicago, Haley and the CTF suffered a series of setbacks in the late 1910s and 1920s, ending what has been called a "golden age" for female teachers. Haley was also an active member of the Women's Suffrage Party of Illinois, linking women's suffrage to her lifelong struggle for teachers' rights. Margaret A. Haley died of a heart attack in Chicago in January 1939.[29]

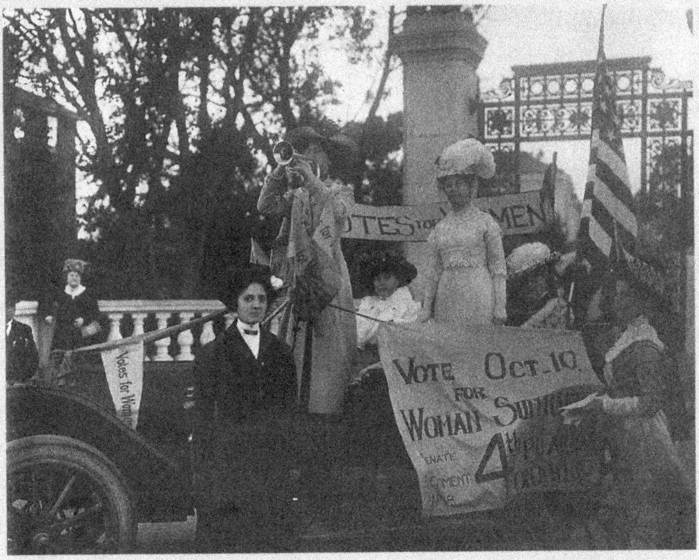

Margaret A. Haley (wearing the plumed hat) in a Women's Suffrage Parade, 1911. Courtesy of the Chicago History Museum (ICHi-01601).

schools by getting large corporations to pay their share of property taxes. The struggle began in 1899, when the Chicago Board of Education reneged on a promised increase in teacher salaries. Inspired by a newspaper story about the Pullman Car Company's evasion of property taxes, Haley successfully took five major utility and street railway companies to court, where a subsequent victory that led to a 1907 tax reassessment that secured nearly $600,000 in back taxes and increased the city's annual tax revenue by $250,000. The union's cause was greatly aided by the 1905 election of Edward F. Dunne, the second Irish Catholic mayor of Chicago, who won office by creating an effective coalition of ethnic blocs and progressive reformers. Haley was a member of Dunne's "kitchen cabinet," his chief advisor on school affairs. With Haley's silent support, Dunne put together an unprecedented and controversial board of education, one that featured several women (including Jane Addams, whom the more combative Haley sarcastically labeled "Gentle Jane") and supporters of the CTF's democratization mission. In 1906, teachers finally received their back pay, a $45 check that provided a significant morale boost. These successes were short-lived, however, as the board's relative radicalism generated a significant backlash, helping Republican Fred Busse defeat Dunne in 1907. The CTF would be on the defensive for the remainder of Haley's life.[30]

The sense of crisis was doubtless sharpened by the 1916 death of Catherine Goggin, whose deft political touch had always complemented Haley's more forceful leadership style. But the reality was that after 1907, the CTF was operating in a much more difficult environment, as the success of the public school movement and new methods of teacher training created greater opportunities for male experts, and conservative business interests moved to counter the CTF's democratic efforts to reshape Chicago's public schools. Things came to a head in 1915, when the Chicago Board of Education created the Loeb Rule, which outlawed ties between public school teachers and organized labor. Sixty-eight teachers were not hired back, including thirty-eight members of the CTF. While the city's teachers initially responded by creating a national union, the American Federation of Teachers (AFT), an organization that was soon dominated by the often male and higher-status high school teachers, the decision ultimately fractured the coalition, and Haley's CTF left the national body in May 1917. Haley remained active in trade union politics, supporting John

Fitzpatrick's candidacy for mayor in the election of 1919, but the CTF never returned to the ranks of organized labor.[31]

These issues were only exacerbated in the late 1920s when the combined forces of the property tax strike and the Great Depression wreaked havoc on the school system. In 1929, the average Chicago elementary school teacher made $2,505 per year, substantially more than the national average, but $250 less than their male compatriots and $800 less than men teaching in the city's high schools. On the eve of the Depression, then, an elementary school teacher earned a relatively comfortable (if not equitable) salary, an achievement shaped by the efforts of the CTF, the AFT, and the more conservative NEA.

All of these gains were threatened by the crisis of the early 1930s. In 1931, Anton Cermak cut teachers' salaries in an effort to avoid complete fiscal collapse. His successor, Edward Kelly, made even more drastic cuts to the board of education's budget in 1933, firing 10 percent of the city's teachers and cutting school finances even further. Many of the city's fourteen thousand teachers were forced to endure repeated "payless paydays," and public school teachers received paychecks on time only three times between January 1931 and May 1933.

Frustrated by a $5 pay raise that had just been granted to school janitors (men with critical ties to the Kelly-Nash machine), teachers and their students finally took to the streets in April 1933. On April 14, five thousand teachers gathered in Grant Park, a demonstration that ended in violence between police and teachers, clashes that featured Irish Americans on both sides. Critically, the teachers had an influential Irish American ally in Helen Maley Hefferan, the "public school Catholic," a former teacher and one of the most active members of the school board. Pressured by Hefferan and public support for the teachers, Kelly soon gave in on backpay, money that was nevertheless slow to make its way to Chicago teachers. It was only in 1934 that they received their money, after Kelly secured a massive loan from the federal government. The Chicago machine could keep its constituents happy only when it received resources from Washington, D.C.[32]

In the final chapter of her autobiography, Margaret Haley argues that Chicago was the proving ground of American democracy, and that her life had been lived at the heart of a forty-year contest between the defenders and exploiters of true popular government. In Haley's opinion, public schools were a particularly important battleground in the war against privilege. Despite the setbacks of the 1920s and 1930s, she remained relatively optimistic about the future: "It is something, after all, to have lived for forty years upon a battleground, to have been even a small part in the gigantic struggle for justice, . . . Fighting Irish I was then, a child of a generation of men and women who had battled for something beyond immediate gain." Her career symbolized both the achievements of and limitations placed on Illinois's Irish American teachers, who seized opportunities to better themselves and their students in Chicago's classrooms in the early twentieth century. These efforts were curtailed in the 1910s and 1920s by a combination of conservative reaction and male privilege, but Irish American women's ultimate success in education was symbolized by the careers of figures such as Catherine Goggin, Margaret Haley, Helen Maley Hefferan, and Amelia Dunne Hookway. The teachers' confrontation with the Kelly-Nash machine in 1933 also highlights another broad issue that has dominated the history of Irish in twentieth-century Chicago: the ambivalent relationship between democracy and the political machine. Nowhere was this tension more evident than in the fraught and complex relationship between the Chicago Irish and African Americans.[33]

The Chicago Irish and Civil Rights

The rise and fall of Edward Kelly illustrated the fact that Irish political success in Chicago depended on relationships with other ethnic and racial groups. From the late nineteenth century onward, there were very few wards in the city where the Irish were in the majority. To be successful, Irish political bosses thus had to be able to distribute patronage effectively, sharing often relatively scarce resources with other communities in return for political support. In this sense, Edward Kelly and Patrick Nash were only the most able and ambitious of a long line of Chicago Irish politicians, men who benefited from their own considerable talents and the dramatic increase in resources provided by the federal government's New Deal policies. By the mid-1930s, it was clear that African Americans held the key to Democratic success in the city, and Kelly moved to create a more stable basis for his administration by securing the support of William Dawson and other black elites. It was the combination of African American political support and federal resources that underlay the success of the Irish political machine between 1933 and 1983.[34]

For all the importance placed on distributing patronage across ethnic and racial lines, Irish Americans benefited disproportionately from their political tribunes, particularly in certain sectors of municipal employment. Tom Donovan, Richard J. Daley's patronage chief, once joked that the mayor's idea of affirmative action was "nine Irishmen and a Swede." This is the kind of hyperbole typical in ethnic humor, but the Irish certainly did well from the machine. In the early 1960s, when Irish Americans constituted about 10 percent of Chicago's population, 24 percent of the city's aldermen, 42 percent of the ward commissioners, and almost 50 percent of the district attorneys were Irish, and 41 of the 72 highest administration positions within the Chicago Police Department were held by Irishmen. The tensions between the need to distribute resources and the inclination to reward Irish American constituents was one of the issues that would ultimately lead to the downfall of the machine in the late 1970s. It was a long run, however, and under Richard J. Daley, these political problems were managed with remarkable effect. Unfortunately, the costs of the ways that they were managed were also considerable.[35]

There was nothing new about tensions between the Irish and African Americans in Chicago. Race relations were transformed by the Great Migration, which saw five hundred thousand African Americans move from the South to Chicago between 1916 and 1970. The war years were particularly important, when restrictions on emigration created greater opportunities for industrial employment for southern migrants in Chicago. And this had dramatic impact: between 1916 and 1919, Chicago's black population rose from 44,000 to 109,000. African American settlement largely was confined to what was called the Black Belt, an area just to the east of South Side Irish neighborhoods including Back of the Yards, Bridgeport, and Canaryville. The unsettled economic transition of the postwar environment sharpened racial tensions across these flashpoint areas, leading to sporadic clashes between gangs of young men. The most serious of these was the infamous Chicago Race Riots of 1919, a murderous series of clashes that ranged across the city for a week, leaving thirty-eight people dead and over five hundred wounded. According to a report put together by Chicago's Commission on Race Riots, approximately 40 percent of the clashes occurred in the white neighborhoods near the stockyards. Not surprisingly, Irish gangs from Bridgeport played prominent roles in the rioting, including

Ragen's Colts and the Hamburg Athletic Club, where seventeen-year-old Richard J. Daley was an active member (he became club president in 1924). Although Daley never admitted that he was involved in the attacks, his most recent biographers have argued that at the very least, the future mayor was close to the center of the violence.[36]

While outbreaks of violence left lasting scars on communal relations in Chicago, most Irish communities did not take to the streets to defend their neighborhoods. Instead, families simply moved to other parts of the city, leaving places like Washington Park with a complex mixture of fear, regret, resentment, and opportunity. In Irish neighborhoods bordering the Black Belt, these changes often occurred with remarkable speed. Between 1916 and 1930, for example, Corpus Christi Church, a few blocks north of Washington Park, went from being "lace curtain" Irish to the heart of Bronzeville. Loath to let Corpus Christi become a black church, Bishop Mundelein sent the Reverend Frank O'Brien to the church in 1924 to "save Corpus Christi for the people who built it." Once on the ground, O'Brien and other local priests decided that the church should minister to African Americans who lived in the area. It would not have mattered; between 1924 and 1928, the remaining white members left. James Farrell's novels echo this same dynamic. In the second book of his *Studs Lonigan* trilogy, *The Young Manhood of Studs Lonigan*, Farrell describes Studs's participation in the race riots and more routine acts of violence against African Americans, Jews, and other ethnic foes. Studs makes clear his disdain for the "lesser" races throughout the books. His father, Patrick Lonigan, has faith that Father Gilhooley will manage to protect the neighborhood, but when the priest celebrates the church's new black parishioners at mass, the Lonigans turn their backs on him, disillusioned by his failure to defend their vision of community. Ultimately, they leave their home for the South Shore, selling their house to a black man and joining the Irish exodus from Washington Park in the 1920s. Farrell's novels thus describe a pattern of ineffectual protest and resentful withdrawal that was characteristic of the Irish response to the growing African American presence in Chicago.[37]

It was World War II that triggered the next flashpoint in race relations, initiating the Second Great Migration, as black workers again moved to the city to take advantage of increased job opportunities. By 1945, 531,000 men and women worked in the munitions industry. The end of the war, however, brought significant challenges, as wartime industries closed and demobilized soldiers returned to the city to work. The combination of economic dislocation and population growth exacerbated long-running housing shortages in the city, an issue that would bedevil the Kelly, Kennelly, and Daley administrations. Relatively liberal on the issue of racial integration, Kelly gave his full support to Elizabeth Wood, the liberal executive secretary of the Chicago Housing Authority, who advocated a gradualist approach to integrated public housing. Controversy first broke out in November 1946 at Airport Homes in West Lawn near Midway Airport, where white residents protested efforts to move black families into the project. Kelly pledged to defend the black residents, saying that "all law-abiding citizens may be assured of their right to live peaceably anywhere in Chicago" and sending the police in to battle with demonstrators. In this case, Kelly's efforts were to no avail, as the black residents left and none would replace them.[38]

Housing was not the only sector where integration efforts triggered controversy. While black students technically had the right to go to school in any of the Chicago public schools, several schools remained firmly set against racial integration. Inspired by an antiblack strike in neighboring Gary, Indiana, white students opposed to black admission walked out of Englewood, Morgan Park, and Calumet High Schools in September 1945. On this occasion, the mayor's efforts to mute the protest were more effective. The veteran Irish boss worked with the city press to downplay the story, and the strikes fell apart quietly and quickly. In a few instances, priests and other Irish tribunes led parish resistance to racial integration, most notably Monsignor Daniel F. Byrnes, the Irish-born priest of Visitation parish in Englewood from 1932 to 1952. Byrnes consistently urged his parishioners to stand firmly against black immigration into their neighborhoods, reminding them "the Vis" was the "largest and greatest parish in the diocese." Controversies over racial integration in 1945 and 1946 only accelerated Mayor Kelly's fall from grace, threatening to fracture the traditional Irish working-class base of the machine.[39]

Monsignor Byrnes's strident opposition to integration was hardly characteristic of the Irish response to integration in Chicago. These issues split congregations and households, divisions that were often framed along generational lines. Writing about his experience growing up in Our Lady of the Angels parish on the

West Side, historian James Barrett describes how he got involved in civil rights and later antiwar activism through parish groups, reflective of a new kind of Catholicism that generated tension with his father, a policeman with more traditional religious views.[40]

These same types of tensions prevailed in St. Sabina's Parish in Auburn-Gresham. Monsignor John A. McMahon, who moved to the far South Side church from an already integrated parish in 1952, attempted to prepare his parishioners for integration so that they could preserve the strength of the parish community. Inspired by Bishop Bernard Shiel, the founder of the Catholic Youth Organization and an outspoken advocate for the marginalized and underprivileged, McMahon formed a number of parish groups that were dedicated to community engagement and social action. Father McMahon also was an active member of Organization of the Southwest Communities, an ecumenical organization that brought Catholic and Protestant pastors into Saul Alinsky's efforts to reduce racial division on the Southwest Side of the city. Although McMahon's efforts were rejected by many of his parishioners and did little to stem the tide of white flight from the parish, his hard work clearly laid the groundwork for St. Sabina's later emergence as a flourishing black-majority church dedicated to social justice issues.[41]

Perhaps the most conspicuous Irish American supporters of civil rights and racial integration in Chicago were nuns. Since the mid-nineteenth century, the sisters of a variety of Catholic orders had provided educational, social, and spiritual care for the city's poor, living among and serving a shifting population of ethnic immigrants and African Americans. These efforts became more pronounced in the 1960s, as inner-city nuns became some of the most forceful advocates for reform. The most celebrated of these figures was Sister Mary William Sullivan, the charismatic director of Marillac House, a settlement house run by the Daughters of Charity in East Garfield Park. Working with sympathetic Catholic leaders such as Monsignor John "Jack" Egan and John A. McDermott, the executive of Chicago's Catholic Interracial Council, Sister Mary William battled Mayor Daley and the establishment to get resources and rights for black communities. On June 12, 1965, she and five other Daughters of Charity were arrested at a well-publicized civil rights demonstration in the Chicago Loop. The arrest shocked nearly everyone, including one desk sergeant, who claimed "that he had never booked a nun before." As historian

Sister Mary William Sullivan, D.C., with Martin Luther King Jr., October 1964.
Courtesy of the Daughters of Charity, Province of St. Louise, St. Louis, Missouri.

Sister Mary William Sullivan (1925–2017)

Born in St. Louis in 1925, Sister Mary William Sullivan was the daughter of William Sullivan of St. Louis and Lillian (O'Meara) Sullivan of County Tipperary, Ireland. She received her BA in education from Fontbonne College (1951) in St. Louis and a master's in social work from the Catholic University of America (1955). Throughout a remarkable seventy-three-year career of service, Sullivan worked in a variety of educational, philanthropic, and social outreach settings in Milwaukee, Chicago, San Francisco, Dallas, Amarillo, Austin, and St. Louis. She is perhaps best known for her civil rights work in Chicago, serving as the director of the Extension Program in Public House (1959–64) and administrator of Marillac House (1964–68). In the latter capacity, she worked closely with Martin Luther King Jr. and local leaders on the Catholic Interracial Council of Chicago. A fierce advocate for community, educational, racial, and social justice, Sullivan described herself as a "large, loud Irish nun sitting on the corner of Jackson and California." She died in July 2017, months after celebrating a remarkable seventy-three years as a Daughter of Charity.[42]

Suellen Hoy makes clear, however, the nuns' commitment to social justice fit into a much longer history of public service in Chicago. Sister Mary William put it more succinctly, quipping, "Sisters have been walking in hospital and school corridors for years . . . and I'm just Irish enough and Chicago enough not to want all that walking to go to waste."[43]

Irish movement from inner city neighborhoods to the suburbs was not a simple matter of white flight from an increasingly racially diverse city. It also reflected a real success story, the growing affluence of third- and fourth-generation Irish Americans, who took advantage of greater capital and postwar federal legislation to buy homes in suburbs such as Arlington Heights, Mount Prospect, Oak Lawn, River Forest, and Wilmette. It is worth noting that Irish Americans were slower to move to the suburbs than other white ethnic groups. In Chicago, many families attempted to re-create their inner-city parish communities in new neighborhoods at the edge of the city. In her model study of St. Sabina's Parish, Eileen McMahon documented parishioners' movement from St. Sabina's to Beverly, where the transplanted families have championed the South Side Irish Parade and other events to recapture the feel of their old lives. In the words of one parishioner, "This area [St. Barnabas Parish in Beverly] was appealing because . . . there were so many people that we knew . . . transplants from Sabina's, Little Flower, Leo, Ethelreds. . . . We felt comfortable coming in here the same way I felt comfortable at St. Sabina's growing up." And yet, move to the suburbs they did. By 1980, the only discernibly Irish neighborhoods in Chicago proper were Beverly, Bridgeport, and Morgan Park.[44]

The postwar movement of Irish Americans to the suburbs had little noticeable impact on the fortunes of Chicago's Irish-dominated political machine. In the wake of Edward Kelly's fall, Cook County Democratic Party leaders decided they needed a reformer and selected Martin Kennelly, a successful businessman (the founder of Allied Van Lines, the famous transport company) and prominent civic leader, who was duly elected mayor of Chicago in 1947. If Kennelly was originally from Bridgeport, he had little else in common with either his predecessor or the man who would succeed him, Richard J. Daley. Kennelly promised to attack the patronage system that lay at the heart of the machine. While Kennelly was an ineffectual administrator (Mathias "Paddy" Bauler, North Side alderman and famous clown prince of Chicago politics, labeled him "Fartin' Martin"), he did attack the patronage system with gusto, appointing an aggressive commission that put real teeth into civil service reform, greatly reducing the number of patronage jobs that ward committeemen and alderman had at their disposal. This earned the new mayor the enmity of influential machine leaders like Daley and Jacob

Arvey. Kennelly damaged his prospects even further by attacking policy wheels and jitney cabs, two powerful institutions in black Chicago that provided much-needed finances for William Dawson and other African American politicians. With Dawson and other machine leaders' support, Daley overthrew Kennelly after his second term, narrowly defeating him in the 1955 mayoral election. Old-style machine politics were back. As Paddy Bauler quipped, "Chicago ain't ready for reform yet."[45]

Richard J. Daley (1902–76) was the mayor of Chicago from 1955 to 1976. A Bridgeport native, Daley rose through the ranks of the Democratic machine, becoming a committeeman of the Eleventh Ward in the late 1940s and chairman of the Cook County Democratic Party in 1953, a position he retained until his death. Daley treasured his Bridgeport roots and traditional Catholic values, returning home most days to have dinner with his wife, Bridgeport native Eleanor Guilfoyle, at their bungalow on South Lowe Avenue. His closest friends were Irish, as were most of his closest advisors, including Northwest Side alderman Tom Keane, a real estate attorney who helped run the City Council throughout the 1960s. According to Milton Rakove, a University of Illinois at Chicago professor and political consultant, Daley viewed the city "as a series of Bridgeports—communities where God-fearing, decent, hard-working people strive to keep the community stable, hold onto the values of their fathers, and fulfill their obligation as citizens to the neighborhood, the *polis*, and the nation." Ironically, the mayor's development policies—which prioritized the Loop and transportation infrastructure projects such as O'Hare International Airport and countless expressways—accelerated the deterioration of the neighborhoods he celebrated.[46]

Daley also enjoyed the trappings of Irishness. He brought back the city's official St. Patrick's Day Parade in 1956, an annual opportunity to celebrate his Irish heritage and display the might of the machine. It was an immediate success, drawing 10,000 marchers and 250,000 spectators that year. Led by the mayor, the parade began at State and Kinzie, moving down State Street until it reached Adams, where the marchers turned west to Old St. Patrick's Church. The march lasted over an hour, featuring "Irish pipe and drum units, and floats bearing Irish colleens, Irish dances, and Gaelic football players. Marchers were carrying blackthorn sticks and shillelaghs and wearing hats festooned with shamrocks." The mayor's favorite song was the nineteenth-century Irish

Mayor Richard J. Daley and Eleanor Daley (*right*) with Michael Howlett, the Illinois secretary of state, and Catherine O'Connell, the St. Patrick's Day Parade queen, 1976. Laszlo Kondor, photographer, MSLASZ13_04_0004_0011_0011, Laszlo Kondor Photograph Collection, Special Collections and University Archives, University of Illinois–Chicago.

air "Garry Owen," and his favorite band was the Shannon Rovers Irish Pipe Band, which he hired to play for Richard Nixon when the president visited the city in 1974. Both his successor, Jane Byrne (1933–2014), and his son, Richard M. Daley (1942–), continued to wield Irish symbols in their political campaigns, which featured shamrocks and slogans like "Erin Go Bragh" (Ireland Forever). For the Daleys, as for so many Irish Americans across Chicago and the region, the markers of Irish identity still mattered.[47]

In the wake of the 1955 election, Daley moved quickly to restore the patronage system, rolling back and ignoring Kennelly's civil service reforms. According to the legendary Chicago journalist Mike Royko in *Boss*, his celebrated biography of the mayor, patronage and nepotism lay at the heart of the machine, and "nobody in the Machine [was] more family conscious than Chairman Daley." Loyalty was nearly as important. Mayor Daley used his position as party chairman to carefully control the selection of candidates at party meetings at the Morrison Hotel in the Loop. Creating slates that balanced the city's shifting ethnic and racial politics, as well as reform and machine agendas, Daley managed to win six mayoral elections, a remarkable achievement that reflected his considerable organizational and political skill. Mirroring national political trends, Daley moved from the left to the right as the 1960s progressed, a shift that Michael Madigan, then a young committeeman from the South Side, called the smartest political move he had ever seen.[48]

While scandals were frequent throughout his long tenure—particularly in the police department—Daley never paid a political price for corruption. Under his management, Chicago provided better public services than most American cities, a reputation that helped Daley become influential on the national scene. This was evident by 1960, when the Chicago mayor played a critical role in the presidential election of John F. Kennedy, the Irish American icon. Kennedy's election-eve visit to Chicago on November 4, 1960, was managed with the full organizational power of the machine: hundreds of thousands of people turned out to view a torchlight parade that proceeded down Michigan Avenue to Chicago Stadium, where nearly thirty thousand attended a rally that featured Daley and over one hundred entertainers. Kennedy received more proof of the machine's value on Election Day, when 89.3 percent of the city's eligible voters were reported to have voted. With Illinois turning out for Kennedy in a tight race, Chicago's Irish political boss played a key role in getting the first Irish Catholic elected president of the United States.[49]

In the political terms of the machine, Richard J. Daley managed the city's racial politics effectively, maintaining working relationships with William Dawson and other black submachine leaders and appealing to black voters without offending key white constituencies. The fact that he won every mayoral election is testament to the fact that he maintained African American voter support, as well as to the weakness of the Republican Party in the city. But in other ways, Daley's tenure sharpened racial tensions in Chicago to deadly effect. In many ways, he continued and accelerated Kennelly's public housing policies, concentrating poor, largely African American families in high-rise buildings firmly within the expanding Black Belt. Daley's ambitious development initiatives—massive construction projects such as the University of Illinois at Chicago's Circle campus and the Dan Ryan Expressway (named after the Irish American former president of the Cook County Board of Commissioners)—disrupted neighborhoods and cordoned off South Side black communities from the rest of the city. Daley did little to address problems in Chicago's public schools, seemingly following the cautionary advice that Edward Kelly had given him in his early years in the machine: "Avoid the public schools. They'll kill you."[50]

After 1963, Daley abandoned any pretense of New Deal politics, positioning himself against black criminality and youth radicalism. These politics were most notably represented by his infamous "Shoot to Kill" speech in April 1968, Daley's heavy-handed order to fire on rioters in west Chicago in the aftermath of the assassination of Martin Luther King. Daley's inability to fathom the demands for change was on full display that same year at the Democratic National Convention, where he unleashed the Chicago police and the National Guard against demonstrators.[51]

The outbreak of the Troubles in Northern Ireland in the late 1960s produced a similar response. The key events occurred in and outside of the city of Derry, where the Royal Ulster Constabulary (the police force in Northern Ireland) and Protestant extremists attacked the participants in controversial civil rights marches in October 1968 and January 1969. The resultant riots dramatically increased political instability in the province, bringing international media attention to the north of Ireland. Not surprisingly, images of beleaguered Ulster Catholics generated widespread sympathy from Irish Americans, who organized the American Congress for Irish Freedom and the National Association for Irish Justice (NAIJ) to raise funds and support. Both organizations had active branches in Chicago.

In August 1969, the NAIJ brought Bernadette Devlin on an American tour. Devlin was a charismatic and outspoken twenty-two-year-old Irish radical who had just been elected to the British Parliament. Irish Americans initially were enthusiastic about Devlin's visit, but she quickly alienated the conservative establishment with searing critiques of American racism. Devlin called Mayor Daley "a racist pig" and declared that she had no interest in meeting the Chicago leader. Daley struck back, recommending that money should be donated to the Irish Red Cross rather than Devlin. When she came to Chicago, only two hundred supporters greeted her at O'Hare Airport. Daley quietly left to spend the weekend at his summer home in Michigan. Daley's disapproval of Devlin and the New Left was clear, but so too was his broad sympathy for Irish nationalism and Northern Irish Catholics. When British soldiers killed thirteen demonstrators at Bloody Sunday in Derry in January 1972, the mayor caused an uproar in the British press by comparing the regiment to Nazi stormtroopers and promising to send $75,000 to the families of victims.[52]

Daley's final years in office were increasingly ineffectual. The aging mayor remained in political control, winning the 1975 election by nearly 58 percent over his Republican opponent. As his election victories showed, the mayor remained remarkably popular until his death. But in other ways, Daley's approach to Chicago politics no longer worked. With a Republican administration in office in Washington, federal resources were not quite so forthcoming. Moreover, the Civil Rights Act of 1964 and other federal statutes limited the machine's ability to dole out favors. Long denied access to certain sectors of municipal employment, African Americans increasingly challenged the discriminatory practices that had been at the heart of patronage politics. In 1970, the Afro-American Patrolmen's League brought suit against the Chicago Police Department, alleging discrimination against black policemen. Six years later, a federal judge ordered the department to hire more African Americans, a ruling that withheld key federal funds from the city. Daley was enraged, but he was unable to get Washington to provide the funds. The environment in Illinois politics was hardly more congenial for the Irish boss. James Thompson, the district attorney for northern Illinois and a future Republican governor, aggressively pursued top members of the Daley machine, convicting key friends and allies such as Matt Danaher and Tom Keane on corruption charges. The times had changed.[53]

Richard J. Daley died of a massive heart attack on December 20, 1976. In some ways, Chicago's political machine died with him. The city has had two more Irish American mayors: Jane Byrne (1979–83) and Richard M. Daley (1989–2011). Although the younger Daley was mayor for twenty-two years, a year longer than his famous father, he presided over a Chicago political scene that had been transformed by dramatic reductions in federal funding, white migration to the suburbs, and Harold Washington's successful 1983 mayoral campaign. Daley certainly shared some of his father's political tendencies, most notably his celebration of Ireland, his focus on business-friendly downtown development policies, and patronage scandals late in his tenure, but the machine he led was no longer the same. In 1993, the *Chicago Tribune*'s John Kass published a story on Richard M. Daley's looming departure from Bridgeport, a story that was getting big play across the city. The article focuses on the degree to which the Bridgeport of Daley's father no longer existed. Irish American families remained, Kass makes clear, living alongside Asian and Hispanic shopkeepers who worked hard and raised their families. But this was not the same Bridgeport. City Hall did not have the same resources to hand out, and both gentrification and urban decay had transformed the neighborhood. Eight months later, the Daleys left for a fashionable development just south of the Loop. Remarkably successful for half a century, Chicago's South Side powerbrokers, men like Edward Kelly and Richard J. Daley, had been unable to protect their constituents from change. Now the Daleys were leaving Bridgeport as well.[54]

CONCLUSION: IRISH IDENTITIES IN CONTEMPORARY ILLINOIS

In spring 1998, an Irish American magazine titled *World of Hibernia* listed the largest St. Patrick's Day festivals in the world. Two of the top ten were in Chicago: the city's official parade, inaugurated by Richard J. Daley in 1956, and a separate South Side parade that dated back to 1953. Both parades now feature thousands of marchers and regularly draw more than two hundred thousand spectators, clear illustrations of the continuing power of Irishness in Illinois.[1]

The dramatic success of Chicago's St. Patrick's Day parades reflects a broader renaissance of Irish cultural expression in the state over the last sixty years. This surge of popular interest in all things Irish has occurred despite a number of seemingly negative trends. Irish immigration continued to decline across the period. Only 6,559 Irish immigrants came to the United States in the 1970s, a number that increased in the 1980s with special visa programs introduced by influential Irish American congressmen in 1986 and 1990. These "new Irish" emigrants settled in urban centers such as New York, Boston, and Chicago, playing vital roles in the formation of vibrant underground communities. That said, their numbers were hardly sufficient to re-create Irish neighborhoods in the city. As traditional Irish urban neighborhoods moved to more homogenous suburbs and the power of the Irish political machine declined in the 1970s and beyond, popular interest in Irish cultural forms like Irish dancing, traditional music, and theater surged, creating Irish institutions that are now renowned around the world. Participating in these Irish cultural networks—whether it's watching the South Side Irish Parade or attending a performance of the Trinity Irish Dancers—has become an important element in what it means to be Irish in Illinois.[2]

One of the first developments in this renaissance occurred in higher education. In 1961, Emmet Larkin and Lawrence McCaffrey, two prominent historians who spent their careers teaching in Chicago, helped found the American Conference for Irish Studies, an organization dedicated to promoting research on Ireland and Irish America. Traditionally looked down upon as subfields of British and American scholarship, the study of Irish and Irish American history and literature mushroomed in the 1960s, providing opportunities for college students to take courses on Irish subjects and travel to the Emerald Isle in increasing numbers. The growing popularity of Irish studies in Illinois was reflected in the creation of academic and study-abroad programs at DePaul University, Illinois State University, Loyola University of Chicago, Northern Illinois University, and Southern Illinois University (SIU) in Carbondale. Irish studies has been particularly vibrant at SIU, which hosted an Irish and Irish Immigration Studies program directed by Charles Fanning, the pioneering scholar of Irish American literature. The American Conference for Irish Studies (ACIS) has grown to become the largest interdisciplinary Irish studies organization in the world. Illinois universities have continued to play an active role. The 2013 ACIS international meeting, hosted by DePaul and Northern Illinois University, brought nearly five hundred scholars to Chicago for four full days of academic presentations and cultural events. It was a far cry from the organization's small beginnings.

This same type of trajectory is evident in a wide range of more popular cultural forms. Irish dancing has become a staple of suburban and city life, with thousands of boys and girls donning traditional Irish costumes and ringleted wigs to practice and perform ceili and step dancing on a weekly basis. The most famous

Lawrence J. McCaffrey (1925–2020)
Lawrence John McCaffrey was a pioneering historian of the Irish in America and one of the cofounders of the American Conference for Irish Studies, the largest interdisciplinary Irish studies organization in the world. Born in Riverdale, Illinois, in 1925, McCaffrey received degrees from St. Ambrose University and Indiana University. He spent most of his academic career at Loyola University in Chicago, from which he retired in 1991. He was the author, coauthor, or editor of twelve books on the Irish and Irish American experiences. A tireless promoter of Irish studies across the Midwest region and nation, McCaffrey was selected to be a member of the Irish American Hall of Fame in 2016.

of the Chicago-based academies is the Trinity Academy of Irish Dance, founded in 1982. After Trinity won a number of awards in world competitions, Artistic Director Mark Howard founded the Trinity Irish Dance Company (1990), whose dancers often have fused traditional Irish dance with contemporary hip-hop and other cultural forms at critically lauded and popular performances. Chicago's Irish dance tradition received even greater international attention in the late 1990s with the popularity of *Riverdance*, an Irish traditional music and dance extravaganza that featured Michael Flatley, a South Side Chicago native who started his career at the Dennehy School of Irish Dance. The show now has been seen by over 25 million people, making it one of the most successful dance productions in world history.[3]

Chicago has also retained its reputation as a center of Irish traditional music, which underwent a second revival in the 1960s with the global success of groups like the Clancy Brothers, the Chieftains, and the Dubliners. The city was home to a lively scene in the 1970s, featuring renowned players like John McGreevy and Liz Carroll on fiddle, Eleanor Neary on piano, and Joe Shannon on uilleann pipes. Much of this was captured by the fieldwork of folklorists Mick Moloney and Miles Krassen, who recorded their music in a National Endowment for the Humanities–funded field study designed to preserve the story of Irish immigrant music in America. Most of the featured artists grew up and learned in South Side Irish homes, playing in sessions in bungalows and local bars with appreciative, if small, audiences. The Grammy-winning fiddler and composer Liz Carroll found inspiration there: "My parents would take me and my brother to see music down on 79th Street, where there used to be a place called Hanley's House of Happiness. They would have a live radio show on Sunday nights with lots of Irish musicians, and I really loved it." The expansion and growth of Irish traditional music in Chicago in more recent times was marked by the foundation of the Irish Music School of Chicago in 2003, dedicated to bringing younger players into contact with an older generation of Irish musicians. Traditional music lovers and performers now have a wealth of options to explore across the city, including active sessions in venues like Chief O'Neill's, the Galway Arms, Lanigan's Irish Pub, and Mrs. Murphy and Sons Irish Bistro.[4]

Many of the city's cultural programs have drawn support from the Irish American Heritage Center, founded in 1976 and located in Irving Park since 1985. The organization has a wide-

Liz Carroll (1956–)

Born on the South Side of Chicago in 1956 to Irish immigrant parents, Liz Carroll is an internationally acclaimed fiddler and composer. In 1974, she won the All-Ireland under-eighteen fiddle championship. She returned to Ireland the following year to win the senior championship, only the second American ever to do so. Carroll has been featured on eleven albums and was the first Irish American traditional musician to be nominated for a Grammy. An award-winning composer, Carroll wrote a companion piece to a 2015 exhibition at the Art Institute of Chicago titled "Ireland: Crossroads of Art and Design, 1690–1840."[5]

ranging mission, providing resources for Irish immigrants and supporting cultural programs on Irish dance, language, and theater. The center has hosted notable performances of Irish plays, including productions by the award-winning Irish Theatre of Chicago (originally the Seanachai Theatre Company), founded in 1993. The increasingly dynamic work of Irish filmmakers has been featured at the Chicago Irish Film Festival since 1999, dedicated to providing Chicago audiences with "a window into the color and complexity of Irish life." Originally located in Beverly, the festival has moved from its South Side roots, catering to citywide audiences at theaters in Logan Square and Noble Square.[6]

If the dynamism and growth of Irish academia, dance, film, music, and theater in Chicago and Illinois have been impressive in recent years, the number of participants in these successful cultural associations pales in comparison with those drawn by the dominant event of Irish expression in the state of Illinois: the St. Patrick's Day parade. The famous procession has a rather strange history in Chicago. The first official city parade was in 1843, but it was banned in 1869, only to be brought back by Mayor Daley in 1956. The parade became an annual celebration for the city's Irish community, quickly establishing itself as one of Chicago's most popular public events. By the early 1960s, city and regional television channels offered up to six hours of coverage of Chicago's St. Patrick's Day parade. Like so many other things in Daley's Chicago, the parade often was seen through political lens, as commentators scanned the review stand to see who was standing next to the mayor and thus currently in his favor. The city's most famous St. Patrick's Day custom, dying the Chicago River green, began in 1961.

Chicago's downtown parade on St. Patrick's Day is an impressive tradition, one of the most popular festivals in the world. The official parade, however popular, has little that makes its distinct from Irish parades in other American cities. What makes Chicago's St. Patrick's Day different is its second, unofficial parade on the same day: the South Side Irish Parade. While there was a long tradition of celebrating St. Patrick's Day along East Seventy-Ninth Street on the South Side, the first Southtown Parade occurred in 1953, a festival that quickly was subsumed by the city's official parade in 1960.

The South Side Parade was revived in 1979 by George Hendry and Pat Coakley, men who had moved from St. Sabina's and the Little Flower in Auburn to Morgan Park as part of the Irish exodus from inner-city parishes. The rebirth of the South Side Irish Parade was an explicit attempt to re-create the sense of community the men had known in their old neighborhoods for their children and their new "green" neighbors. On March 17, 1979, they set off with seventeen children, quickly dubbed the "Wee Folks of Washtenaw and Talman," leading a baby carriage decorated with shamrocks and the flags of the twenty-six counties of the Republic of Ireland down the sidewalks close to their home. Two years later, the South Side Irish Parade moved back to the streets, getting a permit from Mayor Jane Byrne to march down Western Avenue from 103rd Street to 115th. Starting with mass at St. Cajetan Church, the parade reconstructed a self-narrative of the Chicago Irish experience: firemen and policemen, Irish dancers and pipe bands, Boy Scouts and marching bands, unions and politicians. By the late 1990s, the parade was billed as the largest neighborhood-based St. Patrick's Day celebration outside of Dublin, regularly featuring fifteen thousand participants and over two hundred thousand spectators. The dramatic expansion of the parade created real problems, and the event was canceled in 2009 as a result of excessive alcohol consumption and related security concerns. It was revived in 2012, coming back with more participants than ever and a rebranded reputation as a more family-friendly event. In many ways, George Hendry, Pat Coakley, and their successors have succeeded where Irish American politicians failed, recreating the world of the traditional Chicago Irish parish—at least one day each year.[7]

Chicago is hardly the only place in Illinois that celebrates St. Patrick's Day. Marchers turn out by the hundreds of thousands for festivities across the state, including notable parades in Bloomington-Normal, Naperville, Rock Island, Rockford, and Peoria. The Rock Island event bills itself as the nation's only interstate parade, with marchers crossing over the Talbot Bridge to Davenport, Iowa, the traditional home of the largest Irish community in the Quad

Cities. Like their Chicago counterparts, the festivities often attract large crowds. In 2018, nearly twenty-five thousand people attended the thirty-eighth annual parade in Peoria, which made its way through the city center down to the banks of the Illinois River. Nor are these celebrations confined to St. Patrick's Day. Hundreds of communities across the state host Irish festivals throughout the year. Since 1997, for example, Carbondale has hosted the Southern Illinois Irish Festival, a celebration of Irish music and culture. There is no sign that Irishness is fading in Illinois.[8]

In 2010, 1.6 million people in Illinois claimed Irish ancestry. In at least twenty-five counties across the state, between 16 and 20 percent of the population described themselves as Irish. This contemporary portrait of the Irish in Illinois has clear echoes of the past, mirroring the stories featured in this book. Jo Daviess County had the fifth highest percentage of Irish Illinoisans in the state, reflecting both its origins as a heavily Irish mining community and Galena's popularity as a place to escape from the city. Other Illinois counties had similar settlement patterns. Three of the top seven counties on the list, Pope, Grundy, and LaSalle, were home to early Irish communities, the last two largely populated by workers on the Illinois and Michigan Canal. But the contemporary map of Irish Illinois is not just a product of

The St. Patrick Society Grand Parade, Quad Cities. Courtesy of the St. Patrick Society Quad Cities USA.

nineteenth-century migration. Heavy proportions of Irish Americans in DuPage, McHenry, and Will Counties reflect the postwar exodus from Chicago to the suburbs. What is striking, however, is the fact that substantial numbers of people in every part of the state claimed to be Irish. Men and women from Ireland played critical roles in the making of Illinois. Clearly, many remained in the state.[9]

The current popularity of being Irish in Illinois also speaks to the appeal of these stories. Irish settlers were here from the earliest days of European settlement, fighting in a series of wars against Native Americans, struggling against British rule in the American Revolution, and defending the Union in the American Civil War. More Irish immigrants fled to the state to escape the horrors of the Irish famine, and here they dug canals, worked in domestic service, and labored in the meatpacking industry in a rapidly growing Chicago. Faced with often fierce ethnic and religious discrimination, Irish immigrants banded together through the Catholic Church, Irish nationalist organizations like Clan na Gael and the Ancient Order of Hibernians, and the Democratic Party, using their numbers to establish the legitimacy of their presence in the city and the state. By 1890, it had largely worked, and the Irish rose to positions of influence in the Catholic Church, labor unions, and above all, city politics, where the Chicago Irish helped form and run machines that would dominate municipal and state politics in twentieth-century Illinois. Irish success had an immense impact on the modern history of immigration. When new immigrants came to America, it was often Irish America they encountered. While these interactions were often acrimonious and violent, it was the Irish example that mattered in the long run. In this sense, Irish integration and success in Illinois (and the United States) paved the way for future immigrants.

By the early twentieth century, Irish figures had risen to positions of considerable influence in business, politics, and religion. For most Irish men and women, however, the rise to respectability was gradual at best and characterized by struggle. Not all of these fights were with employers or elites; the Irish often struggled against other ethnic or racial groups. The relationship between the Irish and African Americans was particularly fraught in twentieth-century Illinois, especially in Chicago. While some actively fought against racial integration and some community leaders worked hard to smooth transitions in local parish communities, the more characteristic Irish response was flight, as families moved from Bridgeport, Canaryville, and Washington Park to Beverly, Morgan Park, and various Chicago suburbs. Once there, some Irish Americans attempted to re-create and express their attachment to Ireland and being Irish through parades and support for Irish dance, film, traditional music, and theater. The dynamic growth of these organizations is testament to the continuing allure of Irish culture and the influence and success of Irish Americans in Illinois.

What does it mean to be Irish in Illinois today, and what will it mean in the future? There are no simple answers. For many, being Irish is intertwined into the rhythms of everyday life, taking children to Irish dance lessons, going to a popular session at an Irish pub, or watching the Irish soccer team advance in the European Championships or the World Cup. For others, it may be more intermittent, participating in a St. Patrick's Day parade or traveling to Ireland on a family vacation. And for still others, it involves a certain nostalgia, a desire for a simpler time amid the complexity and diversity of contemporary American and Irish life. Whatever form it takes, there is no doubt that Illinois residents will continue to celebrate their attachment to Ireland. In many ways, the strength of that commitment is the real legacy of the Irish in Illinois.

Celebrating Ireland at the Southern Illinois Irish Festival. Courtesy of the Southern Illinois Irish Festival.

For Further Reading

Notes

Bibliography

Index

FOR FURTHER READING

Anyone seeking a better understanding of the Irish in Illinois must begin with the history of Ireland. Many general studies are readily available to both popular and scholarly audiences alike. Thomas Bartlett's *Ireland: A History* (Cambridge, 2010) is an impressive survey of Irish history and culture from the medieval era to the present. Readers will also want to explore older yet valuable perspectives in T. W. Moody and F. X. Martin, ed., *The Course of Irish History* (Cork, 1978); Roy Foster, *Modern Ireland: 1600–1972* (New York, 1989); and Thomas E. Hachey, Joseph M. Hernon Jr., and Lawrence J. McCaffrey, *The Irish Experience: A Concise History* (New York, 1996). For a thoughtful review of new work, see Richard Bourke and Ian McBride, eds., *The Princeton History of Modern Ireland* (Princeton, NJ, 2016).

Few if any events had as dramatic an impact on the history of modern Ireland as the Great Famine. Two books serve as excellent starting points: Peter Gray's *The Irish Famine* (London, 1995), a beautifully illustrated and concise introduction to the subject, and James S. Donnelly Jr.'s *The Great Irish Potato Famine* (Gloucestershire, 2001), a thoughtful synthesis of the best academic work on the Irish famine. A much older yet popular account can be found in Cecil Woodham-Smith, *The Great Hunger: Ireland, 1845–1849* (New York, 1962). Ireland's leading historian of the Irish famine, Cormac Ó Gráda, puts the Irish experience in global context in *Famine: A Short History* (Princeton, NJ, 2010). For an excellent microhistory that details how the famine affected one small community in the west of Ireland, see Robert James Scally, *The End of Hidden Ireland: Rebellion, Famine, and Emigration* (Oxford, 1995).

The broad history of Irish emigration is a vast subject. After all, the modern Irish diaspora spans the globe. Since the 1990s, scholars have intensified their examinations of Irish immigration to New Zealand, Australia, Canada, Brazil, Argentina, and South Africa. Among the first studies to address the totality of this migration was Patrick O'Sullivan's six-volume study of the Irish abroad, *The Irish World Wide: History, Heritage, Identity* (London, 1992). As more comparative scholarship on the Irish diaspora began to emerge, it became clear that the Irish Catholic experience in the United States differed from others. Among the most significant and controversial works to address these issues remains Donald Harmon Akenson's *The Irish Diaspora: A Primer* (Toronto, 1993). For various introductions to the Irish experience in differing settings, see Roger Swift and Sheridan Gilley, *The Irish in Britain, 1815–1939* (Savage, MD, 1989); Bruce S. Elliott, *Irish Migrants in the Canadas: A New Approach* (Montreal, 1988); Malcolm Campbell, *Ireland's New Worlds: Immigrants, Politics, and Society in the United States and Australia, 1815–1922* (Madison, WI, 2008); Donald H. Akenson, *The Irish in South Africa* (Grahamstown, 1990); Helen Kelly, *Irish 'Ingleses': The Irish Immigration Experience in Argentina, 1840–1920* (Dublin, 2009); and Oliver Marshall, *English, Irish and Irish-American Pioneer Settlers in Nineteenth-Century Brazil* (Oxford, 2005).

The Irish American experience nevertheless continues to be the most studied and scrutinized aspect of the diaspora. With good cause. Between the late seventeenth and early twentieth centuries, over 5 million Irish men, women, and children immigrated to the United States. Today an estimated 34 million Americans claim "Irish" as part of their ancestry—more than four times the number of Irish descendants in the rest of the diaspora. For two excellent and readable introductions to the history of Irish America, see Jay P. Dolan, *The Irish Americans: A History* (New York, 2008), and Kevin Kenny, *The American Irish: A History* (New York, 2000). More detailed works have emphasized the importance of Ireland in the making of Irish America. Among the most influential of these, Kerby A. Miller, *Emigrants and Exiles: Ireland and the Irish Exodus to North America* (New York, 1985), argues that premodern Irish cultural worldviews made the transition to American life all the more difficult for many Irish emigrants. Others, such as Lawrence J. McCaffrey, *The Irish Catholic Diaspora in America* (Washington, DC, 1997), emphasize the importance of Catholicism in the Irish American experience. Still others, such as J. J. Lee and Marion R. Casey, ed., *Making the Irish American: History and Heritage of the Irish in the United States* (New York, 2006), argue that the history of Irish America is one of economic and social success—even to the point where that success risks erasing their ethnic identity.

Historians have begun to widen the scope of Irish American studies in recent years. As increasing numbers of American Protestants self-identify as Irish, scholars have written more inclusive histories. For a recent historiographical look at this approach, see Kevin Kenny, ed., *New Directions in Irish-American History* (Madison, WI, 2003). Earlier works that have influenced this trend include Donald Harmon Akenson, *Small Differences: Irish Catholics and Irish Protestants, 1815–1922; An International Perspective* (Montreal, 1988). See also Deirdre Moloney, "Who's Irish? Ethnic Identity and Recent Trends in Irish American History," *Journal of American Ethnic History* 28, no. 4 (Summer 2009): 100–109.

Studies of Irish migration during the colonial and Revolutionary eras have long accounted for multiple religious backgrounds. After all, most eighteenth-century Irish migrants were Presbyterian. For a model study that places Presbyterian migration in an Atlantic World framework, see Patrick Griffin, *The People with No Name: Ireland's Ulster Scots, America's Scots Irish, and the Creation of a British Atlantic World, 1689–1764* (Princeton, NJ, 2001). For an exhaustive and insightful analysis of immigrant correspondence, see Kerby A. Miller, Arnold Schrier, Bruce D. Boling, and David N. Doyle, ed., *Irish Immigrants in the Land of Canaan: Letters and Memoirs from Colonial and Revolutionary America* (New York, 2003). See also Warren R. Hofstra, ed., *Ulster to America: The Scots-Irish Migration Experience, 1680–1930* (Knoxville, TN, 2012). During the American Revolution, Protestant and Catholic migrants could be found on both sides of the Patriot-Loyalist divide. See David Noel Doyle, *Ireland, Irishmen, and Revolutionary America* (Dublin, 1981). For two insightful examinations of the roles that Irish men and women played in the foundation of the United States, see Maurice Bric, *Ireland, Philadelphia, and the Re-invention of America, 1760–1800* (Dublin, 2008), and David A. Wilson, *United Irishmen, United States: Immigrant Radicals in the Early Republic* (Ithaca, NY, 1998).

Historians have focused on nineteenth-century Irish Catholic migration to the United States, which began to outpace that of Irish Protestants during the 1830s. Admittedly, the years prior to the Great Famine (1845–51) have received less attention, and the field is long overdue for a new synthesis. The most readable account for this period continues to be George Potter, *To the Golden Door: The Story of the Irish in Ireland and America* (Boston, 1960). Potter tragically died before he completed the text, which consequently does not contain notes. An older yet relevant work is William Forbes Adams, *Ireland and Irish Emigration to the New World: From 1815 to the Famine* (New Haven, CT, 1932). As for the famine and postfamine years, the aforementioned works by Miller and McCaffrey remain the standards. As these historians have made clear, it was this era that saw the formation of the Irish American stereotype: Catholic, Democratic, and nationalist. In general, Irish women, whose numbers began to outpace that of Irish men during the late nineteenth century, fared better. See Hasia Diner, *Erin's Daughters in America: Irish American Women in the Nineteenth Century* (Baltimore, 1983), and Janet A. Nolan, *Ourselves Alone: Women's Emigration from Ireland, 1885–1920* (Lexington, KY, 1989).

Naturally, region and locale had a very real impact on the Irish Catholic experience in America. A majority carved out new lives in American cities. For some, upward mobility came slowly. The first case study of an Irish ghetto was Oscar Handlin, *Boston's Immigrants: A Study in Acculturation* (Cambridge, MA, 1941). Similar works followed for other Massachusetts communities, such as Stephen Thernstrom, *Poverty and Progress* (Cambridge, MA, 1964), and Timothy Meagher's *Inventing Irish America: Generation, Class, and Ethnic Identity in a New England City, 1880–1928* (South Bend, IN, 2001). Most historians have found that to varying degrees, the Irish fared much better outside of New England. See Dennis Clark, *The Irish in Philadelphia* (Philadelphia, 1973); Earl F. Niehaus, *The Irish in New Orleans* (New York, 1976); Jo Ellen McNergney Vinyard, *The Irish on the Urban*

Frontier: Detroit, 1850–1880 (New York, 1976); Grace McDonald, *History of the Irish in Wisconsin in the Nineteenth Century* (New York, 1976); and Ronald H. Bayer and Timothy Meagher, ed., *The New York Irish* (Baltimore, 1996). The most recent scholarship maintains that the farther west the Irish went, the greater opportunity and material success they found. See David M. Emmons, *Beyond the American Pale: The Irish in the West, 1845–1910* (Norman, OK, 2010), and R. A. Burchell, *The San Francisco Irish, 1848–1880* (Berkeley, CA, 1980).

Turning toward Illinois, only two outdated works address the plight of the Irish in the Prairie State as a whole. Both were written in the early twentieth century, and neither is a full-length study. See P. T. Barry, *The First Irish in Illinois: Reminiscent of Old Kaskaskia Days* (Chicago, 1902), and John P. McGoorty, "The Early Irish of Illinois," *Transactions of the Illinois State Historical Society* 34 (1927): 54–64. Consequently, researchers of the Irish in the Prairie State will find regional histories of immigration to be useful. See Mark Wyman, *Immigrants in the Valley: Irish, Germans, and Americans in the Upper Mississippi Country, 1830–1860* (Carbondale, IL, 1984), and Daniel Elazar, *Cities of the Prairie: The Metropolitan Frontier and American Politics* (New York, 1970).

A scant number of books and articles explore the Irish in downstate communities. An excellent overview can be found in Eileen M. McMahon, "Illinois," in *The Encyclopedia of the Irish in America*, edited by Michael Glazier (Notre Dame, IN, 1999). Two important works have examined the lives of Irish immigrants in Bloomington-Normal: Greg Koos, *Irish Immigrants in McLean County, Illinois* (Bloomington, IN, 2000), and Glenda Riley, "From Ireland to Illinois: Life of Helen Ross Hall," *Illinois Historical Journal* 81, no. 3 (Autumn 1988): 162–80. For a fascinating narrative about Rock Island's most notorious Irish gangster, see Richard Hamer and Roger Ruthhart, *Citadel of Sin: The John Looney Story* (Moline, IL, 2007).

Despite claims that Irish Catholics in America lacked proper farming skills and were "psychologically unsuited for rural America," as Lawrence McCaffrey has argued, a significant minority of Irish immigrants became farmers in the Prairie State. More work remains to be done on this subject. For a genealogy of Irish farmers in central Illinois, see Paul J. Curtin, *West Limerick Roots: The Laurence Curtin Family of Knockbrack, County Limerick, Ireland* (Austin, TX, 1995). Larger explorations of immigrant farming outside of Illinois can be found in Malcolm Campbell, *Ireland's New Worlds: Immigrants, Politics, and Society in the United States and Australia, 1815–1922* (Madison, WI, 2008); Leonard R. Riforgiato, "Bishop John Timon, Archbishop John Hughes, and Irish Colonization: A Clash of Episcopal Views on the Future of the Irish and the Catholic Church in America," in *Immigration to New York*, edited by William Pencak et al. (Cranbury, NJ, 1991); Edward J. Maguire, ed., *Reverend John O'Hanlon's The Irish Emigrant Guide for the United States* (New York, 1976); and James P. Shannon, *Catholic Colonization on the Western Frontier* (New Haven, CT, 1957).

Recent studies of Illinois's Irish during the Civil War include Ryan W. Keating, *Shades of Green: Irish Regiments, American Soldiers, and Local Communities in the Civil War Era* (New York, 2017), and Lawrence J. McCaffrey, "Preserving the Union: Shaping a New Image of Chicago's Irish Catholics and the Civil War," in *Fighting Irish in the American Civil War and the Invasion of Mexico*, edited by Arthur H. Mitchell (Jefferson, NC, 2017).

The overwhelming majority of published works on the Irish in Illinois have focused on Chicago. The starting point for any new research is Lawrence J. McCaffrey, et al., *The Irish in Chicago* (Chicago, 1987). This edited collection contains insightful chapters by leading scholars on the city's Irish population and Catholicism, politics, nationalist organizations, and culture. James R. Barrett's *The Irish Way: Becoming American in the Multiethnic City* (New York, 2012) is another valuable resource. While not an exclusive study of the Windy City, Barrett explores how the Chicago Irish, along with their counterparts in New York and Boston, forged an urban path that ensuing waves of immigrants followed.

The Great Chicago Fire of 1871 and the legend of Mrs. O'Leary's cow have garnered the attention of historians. See Richard F. Bales, "Did the Cow Do It? A New Look at the Cause of the Great Chicago Fire," *Illinois Historical Journal* 90, no. 1 (Spring 1997): 2–24. For overviews of the calamity and its far-reaching consequences, see Ross Miller, *The Great Chicago Fire* (Urbana, IL, 2000), and Karen Sawislak, *Smoldering City: Chicagoans and the Great Fire, 1871–1874* (Chicago, 1995).

Irish Catholicism in Chicago has been well studied. For a general overview, see Ellen Skerrett, "The Catholic Dimension," in *The Irish in Chicago*, edited by Lawrence J. McCaffrey et al. For two recent histories of the diverse impacts nuns have had on Chicago history, see Mary Beth Fraser Connolly, *Women of Faith: The Chicago Sisters of Mercy and the Evolution of a Religious Community* (New York, 2014), and Suellen Hoy, *Good Hearts: Catholic Sisters in Chicago's Past* (Urbana, IL, 2006). For a useful, if more specialized, study, see Ellen Skerrett, "The Irish of Chicago's Hull-House Neighborhood," in *New Perspectives on the Irish Diaspora*, edited by Charles Fanning (Carbondale, IL, 2000). For an excellent study of Catholic integration and Chicago's public schools, see Mimi Cowan, "'We Know Neither Catholics, nor Protestants, nor Free-Thinkers Here': Ethnicity, Religion, and the Chicago Public Schools, 1837–94," in *Religion and Greater Ireland: Christianity and Irish Global Networks, 1750–1950*, edited by Colin Barr and Hilary M. Carey (Montreal, 2015). Historians have also made great strides in exploring the connections between Catholicism and race. For two pioneering studies, see John T. McGreevy, *Parish Boundaries: The Catholic Encounter with Race in the Twentieth-Century Urban North* (Chicago, 1996), and Eileen M. McMahon, *What Parish Are You From? A Chicago Irish Community & Race Relations* (Lexington, KY, 1995).

Scholars have long studied the threads that bound together Irish laborers and nationalists with politics in nineteenth-century Chicago. Readers should begin with Michael F. Funchion, "The Political and Nationalist Dimensions," in *The Irish in Chicago*, edited by Lawrence J. McCaffrey et al. (Urbana, IL, 1987). Funchion observes that Irish politicians did not find success in municipal politics by clustering in ethnic enclaves. Rather, they built coalitions with other immigrant communities. At the street level, as James R. Barrett shows, neighborhood gangs and labor unions became the foundation of Chicago's political machines. Sam Mitrani's *Rise of the Chicago Police Department, 1850–1894* (Urbana, IL, 2013) includes information on the importance of Irish police officers and city politicians. Into the late nineteenth century, labor organizers borrowed tactics from the struggle for Irish independence, such as boycotting. Less controversial than strikes, these methods were often preferred by Irish union leaders with ties to municipal politics. See Richard Schneirov, *Labor and Urban Politics: Class Conflict and the Origins of Modern Liberalism in Chicago, 1864–97* (Urbana, IL, 1998), and Eric L. Hirsch, *Urban Revolt: Ethnic Politics in the Nineteenth-Century Chicago Labor Movement* (Berkeley, CA, 1990).

The threat posed by Irish Catholic political power often led to the growth of nativism in the United States. Surprisingly, little work has been published on the subject for the city of Chicago (or Illinois, for that matter). For the standard work on nativism in American history, see John Higham, *Strangers in the Land: Patterns of American Nativism, 1860–1925* (New Brunswick, NJ, 1955). Another important monograph is the older yet relevant study by Ray Allen Billington, *The Protestant Crusade: A Study of the Origins of American Nativism, 1800–1860* (New York, 1938). In *Paddy and the Republic: Ethnicity and Nationality in Antebellum America* (Middletown, CT, 1986), Dale T. Knobel emphasizes Irish ethnicity over religion as the cause for xenophobia. This is an area where new research is greatly needed.

In Chicago and other cities around the country, Irish Americans countered nativist forces by promoting an independent Ireland. Many found respectability within the social networks offered by nationalist organizations such as Clan na Gael. Gillian O'Brien has explored these and other connections in her evocative study of the murder of Dr. P. H. Cronin, *Blood Runs Green: The Murder That Transfixed Gilded Age Chicago* (Chicago, 2015). Two excellent studies of the broader phenomenon of Irish American nationalism are Thomas N. Brown, *Irish-American Nationalism, 1870–1890* (Philadelphia, 1966), and David Brundage, *Irish Nationalists in America: The Politics of Exile, 1798–1998* (Oxford, 2016). Outside of Chicago, the centennial of Ireland's 1916 Easter Rising gave rise to related studies, including Robert Schmuhl, *Ireland's Exiled Children: America and the Easter Rising* (Oxford, 2016), and Miriam Nyhan Grey, *Ireland's Allies: America and the 1916 Easter Rising* (Dublin, 2016).

Several important studies focus on the roles that Irish women played in Chicago's labor unions and political movements. Without a doubt, the state's most renowned female labor activist was Mary Harris "Mother" Jones. While her life's work took her around the country, biographers remember her experiences in Illinois and Chicago as formative. See Eliott J. Gorn, *Mother Jones: The Most Dangerous Woman in America* (New York, 2001), and Simon Cordery, *Mother Jones: Raising Cain and Consciousness* (Albuquerque, NM, 2010). Likewise, Chicago's Margaret A. Haley became one of America's most influential organizers of teacher unions. See Kate Rousmaniere, *Citizen Teacher: The Life of Margaret Haley* (Albany, NY, 2005), and Robert L. Reid, ed., *Battleground: The Autobiography of Margaret A. Haley* (Urbana, IL, 1982). For a broader examination of this subject, see Janet Nolan, *Servants of the Poor: Teachers and Mobility in Ireland and Irish America* (Notre Dame, IN, 2004).

The political machine built by Irish Democrats in the twentieth century has long attracted scholarly attention. For an important study of reform efforts and municipal politics that led to the big-city machine, see James L. Merriner, *Grafters and Goo Goos: Corruption and Reform in Chicago* (Carbondale, IL, 2004). For a biographical study of Chicago's first machine-style mayor, see Roger Biles, *Big City Boss in Depression and War: Mayor Edward J. Kelly of Chicago* (DeKalb, IL, 1984). The origins and legacies of Richard J. Daley's machine have been examined numerous times. See Adam Cohen and Elizabeth Taylor, *American Pharaoh: Mayor Richard J. Daley; His Battle for Chicago and the Nation* (Boston, 2000); Milton J. Rakove, *Don't Make No Waves—Don't Back No Losers: An Insider's Analysis of the Daley Machine* (Bloomington, IL, 1975); and Mike Royko, *Boss: Richard J. Daley of Chicago* (New York, 1971). Nationally, the most comprehensive work of machine politics remains Stephen Erie, *Rainbow's End: Irish-Americans and the Dilemmas of Urban Machine Politics* (Berkeley, CA, 1988). Erie rejects the conclusions of other studies that argue that the Irish found economic and social mobility in politics. For an excellent study of African American politics that is critical of Erie's ethnic rivalry thesis, see William Grimshaw, *Bitter Fruit: Black Politics and the Chicago Machine, 1931–1991* (Chicago, 1991). See also Daniel Patrick Moynihan, "The Irish," in *Beyond the Melting Pot: Jews, Italians, and Irish of New York City*, edited by Nathan Glazier and Daniel Patrick Moynihan (Cambridge, MA, 1963).

Historians continue to explore the causes and implications of racial animosities between Chicago's Irish and black populations. The essential starting point for any understanding of the African American experience in Chicago is St. Clair Drake and Horace R. Cayton's landmark *Black Metropolis: A Study of Negro Life in a Northern City* (New York, 1945). The most important work on community relations, Arnold R. Hirsch's *Making the Second Ghetto: Race and Housing in Chicago, 1940–60* (Cambridge, 1983), discusses how Irish Catholics strove to prevent African Americans from settling in white ethnic neighborhoods after World War II. For a similar study involving white ethnic Catholics in the urban North, see John T. McGreevy, *Parish Boundaries: The Catholic Encounter with Race in the Twentieth-Century Urban North* (Chicago, 1996). Accounts of the 1919 Race Riot, while not specifically dedicated to an examination of the city's Irish, are must-reads for the subject: David F. Krugler, *1919, the Year of Racial Violence: How African Americans*

Fought Back (Cambridge, 2014), and William M. Tuttle, *Race Riot: Chicago and the Red Summer of 1919* (New York, 1970).

As African Americans increasingly resettled in Chicago's inner city, Irish Americans fled to the suburbs. For an in-depth look at how one South Side neighborhood faced these changes, see Margaret Lee, "Shamrocks and Segregation: The Persistence of Upper-Class Irish Ethnicity in Beverly Hills, Chicago," in *After the Flood: Irish America, 1945–1960*, edited by James S. Rogers and Matthew J. O'Brien (Dublin, 2009). For a broader study of suburbanization in Chicago, see Elaine Lewinnek, *The Working Man's Reward: Chicago's Early Suburbs and the Roots of American Sprawl* (Oxford, 2014).

The Irish certainly left their cultural imprint on Chicago, from St. Patrick's Day parades to Irish music and literature, and it is difficult to imagine the Windy City without the Irish. Literary scholars and historians alike continue to examine the significance that Finley Peter Dunne and James T. Farrell had on Chicago history. See Finley Peter Dunne, *Mr. Dooley and the Chicago Irish: The Autobiography of a Nineteenth-Century Ethnic Group*, edited by Charles Fanning (Washington, DC, 1976); Charles Fanning, *Finley Peter Dunne and Mr. Dooley: The Chicago Years* (Lexington, KY, 1978); and Charles Fanning, "James T. Farrell and Irish-American Fiction," in *The Irish Voice in America: Irish-American Fiction from the 1760s to the 1980s* (Lexington, KY, 1990). For well over a century, Chicagoans of all backgrounds have enjoyed traditional Irish music. See Nicholas Carolan, *A Harvest Saved: Francis O'Neill and Irish Music in Chicago* (Cork, 1997), and Fintan Vallely, *The Companion to Irish Traditional Music* (Cork, 1998). And what would St. Patrick's Day in Chicago be without the dyeing of the Chicago River? For an excellent overview, see Daryl Adair and Mike Cronin, *The Wearing of the Green: A History of St. Patrick's Day* (New York, 2002).

The bulk of new research opportunities lie outside of Chicago, and here scholars will want to begin by consulting general histories of the Prairie State. The most recent of these explores the political, social, and economic development of the state. See Roger Biles, *Illinois: A History of the Land and Its People* (DeKalb, IL, 2005). Other noteworthy syntheses include Richard J. Jensen, *Illinois: A History* (1978; repr., Chicago: 2001), and Robert P. Howard, *Illinois: A History of the Prairie State* (Grand Rapids, MI, 1972). Valuable annotated bibliographies and historiographical essays can be found in Ellen M. Whitney et al., *Illinois History: An Annotated Bibliography* (Westport, CT, 1995), and *Journal of the Illinois State Historical Society*, 111, nos. 1–2 (Spring–Summer 2018).

Many will find useful resources in digitized contemporary histories from the nineteenth century. Examples include John Reynolds, *The Pioneer History of Illinois: Containing the Discovery in 1673, and the History of the Country to the Year 1818, When the State Government Was Organized* (Belleville, IL, 1852); *The History of Jo Daviess County, Illinois* (Chicago, 1878); W. T. Norton, *Centennial History of Madison County,*

Illinois and Its People, 1812–1912, 2 vols. (Chicago, 1912); Henry S. Beebe, *History of Peru* (Peru, IL, 1858); U. J. Hoffman, *History of La Salle County, Illinois*, (Chicago, 1906); W. W. Stevens, *Past and Present of Will County, Illinois* (Chicago: 1907); and Alfred Theodore Andreas, *History of Chicago: From the Earliest Period to the Present Time*, 3 vols. (Chicago, 1886). These are but a few of many readily available works.

Moving forward, historians will want to look in both expected and unexpected places for new information on the Irish of Illinois. Whether researching politics, religion, labor, race, or urban development, they may find references to the Irish in the indexes of many related monographs. An impressive body of work on canal diggers and railroad workers is one good example. See Peter Way, *Common Labor: Workers and the Digging of North American Canals, 1780–1860* (Baltimore, 1993), and Ryan Dearinger, *The Filth of Progress: Immigrants, Americans, and the Building of Canals and Railroads in the West* (Oakland, CA, 2016). Scholars will be able to take a similar approach to Illinois's Irish during the American Civil War. See Mark Hubbard, ed., *Illinois's War: The Civil War in Documents* (Athens, OH, 2013). Beyond this, dozens of relatively untapped historical societies and libraries across the state await the attention of new researchers. The free newspaper database operated by the University of Illinois is an excellent starting place for any history of the Irish in Illinois. For this critical resource, see https://idnc.library.illinois.edu.

NOTES

Introduction

1. Thomas Shaw, *Story of the LaSalle Mission*, 1:15, 23, 27–37, 55, 75; Henry S. Beebe, *History of Peru*, 138; Ryan Dearinger, *The Filth of Progress: Immigrants, Americans, and the Building of Canals and Railroads in the West*, 78; U. J. Hoffman, *History of La Salle County, Illinois*, 189; Eileen M. McMahon, "Canal Diggers, Church Builders: Dispelling Stereotypes of the Irish on the Irish and Michigan Canal Corridor," 52, 58–60, 68–69.

2. Department of the Interior, Census Office, *Report of the Population of the United States at the Eleventh Census, 1890*, 607, 686; Reboot Illinois, "Top 25 Counties in Illinois with the Most Luck o' the Irish," HuffPost, updated December 6, 2017, https://www.huffingtonpost.com/reboot-illinois/top-25-counties-in-illino_b_9491428.html; *Chicago Tribune*, March 15, 2015.

3. See Lawrence J. McCaffrey et al., *The Irish in Chicago* for an excellent introduction to that topic.

4. David Emmons, *Beyond the Pale: The Irish in the American West, 1845–1910.*

5. Jay Dolan, *The Irish Americans: A History*, 303–7.

6. For discussion of this era, see Sean Connolly, *Religion, Law, and Power: The Making of Protestant Ireland, 1660–1760*, particularly 263–313. For more recent narratives, see Jane Ohlmeyer, "Conquest, Civilization, Colonization: Ireland, 1540–1660," and Ultan Gillen, "Ascendancy Ireland, 1660–1800," in Bourke and McBride, *Princeton History of Modern Ireland*, 21–73.

7. Kevin Kenny, *The American Irish: A History*, 7–44. For more specialized scholarship on Ulster, see R. J. Dickson, *Ulster Emigration to Colonial America, 1718–1775*; Patrick Griffin, *The People with No Name: Ireland's Ulster Scots, America's Scots Irish, and the Creation of a British Atlantic World, 1689–1784*; Kerby A. Miller et al., *Irish Immigrants in the Land of Canaan: Letters and Memoirs from Colonial and Revolutionary America*; Maurice Bric, *Ireland, Philadelphia and the Re-invention of America, 1760–1800*; David A. Wilson, *United Irishmen, United States: Immigrant Radicals in the Early Republic*. On 1798 in Ireland, see Thomas Bartlett, ed., *1798: A Bicentenary Perspective*; and Guy Beiner: *Forgetful Remembrance: Social Forgetting and Vernacular Historiography of a Rebellion in Ulster.*

8. Miller, *Emigrants and Exiles: Ireland and the Irish Exodus to North America*, 193–279.

9. John Mitchel, *The Last Conquest of Ireland (Perhaps)*; James S. Donnelly Jr., *The Great Irish Potato Famine*. For a concise and beautifully illustrated introduction to the Irish famine, see Peter Gray, *The Irish Famine*.

10. Kenny, *American Irish*, 131.

11. Kenny, *American Irish*, 7–8, 45–46, 89–90, 131, 181–85, 221–25. See also Hasia Diner, *Erin's Daughters in America: Irish Immigrant Women in the Nineteenth Century*; and Janet Nolan, *Ourselves Alone: Women's Emigration from Ireland, 1885–1920*.

12. "Fact Sheet: Immigrants in Illinois," American Immigration Council, last modified October 4, 2017, https://americanimmigrationcouncil.org/research/immigrants-in-illinois.

1. From Imperial Soldiers to Prairie Patriots

1. David Noel Doyle, "Scots Irish or Scotch Irish?" 151; Kevin Kenny, "Editor's Introduction," 15.

2. The American Bottom was so named because it contained as much as three-quarters of the Illinois Country's American population. See John P. McGoorty, "The Early Irish of Illinois," 59.

3. P. T. Barry, *The First Irish in Illinois: Reminiscent of Old Kaskaskia Days*, 1; McGoorty, "Early Irish," 54. See also Eileen M. McMahon, "Illinois," 401.

4. Harman Murtagh, "Irish Soldiers Abroad, 1600–1800," 294–314; Barry, *First Irish in Illinois*, 1; McGoorty, "Early Irish," 54–55; Roger Biles, *Illinois: A History of the Land and Its People*, 6–8; Michael J. O'Brien, *The McCarthys in Early American History*, 136; Daniel Royot, *Divided Loyalties in a Doomed Empire*, 79.

5. McMahon, "Illinois," 401; Barry, *First Irish*, 2.

6. Nicholas B. Wainwright, *George Croghan: Wilderness Diplomat*, 112–13.

7. Fintan O'Toole, *White Savage: William Johnson and the Invention of America*, 16–47; Richard White, *The Middle Ground: Indians, Empires, and Republics in the Great Lakes Region, 1650–1815*.

8. McGoorty, "Early Irish," 55; Wainwright, *George Croghan*, 201–38. See also Daniel Richter, *Facing East from Indian Country: A Native History of Early America*, 191–211. Fort Kaskaskia was garrisoned by the 18th Royal Irish Infantry following Croghan's negotiations. See Barry, *First Irish*, 2–5.

9. John E. Kleber, *Encyclopedia of Louisville*, 524–25.

10. Wainwright, *George Croghan*, 3–4. See also Albert T. Volwiler, *George Croghan and the Westward Movement, 1741–1782*, 183–88; White, *Middle Ground*, 303–4.

11. Patrick Griffin, "Searching for Independence: Revolutionary Kentucky, Irish American Experience, and Scotch-Irish Myth, 1770s-1790s," 211–32; Bernard W. Sheehan, "'The Famous Hair Buyer General': Henry Hamilton, George Rogers Clark, and the American Indian," 1–28.

12. Biles, *Illinois*, 36–37. See also Lowell H. Harrison, *George Rogers Clark and the War in the West*; William H. English, *Conquest of the Country Northwest of the River Ohio 1778–1783 and Life of General George Rogers Clark.*

13. Barry, *First Irish*, 8; McGoorty, "Early Irish," 55–57; English, quoted in Edward Fitzpatrick, "Early Irish Settlers of Kentucky," 142.

14. McGoorty, "Early Irish," 57–61. Another Irishman, a trader named William Arundel, settled in Cahokia before the 1780s. He, Brady, McCarty, and a handful of hunters were the only white men, aside from French Canadians, residing in the Illinois Territory before Clark's arrival. See Barry, *First Irish*, 9–10; John Reynolds, *The Pioneer History of Illinois: Containing the Discovery in 1673 . . .*, 89–90, 128.

15. Miller et al., *Irish Immigrants in the Land of Canaan*, 552n31; Reynolds, *Pioneer History of Illinois*, 143–44.

16. Biles, *Illinois*, 28–30.

17. "Resident Population and Apportionment of the U.S. House of Representatives: Illinois," U.S. Census Bureau, last modified December 28, 2000 https://www.census.gov/dmd/www/resapport/states/illinois.pdf; Biles, *Illinois*, 32.

18. McGoorty, "Early Irish," 62–63; Barry, *First Irish*, 13–14; Reynolds, *Pioneer History of Illinois*, 116. Information on Edgar's estate can be found in the U.S. Federal Census records of 1820 and 1830. It is unsurprising to find that slaves were residing in southeastern Illinois. Although slavery had been forbidden in the Northwest Ordinance of 1787, it was tolerated through the 1820s. "Attitudes on slavery in Illinois," as Roger Biles has noted, "remained difficult to sort out" through the Civil War. Biles, *Illinois*, 83. See also Biles, 33, 83–101.

19. Reynolds, *Pioneer History*, 185–90, 271–73.

20. Ann Durkin Keating, *Rising Up from Indian Country: The Battle of Fort Dearborn and the Birth of Chicago*, 55–61; Joseph Kirkland, *The Chicago Massacre of 1812*, 151; B. J. Griswold, *The Pictorial History of Fort Wayne, Indiana: A Review of Two Centuries of Occupation . . .*, 1:233; McGoorty, "Early Irish," 63; McMahon, "Illinois," 401.

21. McGoorty, "Early Irish," 62; Reynolds, *Pioneer History*, 205–6.

22. David A. Wilson, *United Irishmen, United States: Immigrant Radicals in the Early Republic*, 43–44; Reynolds, *Pioneer History*, 328–29.

23. Biles, *Illinois*, 33–34.

24. Reynolds, *Pioneer History*, 352–53, 389–90; McGoorty, "Early Irish," 63.

25. McGoorty, "Early Irish," 57–62; Barry, *First Irish*, 13; Reynolds, *Pioneer History*, 152, 361, 378–81. See also Reboot Illinois, "Top 25 Counties in Illinois with the Most Luck o' the Irish," HuffPost, updated December 6, 2017, https://www.huffingtonpost.com/reboot-illinois/top-25-counties-in-illino_b_9491428.html.

26. Barry, *First Irish*, 13–14; Reynolds, *Pioneer History*, 165–66; Mary Nolan, "Honorable James L. D. Morrison," 1–3.

27. Reynolds, *Pioneer History*, 246–47, 386–87, 413; McGoorty, "Early Irish," 63.

28. Biles, *Illinois*, 40–43. See also Alan Taylor, *The Civil War of 1812: American Citizens, British Subjects, Irish Rebels, and Indian Allies*. For an important discussion of race and settler colonialism in the Old Northwest, see Michael Witgen, "Seeing Red: Race, Citizenship, and Indigeneity in the Old Northwest," 581–611.

29. Reynolds, *Pioneer History*, 381–82; Biles, *Illinois*, 43–46.

30. Reynolds, 298–300.

31. *Portrait and Biographical Album of Champaign County, Illinois*, 123–24.

32. Reynolds, *Pioneer History*, 381–87.

33. Jon Musgrave, "American Weekend," *Harrisburg Daily Register*, 6 January 1996; Biles, *Illinois*, 43; Jane H. Adams, *The Transformation of Rural Life: Southern Illinois, 1890–1990*, 43; Reboot Illinois, "Top 25 Counties." This phenomenon is not unique to Illinois. See Kerby A. Miller, "'Scotch-Irish,' 'Black Irish,' and 'Real Irish': Emigrants and Identities in the Old South," 139–59.

34. Grace Partridge Smith, "Four Ballads from 'Egypt,'" 115–19; Reynolds, *Pioneer History*, 202–4; McGoorty, "Early Irish," 59.

35. John W. Allen, *It Happened in Southern Illinois*, 243–44; Bruce L. Cline, *More History, Mystery, and Hauntings of Southern Illinois*, 60.

36. Wilson, *United Irishmen, United States*, 2, 156–57; U.S. 15th Congress, 1817–1819, House Committee on the Public Lands, "Report of the Committee on the Public Lands on Petitions of Irish Emigrant Associations . . . ," 1–2.

37. Richard V. Carpenter and J. W. Kitchell, "The Illinois Constitutional Convention of 1818," 351.

38. Biles, *Illinois*, 45–47; Reynolds, *Pioneer History*, 332, 389–390, 413; Carpenter and Kitchell, "Illinois Constitutional Convention," 407; George Washington Smith, *A History of Southern Illinois: A Narrative Account of Its Historical Progress, Its People, and Its Principal Interests*, 157.

39. Stan J. Hale, ed., *Williamson County Illinois Sesquicentennial History*, 121. See also "Africa History," Williamson County Illinois Historical Society, accessed January 13, 2019, https://www.wcihs.org/history/history-of-the-village-of-africa/.

40. Scholars have already noted the importance of generation in their studies of Irish Catholics. See Timothy J. Meagher, *Inventing Irish America: Generation, Class, and Ethnic Identity in a New England City, 1890–1928.*

41. Reynolds, *Pioneer History*, 272. See also Dale T. Knobel, *Paddy and the Republic: Ethnicity and Nationality in Antebellum America*; Warren R. Hofstra, ed., *Ulster to America: The Scots-Irish Migration Experience, 1680–1830*; Griffin, *People with No Name.*

42. Miller, *Land of Canaan*, 7–8, 609; Reynolds, *Pioneer History*, 86–87, 299, 328–29.

2. From Irish Exiles to Paddy Politicians

1. Throughout this book, we have transcribed quotations as they appeared in the original material and have not corrected any misspellings or grammatical errors.

2. David A. Wilson, *Thomas D'Arcy McGee: The Extreme Moderate, 1857–1868*, 18; George Potter, *To the Golden Door: The Story of the Irish in Ireland and America*, 540–45.

3. Biles, *Illinois*, 62–63. See also Thomas Bartlett, *Ireland: A History*.

4. Biles, *Illinois*, 62–63. See also Richard J. Jensen, *Illinois: A History*.

5. Lawrence J. McCaffrey, "Preserving the Union: Shaping a New Image of Chicago's Irish Catholics and the Civil War," 81.

6. Potter, *Golden Door*, 137–38; Miller, *Emigrants and Exiles*, 252–63; Mark Wyman, *Immigrants in the Valley: Irish, Germans, and Americans in the Upper Mississippi Country, 1830–1860*, 6.

7. Potter, *Golden Door*, 201.

8. Biles, *Illinois*, 79–80; Potter, *Golden Door*, 212, 377; Wyman, *Immigrants in the Valley*, 167. See also *The History of Jo Daviess County, Illinois*; Reboot Illinois, "Top 25 Counties."

9. McMahon, "Illinois," 402.

10. Kerry A. Trask, *Black Hawk: The Battle for the Heart of America*, 95. See also Patrick J. Jung, *The Black Hawk War of 1832*; Biles, *Illinois*, 80–82.

11. Jensen, *Illinois*, 50–57; McMahon, "Illinois," 405.

12. Richard Lawrence Miller, *Lincoln and His World: Prairie Politician, 1834–1842*, 89–91.

13. W. T. Norton, *Centennial History of Madison County, Illinois and Its People, 1812–1912*, 1: 349; Biles, *Illinois*, 86–87; Miller, *Prairie Politician*, 89–91.

14. Richard S. Newman, *The Transformation of American Abolitionism: Fighting Slavery in the Early Republic*; Joanne Pope Melish, *Disowning Slavery: Gradual Emancipation and "Race" in New England, 1780–1860*; Noel Ignatiev, *How the Irish Became White*; David Roediger, *The Wages of Whiteness: Race and the Making of the American Working Class*. For scholars who acknowledge this context, see Angela F. Murphy, *American Slavery, Irish Freedom: Abolition, Immigrant Citizenship, and the Transatlantic Movement for Irish Repeal*; Miller, *Prairie Politician*.

15. Biles, *Illinois*, 72–73; McMahon, "Illinois," 402; Peter Way, *Common Labor: Workers and the Digging of North American Canals, 1780–1860*, 50, 94–95; Wyman, *Immigrants in the Valley*, 80.

16. Dearinger, *Filth of Progress*, 57–106; Way, *Common Labor*, 136–37, 169–71.

17. James Silk Buckingham, *Eastern and Western States of America*, 3:222–23.

18. Francis Grund, *The Americans: In Their Moral, Social, and Political Relations*, 1:90; *Illinois Free Trader* (hereafter *IFT*), February 26, 1841. See, especially, Eileen M. McMahon, "Canal Diggers, Church Builders," 43–81.

19. Way, *Common Labor*, 173; Dearinger, *Filth of Progress*, 58; Potter, *Golden Door*, 201; Chicago Medical Society, *History of Medicine and Surgery and Physicians and Surgeons of Chicago*, 33.

20. Biles, *Illinois*, 73–75; Wyman, *Immigrants in the Valley*, 82; Mathieu W. Billings, "Potent Legacies: The Transformation of Irish American Politics, 1815–1840," 372–75; Way, *Common Labor*, 210–11. See also Catherine Tobin, "The Lowly Muscular Digger: Irish Canal Workers in Nineteenth-Century America."

21. Billings, "Potent Legacies," 250–251; David Noel Doyle, "The Irish in North America, 1776–1845," 187.

22. Billings, "Potent Legacies," 361–64.

23. Billings, "Potent Legacies," 361–421.

24. Fergus O'Ferrall, *Catholic Emancipation: Daniel O'Connell and the Birth of Irish Democracy.*

25. See Alexander Keyssar, *The Right to Vote: The Contested History of Democracy in the United States.*

26. Billings, "Potent Legacies," 382–86. See also Illinois State Historical Library, *Transactions of the Illinois State Historical Society for the Year 1914*, 155, 166.

27. *Chicago American*, May 5, 1840; Billings, "Potent Legacies," 391–93, 402–3.

28. Billings, "Potent Legacies," 361–421.

29. Bessie Louise Pierce, *A History of Chicago*, 1:383, 398; Orestes A. Brownson, "Native Americanism," 8.

30. See, especially, Murphy, *American Slavery, Irish Freedom*; Michael F. Funchion, "The Political and Nationalist Dimensions," 73; Pierce, *History of Chicago*, 1:181. See also the *Chicago Democrat*, March 21, 1843.

31. *IFT*, February 26 and May 14, 1841, July 7 and August 4, 1843.

32. *IFT*, September 22, 1843.

33. *Ottawa Free Trader* (hereafter *OFT*), June 28 and August 29, 1845. Admittedly, the *Free Trader* expressed skepticism prior to O'Connell's "American Eagle" speech. See *OFT*, November 29, 1844. For the most recent interpretation of O'Connell, slavery, and repeal, see Murphy, *American Slavery, Irish Freedom.*

34. See James S. Donnelly Jr., *The Great Irish Potato Famine, 81*; Cecil Woodham-Smith, *The Great Hunger: Ireland, 1845–1849*; Dolan, *Irish Americans*, 67–83; Potter, *Golden Door*, 470; *Juliet Signal* (Joliet, IL), March 23, 1847.

35. Ellen Skerrett, "The Catholic Dimension," 25; Potter, *Golden Door*, 461–62.

36. Wyman, *Immigrants in the Valley*, 83–84; Dearinger, *Filth of Progress*, 64–67; McMahon, "Illinois," 402–3.

37. Hale, *Williamson County*, 276; Beebe, *History of Peru*, 141; W. W. Stevens, *Past and Present of Will County*, 1:123, 253; Pierce, *History of Chicago*, 2:380; Biles, *Illinois*, 62–63.

38. Wyman, *Immigrants in the Valley*, 107–9; Biles, *Illinois*, 69–70.

39. Wyman, *Immigrants in the Valley*, 135.

40. Skerrett, "Catholic Dimension," 22.

41. Mary Beth Fraser Connolly, *Women of Faith: The Chicago Sisters of Mercy and the Evolution of a Religious Community*; Suellen Hoy, *Good Hearts: Catholic Sisters in Chicago's Past*, 36–40.

42. McMahon, "Canal Diggers, Church Builders," 43–81; *IFT*, July 9, 1841; *History of Jo Daviess County*, 257; *History of Grundy County Illinois*, 248; Norton, *Centennial History of Madison County*, 501; Charles Ballance, *The History of Peoria, Illinois*, 114.

43. Wyman, *Immigrants in the Valley*, 136; Skerrett, "Catholic Dimension," 23. See John E. McGirr, *Life of the Rt. Rev. Wm. Quarter, D.D., First Catholic Bishop of Chicago.*

44. Skerrett, "Catholic Dimension," 27–32; Potter, *Golden Door*, 355. Irish Catholics emphasized their Americanism in other communities as well. When the Catholics of Ottawa laid the cornerstone of Trinity Church in 1841, they did so on the Fourth of July. *IFT*, July 9, 1841.

45. Dearinger, *Filth of Progress*, 95–98; Wyman, *Immigrants in the Valley*, 83–84.

46. Dearinger, *Filth of Progress*, 98–99; McMahon, "Illinois," 402.

47. Dearinger, *Filth of Progress*, 99–101; McMahon, "Illinois, 405.

48. Barry, *First Irish*, 14–15; Wyman, *Immigrants in the Valley*, 215.

49. Bruce Levine, "Conservatism, Nativism, and Slavery: Thomas R. Whitney and the Origins of the Know-Nothing Party," 466; Tyler Anbinder, *Nativism and Slavery: The Northern Know Nothings and the Politics of the 1850s*, 72.

50. Louis Vargo, "Abraham Lincoln Prepares to Fight a Saber Duel"; *Sangamon Journal*, September 2, 9, and 16, 1842.

51. Thomas M. Keefe, "Chicago's Flirtation with Political Nativism, 1854–1856," *Records of the American Historical Society of Philadelphia*, 131–58; McCaffrey, "Preserving the Union," 80; John P. Senning, "The Know Nothing Movement in Illinois, 1854–1856," 7–33.

52. Keefe, "Political Nativism," 141–44.

53. Mark Hubbard, ed., *Illinois's War: The Civil War in Documents*, 23–24; Keefe, "Political Nativism," 141–44.

54. Senning, "Know Nothing Movement," 10–11, 17, 22–23; McMahon, "Illinois," 405.

55. McMahon, "Illinois," 403.

56. McMahon, "Illinois," 403.

57. Wyman, *Immigrants in the Valley*, 39–42; Porter quoted in Miller, *Emigrants and Exiles*, 313. Historians have long debated the capabilities of Irish laborers to save money and purchase farms. Contemporary evidence, however, suggests that they did so despite the high costs of land and equipment. See Beebe, *History of Peru*, 141. See also Tobin, "Lowly Muscular Digger"; Way, *Common Labor*; *Juliet Signal*, September 29, 1846; Potter, *To the Golden Door*, 540.

58. For the standard work, see David M. Potter, *The Impending Crisis, 1848–1861.*

59. Potter, *Golden Door*, 621; Robert Walter Johannsen, *Stephen A. Douglas*, 332.

60. Potter, *Golden Door*, 621.

61. *OFT*, October 23, 30 and November 6, 1858; McMahon, "Illinois," 405.

62. See David Brundage, *Irish Nationalists in America: The Politics of Exile, 1798–1998*; R. V. Comerford, *The Fenians in Context: Irish Politics and Society, 1848–82.*

63. *OFT*, November 28, 1863.

64. *OFT*, August 20, 1864. The *Chicago Tribune* reported in 1865 that the police had discovered a diary from the Fenian Fair of 1863 that identified members by name. Most, the paper claimed, were officers in the Union army. See the *Chicago Tribune* (hereafter *CT*), March 20, 1864, September 30 and October 17, 1865; Brundage, *Irish Nationalists*

in America, 102–3; *Rock Island Daily Argus*, December 14, 1865; *OFT*, April 16, 1864; *Cairo Evening Times*, September 4, 1865.

65. *CT*, November 9, 10, 1860; *OFT*, November 10, 1860; Richard H. Steckel, "Migration and Political Conflict: Precincts in the Midwest on the Eve of the Civil War," 583–603.

66. Ryan W. Keating, *Shades of Green: Irish Regiments, American Soldiers, and Local Communities in the Civil War Era*; McCaffrey, "Preserving the Union," 79.

67. Hubbard, *Illinois's War*, 65–66, 125. See also Eileen M. McMahon, "Irish Women in the Civil War," 121–39.

68. Iver Bernstein, *The New York City Draft Riots: Their Significance for American Society and Politics in the Age of the Civil War*; Paul Gilje, *Mobocracy: Popular Disorder in New York City, 1763–1834*, 285–86.

69. Adade Mitchell Wheeler and Marlene Stein Wortman, *The Roads They Made: Women in Illinois History*, 47–48; Hubbard, *Illinois's War*, 59.

70. Hubbard, *Illinois's War*, 93–94; McMahon, "Irish Women in the Civil War," 133–34; Theodore J. Karamanski and Eileen M. McMahon, eds., *Civil War Chicago: Eyewitness to History*, 114–15, 127–39.

71. Robert E. Sterling, "Civil War Draft Resistance in the Middle West"; Karamanski and McMahon, *Civil War Chicago*, 114–15.

72. Keating, *Shades of Green*, 132–154; Karamanski and McMahon, *Civil War Chicago*, 214–15; McCaffrey, "Preserving the Union," 87–88.

73. McCaffrey, "Preserving the Union," 87–88.

74. See, especially, Knobel, *Paddy and the Republic*; Ignatiev, *How the Irish Became White*; Roediger, *Wages of Whiteness*; Matthew Frye Jacobson, *Whiteness of a Different Color: European Immigrants and the Alchemy of Race*. Strong quoted in Kenny, *American Irish*, 117–18.

75. Keating, *Shades of Green*, 212; *CT*, September 30, 1865.

76. McCaffrey, "Preserving the Union," 90–91; Kenny, *American Irish*, 129; Skerrett, "Catholic Dimension," 38; *CT*, March 19, 1867.

3. At the Forefront of the Multiethnic City

1. Finley Peter Dunne, *Mr. Dooley and the Chicago Irish: The Autobiography of a Nineteenth-Century Ethnic Group*, ed. Charles Fanning, xxiv. See also Charles Fanning, *Finley Peter Dunne and Mr. Dooley: The Chicago Years*.

2. Biles, *Illinois*, 71; Potter, *Golden Door*, 173, 202; Lawrence J. McCaffrey, *The Irish Catholic Diaspora in America*, 126–27; Dolan, *Irish Americans*, 157. See also William Cronon, *Nature's Metropolis: Chicago and the Great West*.

3. Dolan, *Irish Americans*, 157.

4. Lawrence J. McCaffrey, "The Irish-American Dimension," 7–8; Potter, *Golden Door*, 530; Eileen M. McMahon, *What Parish Are You From? A Chicago Irish Community & Race Relations*, 10; Dolan, *Irish Americans*, 90.

5. Richard F. Bales, "Did the Cow Do It? A New Look at the Cause of the Great Chicago Fire," 2–24.

6. Karen Sawislak, *Smoldering City: Chicagoans and the Great Fire, 1871–1874*, 44; *Chicago Evening Journal*, quoted in Bales, "Did the Cow Do It?" 24.

7. Skerrett, "Catholic Dimension," 34; "History of Holy Family," Holy Family Church, accessed October 14, 2017, http://www.holyfamilychicago.org/history.htm.

8. Skerrett, "Catholic Dimension," 33–34; Ross Miller, *The Great Chicago Fire*, 47; Dolan, *Irish Americans*, 97; Dunne, *Mr. Dooley and the Chicago Irish*, 32.

9. Emmet Larkin, "The Devotional Revolution in Ireland, 1850–1875," 652; Sean J. Connolly, *Priests and People in Pre-famine Ireland, 1780–1845*, 36; Dolan, *Irish Americans*, 107–34; Wyman, *Immigrants in the Valley*, 135.

10. Skerrett, "Catholic Dimension," 31; Dolan, *Irish Americans*, 107–34; *CT*, November 10, 1878.

11. Dolan, *Irish Americans*, 164–81; Kevin Kenny, *Making Sense of the Molly Maguires*; Thomas N. Brown, *Irish-American Nationalism, 1870–1890*, 46–47.

12. Kyle B. Roberts and Stephen Schloesser, *Crossings and Dwellings: Restored Jesuits, Women Religious, American Experience, 1814–2014*, 320; McCaffrey, "Irish-American Dimension," 12; Thomas M. Mulkerins, *Holy Family Parish: Priests and People*, 476–80.

13. Biles, *Illinois*, 133.

14. Richard Schneirov, *Labor and Urban Politics: Class Conflict and the Origins of Modern Liberalism in Chicago, 1864–97*, 69–76.

15. *Chicago Tribune*, quoted in Gillian O'Brien, *Blood Runs Green: The Murder That Transfixed Gilded Age Chicago*, 10; Schneirov, *Labor and Urban Politics*, 75; Sam Mitrani, *The Rise of the Chicago Police Department, 1850–1894*, 57–71, 112–22; James Dabney McCabe, *The History of the Great Riots: Being a Full and Authentic Account* [. . .] *Molly Maguires*, 369–394; *CT*, July 27, 1877. See also H. W. Bolton, *History of the Second Regiment Illinois Volunteer Infantry from Organization to Muster-Out*.

16. Dolan, *Irish Americans*, 167–69.

17. Schneirov, *Labor and Urban Politics*, 119–35.

18. Schneirov, *Labor and Urban Politics*, 183–205; Mitrani, *Chicago Police Department*, 168; James R. Barrett, *The Irish Way: Becoming American in the Multiethnic City*, 89.

19. Schneirov, *Labor and Urban Politics*, 4; Kenny, *American Irish*, 185–92; Eric L. Hirsch, *Urban Revolt: Ethnic Politics in the Nineteenth-Century Chicago Labor Movement*, 141, 143; David Noel Doyle, "The Irish and American Labour, 1880–1920," 51. For the links between respectability and nationalism in Irish America, see Thomas N. Brown, *Irish-American Nationalism*, 17-41.

20. Finley Peter Dunne, *Mr. Dooley in the Hearts of His Countrymen*, 165.

21. Dolan, *Irish Americans*, 164–181; Eliott J. Gorn, *Mother Jones: The Most Dangerous Woman in America*, 3, 181. See also Simon Cordery, *Mother Jones: Raising Cain and Consciousness*.

22. Gorn, *Mother Jones*; Cordery, *Mother Jones*, 187–92; Dolan, *Irish Americans*, 177–78.

On the museum, see Mother Jones Museum (website), accessed July 24, 2019, www.motherjonesmuseum.org.

23. Mitrani, *Chicago Police Department*, 49, 72–100.

24. Funchion, "Political and Nationalist Dimensions," 62; Barrett, *Irish Way*, 206.

25. Funchion, "Political and Nationalist Dimensions," 62–64; Dunne, *Mr. Dooley and the Chicago Irish*, 217.

26. Mitrani, *Chicago Police Department*, 134–65; Funchion, "Political and Nationalist Dimensions," 80; Dolan, *Irish Americans*, 158.

27. Brown, *Irish-American Nationalism*, 63–83.

28. Brundage, *Irish Nationalists in America*, 111–26; Dolan, *Irish Americans*, 189–99. See also Eric Foner, "Class, Ethnicity, and Radicalism in the Gilded Age: The Land League and Irish America," 150–200.

29. Niall Whelehan, *The Dynamiters: Irish Nationalism and Political Violence in the Wider World, 1867–1900*, 77–78; Brown, *Irish-American Nationalism*, 66; O'Brien, *Blood Runs Green*, 10–19; Ely M. Janis, "Petticoat Revolutionaries: Gender, Ethnic Nationalism, and the Irish Ladies' Land League in the United States," 5–27; *Chicago Daily Tribune*, March 18, 1881.

30. Skerrett, "Catholic Dimension," 29–36.

31. Thomas N. Brown, "The Origins and Character of Irish-American Nationalism," *The Review of Politics*, 334.

32. Whelehan, *Dynamiters*, 99–101. See also Bartlett, *Ireland*, 320–30.

33. O'Brien, *Blood Runs Green*, 62–67; Brundage, *Irish Nationalists in America*, 127–45; Bartlett, *Ireland*, 342–45.

34. O'Brien, *Blood Runs Green*, 56.

35. O'Brien, *Blood Runs Green*.

36. Dunne, *Mr. Dooley and the Chicago Irish*, 296; O'Brien, *Blood Runs Green*, 1.

37. Ellen Skerrett, "The Irish of Chicago's Hull-House Neighborhood," 189–222; History of Holy Family, https://holyfamilychicago.org/history; Farrell, personal correspondence, quoted in Skerrett, 189.

38. Hoy, *Good Hearts*, 35–46; Skerrett "The Irish of Chicago's Hull-House Neighborhood," 189.

39. Deborah A. Skok, *More Than Neighbors: Catholic Settlements and Day Nurseries in Chicago, 1893–1930*.

40. O'Brien, *Blood Runs Green*, 10; Erik Larson, *The Devil in the White City: Murder, Magic, and Madness at the Fair That Changed America*.

41. Funchion, "Political and Nationalist Dimensions," 64; Larson, *Devil in the White City*, 212.

42. Funchion, "Political and Nationalist Dimensions"; Larson, *Devil in the White City*. See also Adam Selzer, *H. H. Holmes: The True History of the White City Devil*.

43. Richard Schneirov, Shelton Stromquist, and Nick Salvatore, eds., *The Pullman Strike and the Crisis of the 1890s: Essays on Labor and Politics*.

44. Dunne, *Mr. Dooley and the Chicago Irish*, 183–89.

45. Barrett, *Irish Way*, 1–2.

46. McCaffrey, *Irish Catholic Diaspora*, 126.

47. Barrett, *Irish Way*, 13–55. Ragen's Colts were named for James Ragen, a prominent Chicago Irish businessman, and his brother Frank, founder of the gang's social athletic club and a future Cook County commissioner.

48. Barrett, *Irish Way*, 13–55.

49. Skerrett, "Catholic Dimension," 39–41; Barrett, *Irish Way*, 57–104.

50. Jay P. Dolan, *The American Catholic Experience: A History from Colonial Times to the Present*, 302; Barrett, *Irish Way*, 71–74; Skerrett, "Catholic Dimension," 46, 49.

51. Skerrett, "Catholic Dimension," 38–55.

52. Mimi Cowan, "'We Know Neither Catholics, nor Protestants, nor Free-Thinkers Here': Ethnicity, Religion, and the Chicago Public Schools, 1837–94," 200.

53. Barrett, *Irish Way*, 57–104 passim; McMahon, *What Parish Are You From?* 22; Skerrett, "Catholic Dimension," 51–52, 55 (emphasis added).

54. Barrett, *Irish Way*, 111–13, 133–38.

55. Barrett, *Irish Way*, 105–08; Kenny, *American Irish*, 191.

56. Barrett, *Irish Way*, 108–11, 128–29.

57. Steven A. Riess, *City Games: The Evolution of American Urban Society and the Rise of Sports*, 95–96; Barrett, *Irish Way*, 26–31.

58. E. Woodrow Eckard, "Anti-Irish Job Discrimination circa 1880: Evidence from Major League Baseball," 407–43.

59. Nicholas Carolan, *A Harvest Saved: Francis O'Neill and Irish Music in Chicago*.

60. McCaffrey, "Irish-American Dimension," 14–15; Barrett, *Irish Way*, 157–72; Patricia L. Ireland, "Blarney Streets: The Staging of Ireland and Irish-America by the Chicago Manuscript Company." See also Irwin J. Cohen, *Comiskey Park*; *Rock Island Argus*, September 4, 1908; *Chicago Eagle*, November 21, 1908; *Rock Island Argus*, December 22, 1919; *Free Trader Journal and Ottawa Fair Dealer*, March 31, 1921.

61. Barrett, *Irish Way*, 195–238.

62. Funchion, "Political and Nationalist Dimensions," 62–64; McCaffrey, *Irish Catholic Diaspora*, 126.

63. Fanning, *Finley Peter Dunne and Mr. Dooley*, 130.

64. Barrett, *Irish Way*, 195–238.

65. Fearghal McGarry, *The Rising: Easter 1916*; Clair Wills, *Dublin, 1916: The Siege of the GPO*; and Charles Townshend, *Easter 1916: The Irish Rebellion*.

66. Thomas J. O'Gorman, *One Hundred Years: A History of the Irish Fellowship Club of Chicago*, 27.

67. Robert Schmuhl, *Ireland's Exiled Children: America and the Easter Rising*, 16, 31–32, 46, 55; Brundage, *Irish Nationalists in America*, 162; Funchion, "Political and Nationalist Dimensions," 77; Barrett, *Irish Way*, 239–79.

68. Barrett, *Irish Way*, 242, 257–63; Skerrett, "Catholic Dimension," 47–48.

69. Barrett, *Irish Way*, 14, 45, 47–50, 273. See also David F. Krugler, *1919, the Year of Racial Violence: How African Americans Fought Back*; and William M. Tuttle, *Race Riot: Chicago and the Red Summer of 1919*.

70. Finley Peter Dunne, *Mr. Dooley's Opinions*, 211–12. See also Cameron McWhirter, *Red Summer: The Summer of 1919 and the Awakening of Black America*.

71. Elaine Lewinnek, *The Working Man's Reward: Chicago's Early Suburbs and the Roots of American Sprawl*.

72. Frederick Lewis Allen, *Only Yesterday: An Informal History of the Nineteen-Twenties*, 215–17.

73. Allen, *Only Yesterday*, 224–29.

74. Barrett, *Irish Way*, 205–7; Douglas Bukowski, *Big Bill Thompson, Chicago, and the Politics of Image*, 43–44.

75. Dunne, *Mr. Dooley and the Chicago Irish*, 142; Barrett, *Irish Way*, 218.

76. Barrett, *Irish Way*, 232–35.

77. Funchion, "Political and Nationalist Dimensions," 78–83; Barrett, *Irish Way*, 195–238 passim.

78. McCaffrey, "Irish-American Dimension," 1–21; Barrett, *Irish Way*, 108–11; Miller, *Emigrants and Exiles*, 495–99.

4. Beyond the South Side

1. McMahon, "Illinois," 403; *Daily Pantagraph*, May 5, 1900, in Koos, *Irish Immigrants in McLean County*, 21; Diner, *Erin's Daughters*, 31–33; Miller, *Emigrants and Exiles*, 581; James Ciment, *Encyclopedia of the Jazz Age: From the End of World War I to the Great Crash*, 2:303.

2. Biles, *Illinois*, 122–23, 140–41.

3. McMahon, "Illinois," 404; Biles, *Illinois*, 124, 130.

4. Steven Barleen, "The Saloon on the Prairie: The Family and the Saloon in Braidwood, Illinois, 1865–1883," 211.

5. Charles L. Lumpkins, *American Pogrom: The East St. Louis Race Riot and Black Politics*, 31.

6. Stephen Freeman, "Organizing the Workers in a Steel Company Town: The Union Movement in Joliet, Illinois, 1870–1920," 5, 16; McMahon, "Illinois," 404.

7. Mike Matejka, "Irish Immigrant Son Patrick Morrissey Built Rail Brotherhood," 55–57.

8. David Markwell, "A Turning Point: The Lasting Impact of the 1898 Virden Mine Riot," *Journal of the Illinois State Historical Society*, 211–27; Biles, *Illinois*, 138.

9. Markwell, "A Turning Point," 226.

10. Biles, *Illinois*, 131; McMahon, "Illinois," 403.

11. Biles, *Illinois*, 140; *Farm, Field, and Stockman*, February 6, 1886; *Chicago Tribune*, July 1, 1990.

12. Paul J. Curtin, *West Limerick Roots: The Laurence Curtin Family of Knockbrack, County Limerick, Ireland*, 131.

13. McCaffrey, *Irish Catholic Diaspora in America*, 139. For recent works that address farming in the Irish diaspora, see Malcom Campbell, *Ireland's New Worlds: Immigrants, Politics, and Society in the United States and Australia, 1815–1922*; McMahon, "Illinois."

14. Biles, *Illinois*, 121.

15. Cynthia L. Baer, "The Labor of Irish Women in Nineteenth-Century Bloomington-Normal: A Portrait Painted through the Writings of Sarah Davis and Helen Ross Hall," in Koos, *Irish Immigrants in McLean County*, 31; Janet Duitsman Cornelius and Martha LaFrenz Kay, *Women of Conscience: Social Reform in Danville, Illinois, 1890–1930*, 105.

16. Glenda Riley, "From Ireland to Illinois: Life of Helen Ross Hall," 162–80.

17. Baer, "Labor of Irish Women," 29–38.

18. McMahon, "Illinois," 403; Mark T. Dunn, "Irish American Organizations in Bloomington in the 1880s," in Koos, *Irish Immigrants in McLean County*, 45–46; Daniel Elazar, *Cities of the Prairie: The Metropolitan Frontier and American Politics*, 174–75.

19. David A. Belden, *Will County*, 16; McMahon, "Illinois," 406; Dunn, "Irish American Organizations in Bloomington," 46.

20. David Francis Sweeney, *The Life of John Lancaster Spalding: First Bishop of Peoria, 1840–1916*; McMahon, "Illinois," 406.

21. Dunn, "Irish American Organizations in Bloomington," 49.

22. *Cairo Evening Bulletin*, April 15 and October 19, 1881; *Ottawa Free Trader*, January 28 and March 4, 18, 1882, and August 25, 1888; Whelehan, *Dynamiters*, 77–78.

23. Dunn, "Irish American Organizations in Bloomington," 43–46; *Bloomington Weekly Pantagraph*, October 9, 16, 23 and December 2, 25, 1885.

24. Dunn, "Irish American Organizations in Bloomington," 45.

25. Biles, *Illinois.*

26. Elazar, *Cities of the Prairie*, 175; *Illinois Daily Argus*, September 18, 1868; *Cairo Evening Bulletin*, February 16 and November 4, 1869; Schnierov, *Labor and Urban Politics*, 134; Dunn, "Irish American Organizations in Bloomington," 40–43.

27. Higham, *Strangers in the Land*, 60–63, 77.

28. Dunn, "Irish American Organizations in Bloomington," 40–43.

29. Higham, *Strangers in the Land*, 68–105; *Warren County Democrat*, November 1, 1900.

30. William Wallace Stevens, *Past and Present of Will County, Illinois*, 253 (emphasis added); *Rock Island Argus*, January 26, 1901; *Illinois State Register*, March 18, 1888.

31. Biles, *Illinois*, 148–64; Amanda Dahlquist, "Legislating Motherhood: The History of Mothers' Aid in Montgomery County," 149.

32. Barleen, "Family and the Saloon in Braidwood," 204, 211–12; Alfred Theodore Andreas, *History of Chicago: From the Earliest Period to the Present Time*, 3:853; *True*

Republican (DeKalb), October 8, 1887, and September 11, 1889; Royal Melendy, "The Saloon in Chicago," 289–306.

33. Barleen, "Family and the Saloon in Braidwood," 198; Newton Bateman, Paul Selby, and Josiah Seymour Currey, eds., *Historical Encyclopedia of Illinois*, 1:358; *Urbana Daily Courier*, January 10, 1910.

34. Cornelius, *Women of Conscience*, 109, 146.

35. Daniel Patrick Moynihan and Nathan Glazer, *Beyond the Melting Pot: The Negroes, Puerto Ricans, Jews, Italians, and Irish of New York City*; McCaffrey, *Irish Catholic Diaspora in America*, 118–19.

36. Christopher K. Hays, "The African American Struggle for Equality and Justice in Cairo, Illinois, 1865–1900," 265–84.

37. *Bloomington Daily Bulletin*, June 5, 1899, in Koos, *Irish Immigrants in McLean County*, 70.

38. Roberta Senechal, *The Sociogenesis of a Race Riot: Springfield, Illinois, 1908*, 2; *Chicago Livestock World*, August 15, 1908.

39. Senechal, *Sociogenesis of a Race Riot*, 204–6. Why Irish Americans had a disproportionate influence on race riots in Springfield and Chicago remains open to debate. Answers may generally be distilled into two categories: economics and politics. Roberta Senechal suggests that politics mattered more, since the Irish of Springfield affiliated more closely with the Democratic Party, while African Americans largely voted Republican. Conversely, in his study of the Chicago Race Riot of 1919, William Tuttle emphasizes economics, noting that the Great Migration caused an "abrupt transformation of a feudal peasantry into an urban proletariat." Tuttle, *Race Riot*, 213. Interestingly, both Senechal and Tuttle accept the notion that long-standing antagonisms over jobs factored into the rioting. It is noteworthy that contemporaries regarded Irish and African Americans as race rivals. As Chicagoan John T. Campbell put it in 1910, "The Negroes and the Irish are inclined to run after the dominant race too much. The Irish, being white are not handicapped on account of color, but beyond that, they are little if any ahead of the Negroes in forwarding their race standing." *Broad Ax* (Chicago), June 11, 1910.

40. Mark Wyman and John W. Muirhead, "Jim Crow Comes to Central Illinois: Racial Segregation in Twentieth-Century Bloomington-Normal," 159; *Weekly Pantagraph*, April 9, 1897.

41. Senechal, *Sociogenesis of a Race Riot*, 108; Lumpkins, *American Pogrom*.

42. Biles, *Illinois*, 184–96; *Daily Illini*, September 22, 1917.

43. Carl R. Weinberg, *Labor, Loyalty, and Rebellion: Southwestern Illinois Coal Miners and World War I*, 36, 49–50.

44. Weinberg, *Labor, Loyalty, and Rebellion*, 40–42, 92, 192.

45. Weinberg, *Labor, Loyalty, and Rebellion*, 88–89.

46. Lumpkins, *American Pogrom*, 96–101.

47. Malcolm McLaughlin, *Power, Community, and Racial Killing in East St. Louis*, 1–5; Lumpkins, *American Pogrom*, 1, 110–26.

48. McLaughlin, *Power, Community, and Racial Killing*, 110–11; Lumpkins, *American Pogrom*, 27–30, 93.

49. Lumpkins, *American Pogrom*, 110.

50. Michael Doorley, *Irish-American Diaspora Nationalism: The Friends of Irish Freedom, 1916–1935*; James P. Walsh, "De Valera in the United States, 1919," 96; *Champaign Daily News*, October 23, 1919; *Illinois State Journal*, October 22, 1919; Dolan, *Irish Americans*, 203–4; Kenny, *American Irish*, 197.

51. Biles, *Illinois*, 203–4, 208–9.

52. Cornelius, *Women of Conscience*, 109.

53. Richard Hamer and Roger Ruthhart, *Citadel of Sin: The John Looney Story*, 18–19; Biles, *Illinois*, 206–8.

54. Hamer and Ruthhart, *Citadel of Sin*, 65–114.

55. Hamer and Ruthhart, *Citadel of Sin*, 5, 14–23, 25–46, 55–112.

56. H. W. Brands, *Reagan: The Life*, 10–11; Biles, *Illinois*, 212; Ronald Reagan and Richard G. Hubler, *Where's the Rest of Me?*, 26–41; Norman E. Wymbs, *A Place to Go Back To: Ronald Reagan in Dixon, Illinois*.

57. Biles, *Illinois*, 224; Victor Hicken, "Mine Union Radicalism in Macoupin and Montgomery Counties, IL," Illinois Labor History Society, 1997, http://www.illinoislaborhistory.org/labor-history-articles/mine-union-radicalism-in-macoupin-and-montgomery-counties-il; Memoir of J. R. Fitzpatrick, Archives/Special Collections, Norris L. Brookens Library, University of Illinois-Springfield/Illinois Digital Archives, 1980, 40, http://www.idaillinois.org/digital/collection/uis/id/2045/rec/19.

58. Biles, *Illinois*, 212–20; Reagan, *Where's the Rest of Me?*, 52–53; Wymbs, *A Place to Go Back To*, 18.

59. Biles, *Illinois*, 228–47; T. J. Slattery, *Rock Island: Arsenal for Democracy*, 15.

60. Thomas J. Shelley, "Twentieth Century American Catholicism and Irish Americans," 597.

61. Steven Ewing and John B. Lundstrom, *Fateful Rendezvous: The Life of Butch O'Hare*.

62. Jeannine Basinger, *The World War II Combat Film: Anatomy of a Genre*.

63. Elazar, *Cities on the Prairie*, 179.

64. McCaffrey, *Catholic Diaspora in America*, 1; *Diocese of Rockford, 1908–2008: Our History*, 38–44.

65. Matthew O'Brien, "'Hibernians on the March': Irish-American Ethnicity and the Cold War," 57–70; *Chicago Tribune*, March 18, 1956.

66. *Sycamore Tribune*, March 15, 1946, and January 31, 1947; *Daily Illini*, March 9, 1947; *Farmer's Weekly Review*, March 15, 1950. These types of events only increased across

the decade, reinforcing the notion that Irish Americans were now firmly ensconced in the American landscape.

5. A South Side Empire?

1. James T. Farrell, *Young Manhood of Studs Lonigan*, 373; Charles Fanning, *The Irish Voice in America*, 257–91.

2. Roger Biles, *Big City Boss in Depression and War: Mayor Edward J. Kelly of Chicago.*

3. Kenny, *American Irish*, 184; John T. McGreevy, *Parish Boundaries: The Catholic Encounter with Race in the Twentieth-Century Urban North*, 10; Eileen McMahon, *What Parish Are You From? A Chicago Irish Community and Race Relations*; Skerrett, "Catholic Dimension," 22–60.

4. Skerrett, "Catholic Dimension," 53.

5. Fanning, *Irish Voice in America*, 257–91; "James T. Farrell," Chicago Literary Hall of Fame, accessed July 17, 2019, https://chicagoliteraryhof.org/inductees/profile/james-t.-farrell.

6. Farrell, *Judgment Day*, 100–103, 173–76, 305–8, 418–65.

7. Biles, *Big City Boss*, 17–49; Paul Green, "Kelly-Nash Machine," *Encyclopedia of Chicago*, last modified October 11, 2016, http://www.encyclopedia.chicagohistory.org/pages/686.html.

8. Paul Green, "Kelly-Nash Machine," *Encyclopedia of Chicago*; "King-Nash House," Chicago Landmarks, accessed July 17, 2019, http://www.ci.chi.il.us/Landmarks/K/KingNashHouse.html.

9. Charles Fanning, "Dueling Cultures: Ireland and Irish America at the Chicago World's Fairs of 1933 and 1934," 94–110.

10. Biles, *Big City Boss*, 89–102; 133–51; Adam Cohen and Elizabeth Taylor, *American Pharaoh: Mayor Richard J. Daley; His Battle for Chicago and the Nation*, 56–61.

11. William Grimshaw, *Bitter Fruit: Black Politics and the Chicago Machine, 1931–1991*, 69–87; Biles, *Big City Boss*, 92–94. See also *Chicago Defender*, October 13 and 20, 1934. For the African American experience in Chicago, the indispensable starting point is St. Clair Drake and Horace R. Clayton, *Black Metropolis: A Study of Negro Life in a Northern City.*

12. Barrett, *Irish Way.*

13. Biles, *Big City Boss*, 21–27.

14. Barrett, *Irish Way*, 236–37; Stephen Erie, *Rainbow's End: Irish-Americans and the Dilemmas of Urban Machine Politics*, 129; McMahon, *What Parish Are You From?*, 56.

15. Farrell, *Judgment Day*, 3–21; Fanning, *Irish Voice in America*, 276; Farrell, "Jim O'Neill," 57–63.

16. *Chicago Tribune*, July 23, 1937; Biles, *Big City Boss*, 61–64; Donald G. Sofchalk, "The Chicago Memorial Day Incident: An Episode in Mass Action," 3–43.

17. Biles, *Big City Boss*, 157.

18. Grimshaw, *Bitter Fruit*, 57. For the story of public housing in Chicago, see Arnold R. Hirsch, *Making the Second Ghetto: Race and Housing in Chicago, 1940–1960.*

19. *Chicago Tribune*, October 21, 24, 1950; Biles, *Big City Boss*, 152–59.

20. Roger Faherty Papers, Chicago History Museum; O'Gorman, *One Hundred Years*, 3–6, 12.

21. Faherty Papers, Box 2; O'Gorman, *One Hundred Years*, 48–51; *Chicago Herald and Examiner*, January 22, 1928; Francis M. Carroll, "The Irish Free State and Public Diplomacy: The First Official Visit of William T. Cosgrave to the United States," 86–87.

22. O'Gorman, *One Hundred Years*, 86.

23. Faherty Papers, Box 1; Irish Fellowship Club of Chicago, *Irish Fellowship Club of Chicago: Its History and Objectives, 1902–1953*.

24. Skerrett, "Catholic Dimension," 46.

25. Janet Nolan, *Servants of the Poor: Teachers and Mobility in Ireland and Irish America*, 85–88; Ella Flagg Young, "In Memoriam," 35.

26. Nolan, *Servants of the Poor*, 92; McMahon, *What Parish Are You From?*, 69.

27. Kate Rousmaniere, *Citizen Teacher: The Life of Margaret Haley*, 45–48. On Goggin and Haley, see Tara McCarthy, *Respectability and Reform: Irish-American Women's Activism, 1880–1920*, 48–55.

28. Robert L. Reid, ed., *Battleground: The Autobiography of Margaret A. Haley*, 8, 45.

29. Reid, *Battleground*; Nolan, *Servants of the Poor*, 85–88.

30. Reid, *Battleground*, 105.

31. *Chicago Tribune*, September 2, 1915, and June 28, 1916; Mary J. Herrick, *Chicago Public Schools: A Social and Political History*, 128, 238; Reid, *Battleground*, xxviii–xxix.

32. Nolan, *Servants of the Poor*, 118–21; Biles, *Big City Boss*, 25–26.

33. Reid, *Battleground*, 270–76.

34. Grimshaw, *Bitter Fruit*, 47–166.

35. Dolan, *Irish Americans*, 289; Kenny, *Irish America*, 239.

36. Cohen and Taylor, *American Pharaoh*, 28–35; Barrett, *Irish Way*, 41–50; Krugler, *1919, The Year of Racial Violence*, 99–130; Mike Royko, *Boss: Richard J. Daley of Chicago*, 28–31.

37. Timothy B. Neary, *Crossing Parish Boundaries: Race, Sports, and Catholic Youth, 1914–1954*, 31–35; Farrell, *Studs Lonigan*, 320–47; Skerrett, "Catholic Dimension," 52.

38. It should be noted that some contemporaries were quite critical of Mayor Kelly's approach to housing. Earl B. Dickerson, a former Chicago ward leader passed over by Kelly in favor of Dawson, reputedly because of Dickerson's independence, argued that the mayor was just another figure who typically "winked at" housing discrimination. See Studs Terkel, *Hard Times: An Oral History of the Great Depression*, 447–49.

39. Biles, *Big City Boss*, 136–37; Skerrett, "Catholic Dimension," 52.

40. James R. Barrett, "The Blessed Virgin Made Me a Socialist: An Experiment in Catholic Autobiography and the Historical Understanding of Race and Class," 122–31.

41. McMahon, *What Parish Are You From?*, 116–56.

42. "In Memoriam: Sister Mary William Sullivan, D.C.," accessed September 15, 2019, https://daughtersofcharity.org/obituaries/in-memoriam-sister-mary-william-sullivan-d-c/; Hoy, *Good Hearts*, 143–46.

43. Hoy, *Good Hearts*, 71. For a longer history of nuns' work with African Americans in Chicago, see Hoy, *Good Hearts*, 71–153.

44. McMahon, *What Parish Are You From?*, 182–83; Kenny, *American Irish*, 225–26.

45. *Chicago Tribune*, quoted in Cohen and Taylor, *American Pharoah*, 141.

46. Milton J. Rakove, *Don't Make No Waves—Don't Back No Losers: An Insider's Analysis of the Daley Machine*, 63.

47. *Chicago Tribune*, March 18, 1956. On the persistence of Irish identity in Chicago, see Margaret Lee, "Shamrocks and Segregation: The Persistence of Upper-Class Irish Ethnicity in Beverly Hills, Chicago," 71–86.

48. Royko, *Boss*, 75; Grimshaw, *Bitter Fruit*, 21.

49. Cohen and Taylor, *American Pharaoh*, 260–70.

50. Cohen and Taylor, *American Pharaoh*, 286.

51. *Washington Post*, April 16, 1968. See also Grimshaw, *Bitter Fruit*, 116; Royko, *Boss*, 169.

52. *Chicago Daily News*, August 28, 1969; Matthew J. O'Brien, "Irish America, Race, and Bernadette Devlin's 1969 American Tour," 84–101; Andrew J. Wilson, *Irish America and the Ulster Conflict, 1968–1995*, 34–35; Tara Keenan-Thomson, "'Fidel Castro in a Mini-Skirt': Bernadette Devlin's First US Tour"; *Chicago Tribune*, February 1, 1972.

53. Cohen and Taylor, *American Pharaoh*, 529–58.

54. *Chicago Tribune*, April 4, 1993.

Conclusion

1. There is a third, smaller parade in the Norwood Park neighborhood called the Northwest Side Irish parade (1993 to the present).

2. Scott S. Smith, "Parade Watching," 22; Daryl Adair and Mike Cronin, *The Wearing of the Green: A History of St. Patrick's Day*, 210; Kenny, *American Irish*, 223.

3. Trinity Irish Dance Company website, accessed April 30, 2020, http://www.trinity irishdancecompany.com.

4. *Chicago Tribune*, March 9, 2015; Fintan Vallely, *The Companion to Irish Traditional Music*.

5. Liz Carroll's website, accessed May 2, 2020, http://www.lizcarroll.com.

6. Irish Theatre of Chicago, accessed October 27, 2017, http://www.irishtheatre.org; Chicago Irish Film Festival, accessed January 25, 2020, http://www.chicagoirishfilm-festival.com/.

7. South Side Irish Parade, accessed May 2, 2020, http://www.southsideirishparade .org; *Chicago Tribune*, March 12, 2015; Adair and Cronin, *Wearing of the Green*, 156, 215.

8. *Chicago Tribune*, March 18, 1956; Adair and Cronin, *Wearing of the Green*, 156, 167.

9. Reboot Illinois, "Top 25 Counties."

BIBLIOGRAPHY

Archival Sources

Chicago

CHICAGO HISTORY MUSEUM

Roger Faherty Papers

NEWBERRY LIBRARY

James T. Farrell Papers

Ottawa

LASALLE COUNTY COURTHOUSE

LaSalle County Court Records, 1831–62

Springfield

UNIVERSITY OF ILLINOIS–SPRINGFIELD, NORRIS L. BROOKENS LIBRARY

Memoir of J. R. Fitzpatrick

Government Publications

Department of the Interior, Census Office. *Report of the Population of the United States at the Eleventh Census, 1890*. Washington, DC: Government Printing Office, 1895–97.

U.S. 15th Congress, House Committee on Public Lands. "Report of the Committee on the Public Lands on Petitions of Irish Emigrant Associations of New York, Philadelphia, Baltimore, and Pittsburgh." Washington, DC, 1818.

Newspapers

Bloomington Weekly Pantagraph
Broad Ax (Chicago)
Cairo Evening Times
Chicago American
Chicago Defender

Chicago Democrat
Chicago Livestock World
Chicago Tribune
Daily Illini
Farm, Field, and Stockman
Farmer's Weekly Review
Free Trader Journal and Ottawa Fair Dealer
Harrisburg Daily Register
Illinois Free Trader (Ottawa)
Juliet Signal (Joliet)
New York Times
Ottawa Free Trader
Rock Island Daily Argus
Sangamon Journal (Springfield)
Sycamore Journal
Washington Post

Secondary Sources

Adair, Daryl, and Mike Cronin. *The Wearing of the Green: A History of St. Patrick's Day*. New York: Routledge, 2001.

Adams, Jane H. *The Transformation of Rural Life: Southern Illinois, 1890–1990*. Chapel Hill: University of North Carolina Press, 1994.

Allen, Frederick Lewis. *Only Yesterday: An Informal History of the Nineteen-Twenties.* New York: Harper, 1931.

Allen, John W. *It Happened in Southern Illinois.* 1968. Reprint, Carbondale: Southern Illinois University Press, 2010.

Anbinder, Tyler. *Nativism and Slavery: The Northern Know Nothings and the Politics of the 1850s.* Oxford: Oxford University Press, 1992.

Andreas, Alfred Theodore. *History of Chicago: From the Earliest Period to the Present Time.* 3 vols. Chicago: A. T. Andreas, 1886.

Avella, Steven. *The Confident Church: Catholic Leadership and Life in Chicago, 1940 to 1965.* South Bend, IN: University of Notre Dame Press, 1993.

Baer, Cynthia L. "The Labor of Irish Women in Nineteenth-Century Bloomington-Normal: A Portrait Painted through the Writings of Sarah Davis and Helen Ross Hall." In Koos, *Immigrants in McLean County*, 29–38.

Bales, Richard F. "Did the Cow Do It? A New Look at the Cause of the Great Chicago Fire." *Illinois Historical Journal* 90, no. 1 (Spring 1997): 2–24.

Ballance, Charles. *The History of Peoria, Illinois.* Peoria: N. C. Nason, 1870.

Barleen, Steven. "The Saloon on the Prairie: The Family and the Saloon in Braidwood, Illinois, 1865–1883." *Journal of the Illinois State Historical Society* 106, no. 2 (Summer 2013): 193–223.

Barr, Colin, and Hilary M. Carey, eds. *Religion and Greater Ireland: Christianity and Irish Global Networks, 1750–1950*. Montreal: McGill-Queen's University Press, 2015.

Barrett, James R. "The Blessed Virgin Made Me a Socialist: An Experiment in Catholic Autobiography and the Historical Understanding of Race and Class." In *Faith and the Historian: Catholic Perspectives*, edited by Nick Salvatore, 117–47. Urbana: University of Illinois Press, 2001.

———. *The Irish Way: Becoming American in the Multiethnic City*. New York: Penguin Press, 2012.

———. *Work and Community in the Jungle: Chicago's Packinghouse Workers, 1894–1922*. Urbana: University of Illinois Press, 1987.

Barry, P. T. *The First Irish in Illinois: Reminiscent of Old Kaskaskia Days*. Chicago: Chicago Newspaper Union, 1902.

Bartlett, Thomas, ed. *1798: A Bicentenary Perspective*. Dublin: Four Courts Press, 2003.

———. *Ireland: A History*. Cambridge: Cambridge University Press, 2010.

Basinger, Jeannine. *The World War II Combat Film: Anatomy of a Genre*. Middletown, CT: Wesleyan University Press, 2003.

Bateman, Newton, Paul Selby, and Josiah Seymour Currey, eds. *Historical Encyclopedia of Illinois*. 2 vols. Chicago: Munsell Publishing, 1921.

Beebe, Henry S. *History of Peru*. Peru, IL: J. F. Linton, 1858.

Beiner, Guy. *Forgetful Remembrance: Social Forgetting and Vernacular Historiography of a Rebellion in Ulster*. Oxford: Oxford University Press, 2018.

Belden, David A. *Will County*. Chicago: Arcadia Publishing, 2009.

Bernstein, Iver. *The New York City Draft Riots: Their Significance for American Society and Politics in the Age of the Civil War*. New York: Oxford University Press, 1990.

Biles, Roger. *Big City Boss in Depression and War: Mayor Edward J. Kelly of Chicago*. DeKalb: Northern Illinois University Press, 1984.

———. *Illinois: A History of the Land and Its People*. DeKalb: Northern Illinois University Press, 2005.

Billings, Mathieu W. "Potent Legacies: The Transformation of Irish American Politics, 1815–1840." PhD diss., Northern Illinois University, 2016.

Bodnar, John. *The Transplanted: A History of Immigrants in Urban America*. Bloomington: University of Indiana Press, 1985.

Bolton, H. W. *History of the Second Regiment Illinois Volunteer Infantry from Organization to Muster-Out*. Chicago: R. R. Donnelley & Sons, 1899.

Bourke, Richard, ed. *The Princeton History of Modern Ireland*. Princeton, NJ: Princeton University Press, 2016.

Brands, H. W. *Reagan: The Life*. New York: Anchor Books, 2016.

Bric, Maurice. *Ireland, Philadelphia, and the Re-invention of America, 1760–1800*. Dublin: Four Courts Press, 2008.

Brown, Thomas N. *Irish-American Nationalism, 1870–1890*. Philadelphia: J. B. Lippincott, 1966.

———. "The Origins and Character of Irish-American Nationalism." *Review of Politics* 18, no. 3 (July 1956): 327–58.

Brownson, Orestes A. "Native Americanism." *Brownson's Quarterly Review* 2 (January 1845): 76–98.

Brundage, David. *Irish Nationalists in America: The Politics of Exile, 1798–1998*. Oxford: Oxford University Press, 2016.

Buckingham, James Silk. *Eastern and Western States of America*. 3 vols. London: Fisher, Son, 1842.

Bukowski, Douglas. *Big Bill Thompson, Chicago, and the Politics of Image*. Urbana: University of Illinois Press, 1998.

Byrne, Jane. *My Chicago*. New York: W. W. Norton, 1992.

Campbell, Malcolm. *Ireland's New Worlds: Immigrants, Politics, and Society in the United States and Australia, 1815–1922*. Madison: University of Wisconsin Press, 2008.

Carolan, Nicholas. *A Harvest Saved: Francis O'Neill and Irish Music in Chicago*. Cork, Ireland: Ossian Publications, 1997.

Carroll, Francis M. "The Irish Free State and Public Diplomacy: The First Official Visit of William T. Cosgrave to the United States." *New Hibernia Review* 16, no. 2 (Summer 2012): 77–97.

Carpenter, Richard V., and J. W. Kitchell. "The Illinois Constitutional Convention of 1818." *Journal of the Illinois State Historical Society* 6, no. 3 (October 1913): 327–424.

Chicago Medical Society. *History of Medicine and Surgery and Physicians and Surgeons of Chicago*. Chicago: Biographical Publishing Corporation, 1922.

Ciment, James. *Encyclopedia of the Jazz Age: From the End of World War I to the Great Crash*. 2 vols. New York: Routledge, 2008.

Cline, Bruce L. *More History, Mystery, and Hauntings of Southern Illinois*. Rockford, IL: Black Oak Media, 2011.

Cohen, Adam, and Elizabeth Taylor. *American Pharaoh: Mayor Richard J. Daley; His Battle for Chicago and the Nation*. Boston: Little, Brown, 2000.

Cohen, Irwin J. *Comiskey Park*. Charleston, SC: Arcadia, 2004.

Cohen, Lizabeth. *Making a New Deal: Industrial Workers in Chicago, 1919–39*. Cambridge: Cambridge University Press, 1990.

Comerford, R. V. *The Fenians in Context: Irish Politics and Society, 1848–82*. Dublin: Wolfhound Press, 1985.

Connolly, Mary Beth Fraser. *Women of Faith: The Chicago Sisters of Mercy and the Evolution of a Religious Community*. New York: Fordham University Press, 2014.

Connolly, Sean J. *Priests and People in Pre-famine Ireland, 1780–1845*. Dublin: Gill & MacMillan, 1982.

———. *Religion, Law, and Power: The Making of Protestant Ireland, 1660–1760.* Oxford: Clarendon Press, 1993.

Cordery, Simon. *Mother Jones: Raising Cain and Consciousness.* Albuquerque: University of New Mexico Press, 2010.

Cornelius, Janet Duitsman, and Martha LaFrenz Kay. *Women of Conscience: Social Reform in Danville, Illinois, 1890–1930.* Columbia: University of South Carolina Press, 2008.

Cowan, Mimi. "'We Know Neither Catholics, nor Protestants, nor Free-Thinkers Here': Ethnicity, Religion, and the Chicago Public Schools, 1837–94." In *Religion and Greater Ireland: Christianity and Irish Global Networks, 1750–1950*, edited by Colin Barr and Hilary M. Carey, 187–205. Montreal: McGill-Queen's University Press, 2016.

Cronon, William. *Nature's Metropolis: Chicago and the Great West.* New York: W. W. Norton, 1991.

Curtin, Paul J. *West Limerick Roots: The Laurence Curtin Family of Knockbrack, County Limerick, Ireland.* Austin, TX: P. J. Curtin, 1995.

Dahlquist, Amanda. "Legislating Motherhood: The History of Mothers' Aid in Montgomery County." *Journal of the Illinois State Historical Society* 106, no. 1 (Spring 2013): 129–54.

Dearinger, Ryan. *The Filth of Progress: Immigrants, Americans, and the Building of Canals and Railroads in the West.* Oakland: University of California Press, 2016.

Dickson, R. J. *Ulster Emigration to Colonial America, 1718–1775.* London: Routledge and Kegan Paul, 1966.

Diner, Hasia. *Erin's Daughters in America: Irish Immigrant Women in the Nineteenth Century.* Baltimore: Johns Hopkins University Press, 1983.

The Diocese of Rockford, 1908–2008: Our History. Strasbourg: Editions du Signe, 2007.

Dolan, Jay. *The American Catholic Experience: A History from Colonial Times to the Present.* Garden City, NY: Doubleday, 1985.

———. *The Irish Americans: A History.* New York: Bloomsbury Press, 2008.

Donnelly, James S., Jr. *The Great Irish Potato Famine.* Gloucestershire: Sutton, 2001.

Doorley, Michael. *Irish-American Diaspora Nationalism: The Friends of Irish Freedom, 1916–1935.* Dublin: Four Courts Press, 2005.

Doyle, David Noel. "The Irish and American Labour, 1880–1920." *Saothar* 1, no. 1 (May 1975): 42–53.

———. "The Irish in North America, 1776–1845." In Lee and Casey, *Making the Irish American*, 171–212.

———. "Scots Irish or Scotch Irish?" In Lee and Casey, *Making the Irish American*, 151–70.

Drake, St. Clair, and Horace R. Clayton. *Black Metropolis: A Study of Negro Life in a Northern City.* Chicago: University of Chicago Press, 1993.

Dunn, Mark T. "Irish American Organizations in Bloomington in the 1880s." In Koos, *Irish Immigrants in McLean County*, 39–53.

Dunne, Finley Peter. *Mr. Dooley and the Chicago Irish: The Autobiography of a Nineteenth-Century Ethnic Group.* Edited by Charles Fanning. Washington, DC: Catholic University of America Press, 1976.

———. *Mr. Dooley in the Hearts of His Countrymen.* Boston: Small, Maynard, 1899.

———. *Mr. Dooley's Opinions.* New York: R. H. Russell, 1901.

Eckard, E. Woodrow. "Anti-Irish Job Discrimination circa 1880: Evidence from Major League Baseball." *Social Science History* 34, no. 4 (Winter 2010): 407–43.

Elazar, Daniel. *Cities of the Prairie: The Metropolitan Frontier and American Politics.* New York: Basic Books, 1970.

Emmons, David. *Beyond the Pale: The Irish in the American West, 1845–1910.* Norman: University of Oklahoma Press, 2010.

English, William H. *Conquest of the Country Northwest of the River Ohio, 1778–1783; and Life of Gen. George Rogers Clark.* Indianapolis: Bowen-Merrill, 1896.

Erie, Stephen. *Rainbow's End: Irish-Americans and the Dilemmas of Urban Machine Politics.* Berkeley: University of California Press, 1988.

Ewing, Steven, and John B. Lundstrom. *Fateful Rendezvous: The Life of Butch O'Hare.* Annapolis, MD: Naval Institute Press, 2012.

Fanning, Charles. "Dueling Cultures: Ireland and Irish-America at the Chicago World's Fairs of 1933 and 1934." *New Hibernia Review* 15, no. 3 (Winter 2011): 94–110.

———. *Finley Peter Dunne and Mr. Dooley: The Chicago Years.* Lexington: University Press of Kentucky, 1978.

———. *The Irish Voice in America: Irish-American Fiction from the 1760s to the 1980s.* Lexington: University Press of Kentucky, 1990.

Farrell, James T. *Chicago Stories.* Edited by Charles Fanning. Chicago: University of Illinois Press, 1998.

———. *Judgment Day.* In *Studs Lonigan.* New York: Random House, 1938.

———. *Young Lonigan.* In *Studs Lonigan.* New York: Random House, 1938.

———. *The Young Manhood of Studs Lonigan.* In *Studs Lonigan.* New York: Random House, 1938.

Fitzpatrick, Edward. "Early Irish Settlers of Kentucky." *Journal of the American Irish Historical Society* 2 (1899): 139–44.

Foner, Eric. "Class, Ethnicity, and Radicalism in the Gilded Age: The Land League and Irish America." In *Politics and Ideology in the Age of the Civil War*, edited by Eric Foner, 150–200. New York: Oxford University Press, 1980.

Freeman, Stephen. "Organizing the Workers in a Steel Company Town: The Union Movement in Joliet, Illinois, 1870–1920." *Illinois Historical Journal* 79 (1986): 2–28.

Funchion, Michael. "The Political and Nationalist Dimensions." In McCaffrey et al., *The Irish in Chicago*, 61–97.

Gilje, Paul. *Mobocracy: Popular Disorder in New York City, 1763–1834.* Chapel Hill: University of North Carolina Press, 1987.

Gillen, Ultan. "Ascendancy Ireland, 1660–1860." In Bourke, *Princeton History of Modern Ireland*, 48–73.

Glazier, Michael, ed. *The Encyclopedia of the Irish in America*. Notre Dame, IN: University of Notre Dame Press, 1999.

Gorn, Eliott J. *Mother Jones: The Most Dangerous Woman in America*. New York: Hill and Wang, 2001.

Gray, Peter. *The Irish Famine*. London: Harry N. Abrams, 1995.

Griffin, Patrick. *The People with No Name: Ireland's Ulster Scots, America's Scots Irish, and the Creation of a British Atlantic World, 1689–1764*. Princeton, NJ: Princeton University Press, 2001.

———. "Searching for Independence: Revolutionary Kentucky, Irish American Experience, and Scotch-Irish Myth, 1770s-1790s." In *Ulster to America: The Scots-Irish Migration Experience, 1680–1830*, edited by Warren R. Hofstra, 211–32. Knoxville: University of Tennessee Press, 2012.

Grimshaw, William J. *Bitter Fruit: Black Politics and the Chicago Machine, 1931–1991*. Chicago: University of Chicago Press, 1992.

Griswold, B. J. *The Pictorial History of Fort Wayne, Indiana: A Review of Two Centuries of Occupation of the Region about the Head of the Maumee River*. 2 vols. Chicago: Robert O. Law, 1917.

Grund, Francis. *The Americans: In Their Moral, Social, and Political Relations*. 2 vols. London: Longman et al., 1837.

Guglielmo, Thomas A. *White upon Arrival: Italians, Race, Color, and Power in Chicago, 1890–1945*. Oxford: Oxford University Press, 2004.

Hale, Stan J., ed. *Williamson County Illinois Sesquicentennial History*. Paducah, KY: Turner Company, 1993.

Hamer, Richard, and Roger Ruthhart. *Citadel of Sin: The John Looney Story*. Moline, IL: Moline Dispatch, 2007.

Handlin, Oscar. *The Uprooted: The Epic Story of the Great Migrations That Made the American People*. Philadelphia: University of Pennsylvania Press, 1952.

Harrison, Lowell H. *George Rogers Clark and the War in the West*. Lexington: University of Kentucky Press, 2014.

Hays, Christopher K. "The African American Struggle for Equality and Justice in Cairo, Illinois, 1865–1900." *Illinois Historical Journal* 90, no. 4 (Winter 1997): 265–84.

Herrick, Mary J. *Chicago Public Schools: A Social and Political History*. Beverly Hills, CA: Sage Publications, 1970.

Hicken, Victor. "Mine Union Radicalism in Macoupin and Montgomery Counties, IL." Illinois Labor History Society. 1997. http://www.illinoislaborhistory.org/labor-history-articles/mine-union-radicalism-in-macoupin-and-montgomery-counties-il.

Higham, John. *Strangers in the Land: Patterns of American Nativism, 1860–1925*. New Brunswick, NJ: Rutgers University Press, 1955.

Hirsch, Arnold. *Making the Second Ghetto: Race and Housing in Chicago, 1940–1960.* Cambridge: Cambridge University Press, 1983.

Hirsch, Eric L. *Urban Revolt: Ethnic Politics in the Nineteenth-Century Chicago Labor Movement.* Berkeley: University of California Press, 1990.

History of Grundy County Illinois. Chicago: O. L. Baskin, 1882.

The History of Jo Daviess County, Illinois. Chicago: H. F. Kett, 1878.

Hoffman, U. J. *History of La Salle County, Illinois.* Chicago: S. J. Clarke, 1906.

Hofstra, Warren R., ed. *Ulster to America: The Scots-Irish Migration Experience, 1680–1830.* Knoxville: University of Tennessee Press, 2012.

Hoy, Sue Ellen. *Good Hearts: Catholic Sisters in Chicago's Past.* Urbana: University of Illinois Press, 2006.

———. "Lives on the Color Line: Catholic Sisters and African Americans in Chicago, 1890s–1960s." *U.S. Catholic Historian* 22, no. 1 (Winter 2004): 67–91.

———. "No Color Line at Loretto Academy: Catholic Sisters and African Americans on Chicago's South Side." *Journal of Women's History* 14, no. 1 (Spring 2002): 8–33.

———. "Walking Nuns: Chicago's Irish Sisters of Mercy." In *At the Crossroads: Old Saint Patrick's and the Chicago Irish*, edited by Ellen Skerrett, 39–51. Chicago: Wild Onion Books, 1997.

Hubbard, Mark, ed. *Illinois's War: The Civil War in Documents.* Athens: Ohio University Press, 2013.

Ignatiev, Noel. *How the Irish Became White.* New York: Routledge, 1995.

Illinois State Historical Library. *Transactions of the Illinois State Historical Society for the Year 1914.* Springfield: Illinois State Journal, 1915.

Innis-Jimenez, Michael. *Steel Barrio: The Great Mexican Migration to South Chicago, 1915–1940.* New York: New York University Press, 2013.

Ireland, Patricia, L. "Blarney Streets: The Staging of Ireland and Irish-America by the Chicago Manuscript Company." PhD diss., Southern Illinois University, 1998.

Irish Fellowship Club of Chicago. *Irish Fellowship Club of Chicago: Its History and Objectives, 1902–1953.* Chicago: Irish Fellowship Club of Chicago, 1963.

Jacobson, Matthew Frye. *Whiteness of a Different Color: European Immigrants and the Alchemy of Race.* Cambridge: Harvard University Press, 1998.

Janis, Ely M. "Petticoat Revolutionaries: Gender, Ethnic Nationalism, and the Irish Ladies' Land League in the United States." *Journal of American Ethnic History* 27, no. 2 (Winter 2008): 5–27.

Jensen, Richard J. *Illinois: A History.* 1978. Reprint, Chicago: University of Chicago Press, 2001.

Johannsen, Robert Walter. *Stephen A. Douglas.* 1973. Reprint, Urbana: University of Illinois Press, 1997.

Jung, Patrick J. *The Black Hawk War of 1832.* Norman: University of Oklahoma Press, 2008.

Kantowicz, Edward R. *Corporation Sole: Cardinal Mundelein and Chicago Catholicism.* South Bend, IN: University of Notre Dame Press, 1983.

Karamanski, Theodore J., and Eileen M. McMahon, eds. *Civil War Chicago: Eyewitness to History.* Athens: Ohio University Press, 2014.

Keating, Anne Durkin. *Rising Up from Indian Country: The Battle of Fort Dearborn and the Birth of Chicago.* Chicago: University of Chicago Press, 2014.

Keating, Ryan W. *Shades of Green: Irish Regiments, American Soldiers, and Local Communities in the Civil War Era.* New York: Fordham University Press, 2017.

Keefe, Thomas M. "Chicago's Flirtation with Political Nativism, 1854–1856." *Records of the American Historical Society of Philadelphia* 82 (1971): 131–58.

Keenan-Thomson, Tara. "'Fidel Castro in a Mini-Skirt': Bernadette Devlin's First US Tour." *History Ireland* 17, no. 4 (July–August 2009).

Kenny, Kevin. *The American Irish: A History.* New York: Longman, 2000.

———. "Editor's Introduction." In *New Directions in Irish-American History*, edited by Kevin Kenny, 13–16. Madison: University of Wisconsin Press, 2003.

———. *Making Sense of the Molly Maguires.* Oxford: Oxford University Press, 1998.

Keyssar, Alexander. *The Right to Vote: The Contested History of Democracy in the United States.* New York: Basic Books, 2001.

Kirkland, Joseph. *The Chicago Massacre of 1812: With Illustrations and Historical Documents.* Chicago: Dibble Publishing Company, 1893.

Kleber, John E. *Encyclopedia of Louisville.* Lexington: University of Kentucky Press, 2000.

Knobel, Dale T. *Paddy and the Republic: Ethnicity and Nationality in Antebellum America.* Middletown, CT: Wesleyan University Press, 1986.

Koos, Greg. *Irish Immigrants in McLean County, Illinois.* Bloomington, IL: McLean County Historical Society, 2000.

Krugler, David F. *1919, the Year of Racial Violence: How African Americans Fought Back.* Cambridge: Cambridge University Press, 2014.

Larkin, Emmet. "The Devotional Revolution in Ireland, 1850–1875." *American Historical Review* 77, no. 3 (June 1972): 625–52.

Larson, Erik. *The Devil in the White City: Murder, Magic, and Madness at the Fair That Changed America.* New York: Vintage Books, 2004.

Lee, Joseph, and Marion R. Casey, eds. *Making the Irish American: History and Heritage of the Irish in the United States.* New York: New York University Press, 2008.

Lee, Margaret. "Shamrocks and Segregation: The Persistence of Upper-Class Irish Ethnicity in Beverly Hills, Chicago." In *After the Flood*, edited by Matthew J. O'Brien and James S. Rogers, 71–86. Dublin: Irish Academic Press, 2009.

Levine, Bruce. "Conservatism, Nativism, and Slavery: Thomas R. Whitney and the Origins of the Know-Nothing Party." *Journal of American History* 88, no. 2 (September 2001): 455–88.

Lewinnek, Elaine. *The Working Man's Reward: Chicago's Early Suburbs and the Roots of American Sprawl.* Oxford: Oxford University Press, 2014.

Lumpkins, Charles L. *American Pogrom: The East St. Louis Race Riot and Black Politics.* Athens: Ohio University Press, 2008.

Markwell, David. "A Turning Point: The Lasting Impact of the 1898 Virden Mine Riot." *Journal of the Illinois State Historical Society* 99, no. 3 (Winter 2007): 211–27.

Matejka, Mike. "Irish Immigrant Son Patrick Morrissey Built Rail Brotherhood." In Koos, *Irish Immigrants in McLean County*, 55–57.

McCabe, James Dabney. *The History of the Great Riots: Being a Full and Authentic Account . . . Molly Maguires.* Philadelphia: National, 1877.

McCaffrey, Lawrence J. "The Irish-American Dimension." In McCaffrey et al., *The Irish in Chicago*, 7–8.

———. *The Irish Catholic Diaspora in America.* Washington, DC: Catholic University of America Press, 1976.

———. "Preserving the Union: Shaping a New Image of Chicago's Irish Catholics and the Civil War." In Mitchell, *Fighting Irish*, 78–95.

McCaffrey, Lawrence J., Ellen Skerrett, Michael F. Funchion, and Charles Fanning. *The Irish in Chicago.* Urbana: University of Illinois Press, 1987.

McCarthy, Tara. *Respectability and Reform: Irish-American Women's Activism, 1880–1920.* Syracuse, NY: Syracuse University Press, 2018.

McGarry, Fearghal. *The Rising: Easter 1916.* New York: Oxford University Press, 2010.

McGee, Thomas D'Arcy, and Seán Virgo. *Selected Verse of Thomas D'Arcy McGee.* Toronto: Exile Editions, 1991.

McGirr, John E. *Life of the Rt. Rev. Wm. Quarter, D.D., First Catholic Bishop of Chicago.* New York: Sadlier, 1850.

McGoorty, John P. "The Early Irish of Illinois." *Transactions of the Illinois State Historical Society* 34 (1927): 54–64.

McGreevy, John T. *Parish Boundaries: The Catholic Encounter with Race in the Twentieth-Century Urban North.* Chicago: University of Chicago Press, 1996.

McLaughlin, Malcolm. *Power, Community, and Racial Killing in East St. Louis.* New York: Palgrave MacMillan, 2005.

McMahon, Eileen M. "Canal Diggers, Church Builders: Dispelling Stereotypes of the Irish on the Irish and Michigan Corridor." *Journal of the Illinois State Historical Society* 111, no. 4 (Winter 2018): 43–81.

———. "Illinois." In *The Encyclopedia of the Irish in America*, edited by Michael Glazier, 401–6. Notre Dame, IN: University of Notre Dame Press, 1999.

———. "Irish Women in the Civil War." In Mitchell, *Fighting Irish*, 121–39.

———. *What Parish Are You From? A Chicago Irish Community & Race Relations.* Lexington: University Press of Kentucky, 1995.

McWhirter, Cameron. *Red Summer: The Summer of 1919 and the Awakening of Black America.* New York: Henry Holt, 2011.

Meagher, Timothy J. *Inventing Irish America: Generation, Class, and Ethnic Identity in a New England City, 1890–1928.* Notre Dame, IN: University of Notre Dame Press, 2001.

Melendy, Royal. "The Saloon in Chicago." *American Journal of Sociology* 6 (November 1900): 289–306.

Melish, Joann Pope. *Disowning Slavery: Gradual Emancipation and "Race" in New England, 1780–1860.* Ithaca, NY: Cornell University Press, 1998.

Miller, Kerby A. *Emigrants and Exiles: Ireland and the Irish Exodus to North America.* Oxford: Oxford University Press, 1985.

———. "'Scotch-Irish,' 'Black Irish,' and 'Real Irish': Emigrants and Identities in the Old South." In Kerby A. Miller, *Ireland and Irish America: Culture, Class, and Transatlantic Migration*, 139–59. Dublin: Field Day Publications, 2008.

Miller, Kerby, Arnold Schrier, Bruce D. Boling, and David N. Doyle, eds. *Irish Immigrants in the Land of Canaan: Letters and Memoirs from Colonial and Revolutionary America, 1675–1815.* Oxford: Oxford University Press, 2003.

Miller, Richard Lawrence. *Lincoln and His World: Prairie Politician, 1834–1842.* Mechanicsburg, PA: Stackpole Books, 2008.

Miller, Ross. *The Great Chicago Fire.* Urbana: University of Illinois Press, 2000.

Mitchel, John. *The Last Conquest of Ireland (Perhaps).* New York, 1860.

Mitchell, Arthur H., ed. *Fighting Irish in the American Civil War and the Invasion of Mexico.* Jefferson, NC: McFarland, 2017.

Mitrani, Sam. *The Rise of the Chicago Police Department, 1850–1894.* Urbana: University of Illinois Press, 2013.

Moynihan, Daniel Patrick, and Nathan Glazer. *Beyond the Melting Pot: The Negroes, Puerto Ricans, Jews, Italians, and Irish of New York City.* Cambridge, MA: MIT Press, 1963.

Mulkerins, Thomas M. *Holy Family Parish: Priests and People.* Chicago: Universal Press, 1923.

Murphy, Angela F. *American Slavery, Irish Freedom: Abolition, Immigrant Citizenship, and the Transatlantic Movement for Irish Repeal.* Baton Rouge: Louisiana State University Press, 2010.

Murtagh, Harman. "Irish Soldiers Abroad, 1600–1800." In *A Military History of Ireland*, edited by Thomas Bartlett and Keith Jeffery, 294–314. Cambridge: Cambridge University Press, 1996.

Neary, Timothy B. *Crossing Parish Boundaries: Race, Sports, and Catholic Youth, 1914–1954.* Chicago: University of Chicago Press, 2016.

Newman, Richard S. *The Transformation of American Abolitionism: Fighting Slavery in the Early Republic.* Chapel Hill: University of North Carolina Press, 2002.

Ngai, Mae. *Impossible Subjects: Illegal Aliens and the Making of Modern America.* Princeton: Princeton University Press, 2004.

Nolan, Janet. *Ourselves Alone: Women's Emigration from Ireland, 1885–1920.* Lexington: University Press of Kentucky, 1989.

———. *Servants of the Poor: Teachers and Mobility in Ireland and Irish America*. Notre Dame, IN: University of Notre Dame Press, 2004.

Nolan, Mary. "Honorable James L. D. Morrison." *Central Magazine* 4, no. 1 (January 1874): 1–3.

Norton, W. T. *Centennial History of Madison County, Illinois and Its People, 1812–1912*. 2 vols. Chicago: Lewis Publishing, 1912.

O'Brien, Gillian. *Blood Runs Green: The Murder That Transfixed Gilded Age Chicago*. Chicago: University of Chicago Press, 2015.

O'Brien, Matthew J. "'Hibernians on the March': Irish-American Ethnicity and the Cold War." In *After the Flood*, edited by Matthew O'Brien and James S. Rogers, 57–70. Dublin: Irish Academic Press, 2009.

———. "Irish America, Race, and Bernadette Devlin's 1969 American Tour." *New Hibernia Review* 14, no. 2 (Summer 2010): 84–101.

O'Brien, Michael J. *The McCarthys in Early American History*. New York: Dodd, Mead, 1921.

O'Ferrall, Fergus. *Catholic Emancipation: Daniel O'Connell and the Birth of Irish Democracy*. Dublin: Gill and MacMillan, 1985.

O'Gorman, Thomas J. *One Hundred Years: A History of the Irish Fellowship Club of Chicago*. Chicago, 2001.

O'Toole, Fintan. *White Savage: William Johnson and the Invention of America*. New York: Farrar, Straus, and Giroux, 2005.

Ohlmeyer, Jane. "Conquest, Civilization, Colonization: Ireland, 1540–1660." In Bourke, *Princeton History of Modern Ireland*, 21–47.

Pierce, Bessie Louise. *A History of Chicago*. Vol. 1, *The Beginning of a City, 1673–1848*. Chicago: University of Chicago Press, 1937.

Portrait and Biographical Album of Champaign County, Illinois. Chicago: Chapman Brothers, 1887.

Potter, David M. *The Impending Crisis, 1848–1861*. New York: Harper & Row, 1976.

Potter, George. *To the Golden Door: The Story of the Irish in Ireland and America*. Boston: Little, Brown, 1960.

Rakove, Milton. *Don't Make No Waves—Don't Back No Losers: An Insider's Analysis of the Daley Machine*. Bloomington: Indiana University Press, 1975.

Reagan, Ronald, and Richard G. Hubler. *Where's the Rest of Me?* New York: Duell and Sons, 1965.

Reid, Robert L., ed. *Battleground: The Autobiography of Margaret A. Haley*. Urbana: University of Illinois Press, 1982.

Reynolds, John. *The Pioneer History of Illinois: Containing the Discovery, in 1673, and the History of the Country to the Year 1818, When the State Government Was Organized*. Belleville, IL: N. A. Randall, 1852.

Richter, Daniel K. *Facing East from Indian Country: A Native History of Early America*. Cambridge, MA: Harvard University Press, 2001.

Riess, Steven A. *City Games: The Evolution of American Urban Society and the Rise of Sports.* Urbana: University of Illinois Press, 1991.

Riley, Glenda. "From Ireland to Illinois: Life of Helen Ross Hall." *Illinois Historical Journal* 81, no. 3 (Autumn 1988): 162–80.

Roberts, Kyle B., and Stephen Schloesser. *Crossings and Dwellings: Restored Jesuits, Women Religious, American Experience, 1814–2014.* Boston: Brill, 2017.

Roediger, David. *The Wages of Whiteness: Race and the Making of the American Working Class.* New York: Verso, 1991.

Rogers, James Silas, and Matthew O'Brien. *After the Flood: Irish America, 1945–1960.* Dublin: Irish Academic Press, 2009.

Rousmaniere, Kate. *Citizen Teacher: The Life of Margaret Haley.* Albany: State University of New York Press, 2005.

Royko, Mike. *Boss: Richard J. Daley of Chicago.* New York: Penguin Books, 1971.

Royot, Daniel. *Divided Loyalties in a Doomed Empire: The French in the West to the Lewis and Clark Expedition.* Newark: University of Delaware Press, 2007.

Sawislak, Karen. *Smoldering City: Chicagoans and the Great Fire, 1871–1874.* Chicago: University of Chicago Press, 1995.

Schmuhl, Robert. *Ireland's Exiled Children: America and the Easter Rising.* Oxford: Oxford University Press, 2016.

Schneirov, Richard. *Labor and Urban Politics: Class Conflict and the Origins of Modern Liberalism in Chicago, 1864–97.* Urbana: University of Illinois Press, 1998.

Schneirov, Richard, and John B. Jentz. *Chicago in the Age of Capital: Class, Politics, and Democracy in the Civil War and Reconstruction.* Urbana: University of Illinois Press, 2012.

Schneirov, Richard, Shelton Stromquist, and Nick Salvatore, eds. *The Pullman Strike and the Crisis of the 1890s: Essays on Labor and Politics.* Urbana: University of Illinois Press, 1999.

Selzer, Adam. *H. H. Holmes: The True History of the White City Devil.* New York: Skyhorse, 2017.

Senechal, Roberta. *The Sociogenesis of a Race Riot: Springfield, Illinois, 1908.* Urbana: University of Illinois Press, 1990.

Senning, John P. "The Know Nothing Movement in Illinois, 1854–1856." *Journal of the Illinois State Historical Society* 7, no. 1 (April 1914): 7–33.

Shaw, Thomas. *Story of the LaSalle Mission.* 2 vols. Chicago: M. A. Donahue, n.d.

Sheehan, Bernard W. "'The Famous Hair Buyer General': Henry Hamilton, George Rogers Clark, and the American Indian." *Indiana Magazine of History* 79, no. 1 (1983): 1–28.

Shelley, Thomas J. "Twentieth-Century American Catholicism and Irish Americans." In Lee and Casey, *Making the Irish American*, 574–608.

Skerrett, Ellen. "The Catholic Dimension." In McCaffrey et al., *The Irish in Chicago*, 22–60.

———. "The Irish of Chicago's Hull-House Neighborhood." In *New Perspectives on the Irish Diaspora*, edited by Charles Fanning, 189–222. Carbondale: Southern Illinois University Press, 2000.

Skok, Deborah A. *More Than Neighbors: Catholic Settlements and Day Nurseries in Chicago, 1893–1930*. DeKalb: Northern Illinois University Press, 2007.

Slattery, T. J. *Rock Island: Arsenal for Democracy.* Rock Island: Arsenal Historical Society, 1995.

Smith, George Washington. *A History of Southern Illinois: A Narrative Account of Its Historical Progress, Its People, and Its Principal Interests.* Chicago: Lewis Publishing, 1912.

Smith, Grace Partridge. "Four Ballads from 'Egypt.'" *Hoosier Folklore* 5, no. 3 (September 1946): 115–19.

Smith, Scott S. "Parade Watching." *World of Hibernia* 3, no. 4 (Spring 1998): 22.

Sofchalk, Donald G. "The Chicago Memorial Day Incident: An Episode in Mass Action." *Labor History* 6 (Winter 1965): 3–43.

Steckel, Richard H. "Migration and Political Conflict: Precincts in the Midwest on the Eve of the Civil War." *Journal of Interdisciplinary History* 28, no. 4 (Spring 1998): 583–603.

Sterling, Robert E. "Civil War Draft Resistance in the Middle West." PhD diss., Northern Illinois University, 1974.

Stevens, W. W. *Past and Present of Will County, Illinois.* Chicago: S. J. Clark, 1907.

Sweeney, David Francis. *The Life of John Lancaster Spalding: First Bishop of Peoria, 1840–1916.* New York: Herder and Herder, 1965.

Taylor, Alan. *The Civil War of 1812: American Citizens, British Subjects, Irish Rebels, and Indian Allies.* New York: Alfred A. Knopf, 2010.

Terkel, Studs. *Hard Times: An Oral History of the Great Depression.* New York: Pantheon Books, 1970.

Tobin, Catherine. "The Lowly Muscular Digger: Irish Canal Workers in Nineteenth-Century America." PhD diss., University of Notre Dame, 1987.

Townshend, Charles. *Easter 1916: The Irish Rebellion.* Lanham, MD: Ivan Dee, 2006.

Trask, Kerry A. *Black Hawk: The Battle for the Heart of America.* New York: Henry Holt, 2006.

Tuttle, William M. *Race Riot: Chicago and the Red Summer of 1919.* New York: Atheneum, 1970.

Vallely, Fintan. *The Companion to Irish Traditional Music.* Cork, Ireland: Cork University Press, 1998.

Vargo, Louis. "Abraham Lincoln Prepares to Fight a Saber Duel." *Civil War Times* (February 2002).

Volwiler, Albert T. *George Croghan and the Westward Movement, 1741–1782.* Cleveland: Arthur H. Clark, 1986.

Wainwright, Nicholas B. *George Croghan: Wilderness Diplomat.* Chapel Hill: University of North Carolina Press, 1959.

Walsh, James P. "De Valera in the United States, 1919." *Records of the American Catholic Historical Society of Philadelphia* 73, no. 3 (December 1962): 92–107.

Way, Peter. *Common Labor: Workers and the Digging of North American Canals, 1780–1860.* Baltimore: Johns Hopkins University Press, 1993.

Weinberg, Carl R. *Labor, Loyalty, and Rebellion: Southwestern Illinois Coal Miners and World War I.* Carbondale: Southern Illinois University Press, 2005.

Wheeler, Adade Mitchell, and Marlene Stein Wortman. *The Roads They Made: Women in Illinois History.* Chicago: Charles H. Kerr, 1977.

Whelehan, Niall. *The Dynamiters: Irish Nationalism and Political Violence in the Wider World, 1867–1900.* Cambridge: Cambridge University Press, 2012.

White, Richard. *The Middle Ground: Indians, Empires, and Republics in the Great Lakes Region, 1650–1815.* Cambridge: Cambridge University Press, 1991.

Wills, Clair. *Dublin, 1916: The Siege of the GPO.* Cambridge, MA: Harvard University Press, 2009.

Wilson, Andrew J. *Irish America and the Ulster Conflict, 1968–1995.* Washington, DC: Catholic University of America Press, 1995.

Wilson, David A. *Thomas D'Arcy McGee: The Extreme Moderate, 1857–1868.* Montreal: McGill-Queen's University Press, 2013.

———. *United Irishmen, United States: Immigrant Radicals in the Early Republic* Ithaca, NY: Cornell University Press, 1998.

Witgen, Michael. "Seeing Red: Race, Citizenship, and Indigeneity in the Old Northwest." *Journal of the Early Republic* 38, no. 4 (Winter 2018): 581–611.

Woodham-Smith, Cecil. *The Great Hunger: Ireland, 1845–1849.* New York: Old Town Books, 1962.

Wyman, Mark. *Immigrants in the Valley: Irish, Germans, and Americans in the Upper Mississippi Country, 1830–1860.* 1984. Reprint, Carbondale: Southern Illinois University Press, 2016.

Wyman, Mark, and John W. Muirhead. "Jim Crow Comes to Central Illinois: Racial Segregation in Twentieth-Century Bloomington-Normal." *Journal of the Illinois State Historical Society* 110, no. 2 (Summer 2017): 154–82.

Wymbs, Norman E. *A Place to Go Back To: Ronald Reagan in Dixon, Illinois.* New York: Vantage Press, 1987.

Young, Ella Flagg. "In Memoriam." In "Report of the Superintendent of Schools," *Public Schools of the City of Chicago: Sixty-First Annual Report of the Board of Education for the Year Ending June 30, 1915.* Chicago, n.d.

INDEX OF SURNAMES

Surnames have long been integral to the academic, genealogical, and family histories of Ireland and the Irish diaspora. Ireland was among the first places in the world where a system of hereditary surnames developed, and historians often use surname analysis, in conjunction with contemporary sources, to determine an individual's region or county of nativity. Such is the case with *The Irish in Illinois*. The following index is intended as a research guide. It includes surnames cited within the pages of this text. Each is a name commonly found in Ireland (Edward MacLysaght, *The Surnames of Ireland* [1985; repr., Dublin: Irish Academic Press, 1999]). It is our hope that this index, in conjunction with this volume, will facilitate new learning on the Irish in the Prairie State and beyond.

INDEX OF SUBJECTS

Page numbers in italics indicate illustrations.

MATHIEU W. BILLINGS is an associate faculty adjunct in the Department of History and Political Science at the University of Indianapolis.

SEAN FARRELL is a professor of history at Northern Illinois University. A past president of the American Conference for Irish Studies, he is the author of *Rituals and Riots: Sectarian Violence and Political Culture in Ulster, 1784–1886* and has published a number of articles and books on nineteenth-century Irish history.